GREEN EARTH RESOURCE GUIDE

by Cheryl Gorder

A comprehensive guide about environmentally-friendly services and products:

BOOKS
CLEAN AIR, CLEAN WATER
ECO-TOURISM
EDUCATIONAL MATERIALS
ENERGY CONSERVATION
MAGAZINES, NEWSLETTERS & BROCHURES
SEMINARS, WORKSHOPS & SPEAKERS
HOUSEHOLD & PERSONAL CARE PRODUCTS
ORGANIZATIONS
ORGANICALLY GROWN
RECYCLING
PAPER PRODUCTS
BABY & CHILDREN'S PRODUCTS
ENVIRONMENTAL INVESTING

Green Earth Resource Guide

Published by:

BLUE BIRD PUBLISHING
1713 East Broadway #306
Tempe AZ 85282
(602) 968-4088
FAX (602) 983-7319
Toll-free credit card orders
1-800-654-1993

Cover Art by Itoko Maeno

Library of Congress Cataloging-in-Publication Data

Gorder, Cheryl, 1952-
    Green earth resource guide : a comprehensive guide about
  environmentally-friendly ... / by Cheryl Gorder.
          p.   cm.
    Includes indexes.
    ISBN 0-933025-23-8 : $12.95
    1. Environmental protection--Citizen participation.
  2. Environmental protection--Equipment and supplies.   3. Consumer
education.   I. Title.
TD171.7.G68   1990
  363.7'0525--dc20   90-27726
                                                          CIP

TABLE OF CONTENTS

4

INTRODUCTION

This book emphasizes positive steps we can take to help the planet. Although there are a few books listed that explain our environmental problems—and indeed we should absorb that important information—most of the listing are for products and services that will help use make steps in the right direction.

Basically, being environmentally sensitive consists of 5 steps:

1. Acknowledging that the problems are real.
2. Gaining information about the problems.
3. Gaining information about positive solutions.
4. Changing personal habits and buying habits.
5. Encouraging others to do the same.

This book can help in all five steps.

LET'S KEEP "EARTH DAY EVERY DAY !!"

For Better or Worse ©1990 Lynn Johnson.
Reprinted with permission of Universal Press Syndicate. All rights reserved

★ **Introduction**

ABOUT THE AUTHOR

Cheryl Gorder has been addressing issues that concern us all: homelessness, parenting, and education. Her book *Homeless: Without Addresses in America* won a Benjamin Franklin Award in 1989. Another one of her books, *Home Schools: An Alternative* has been a homeschooling bestseller and is now available in its third edition.

She has previously compiled other resource guides: *Home Education Resource Guide* and *Home Business Resource Guide*. She decided to do this *Green Earth Resource Guide* after parents and librarians asked her to do so.

ACKNOWLEDGMENTS

We gratefully acknowledge the following contributors: Itoko Maeno for her exquisite cover art; Tribune Newspapers of Arizona for the article "Investing in Ecology;" Rainforest Action Movement for "Seven Things You Can Do To Save the Rainforests;" the Picture Cube; Tribune Media Services & United Press Syndicate. We would also like to thank the hundreds of businesses and organizations that provided information and products that were reviewed for this book.

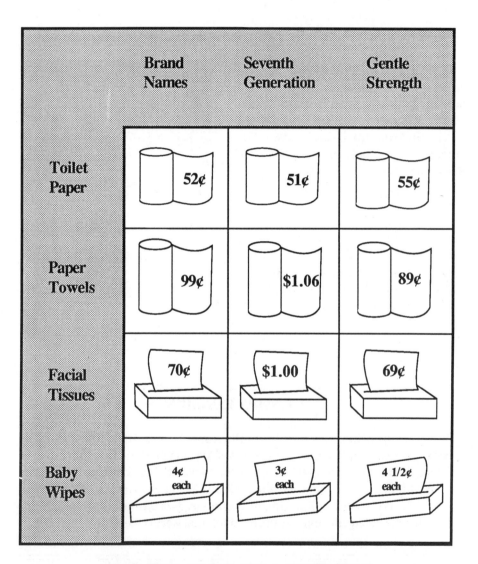

	Brand Names	Seventh Generation	Gentle Strength
Toilet Paper	52¢	51¢	55¢
Paper Towels	99¢	$1.06	89¢
Facial Tissues	70¢	$1.00	69¢
Baby Wipes	4¢ each	3¢ each	4 1/2¢ each

COST COMPARISON

 Investing in Ecology

Investing in Ecology:
Costly 'Green' Goods Pay Off
by Clint Williams

Reprinted by permission of the Tribune Newspapers, Arizona

If you've heard it once in the last year, you've heard it a zillion times: "Save the planet. Save the planet."

Fine idea, you say. But how much extra is this saving the planet stuff going to cost?

About $155 a year, according to a survey of some common household items and their environment-friendly counterparts. That price tag is based on the price difference between commercial brand-name toilet paper, dishwasher soap and laundry powder and the so-called "green" versions. The annual cost difference is also based on the assumption that in the course of a year a typical family uses 200 rolls of toilet paper, does 365 loads of laundry and 365 loads of dishes.

Although you pay a premium for green products, the money spent now, proponents say, means savings in energy, disposal costs and pollution cleanup costs.

"A simple roll of toilet paper deals with a whole variety of environmental issues," says Jeffrey Hollander, chief executive officer of Seventh Generation, a Vermont-based mail order company that specializes in green goods. (Seventh Generation products found in this book.)

The toilet paper most of us use is made from virgin paper that is bleached with chlorine to make it whiter. Additionally, it may be dyed so that it better matches your bathroom decor.

Making toilet paper from virgin paper uses more energy—not to mention trees—than using recycled paper. Chlorine bleaching pumps a variety of cancer-causing by-products into the air and water.

Environmentally-friendly toilet paper (and other paper products) is made from unbleached, recycled paper.

The toilet paper sold by Seventh Generation is a result of a two-year product development process with a paper manufacturer, Hollender says.

"Part of our effort, and part of our expense, is working with industry to get them to change the way they do things," Hollender says.

Increased use of recycled paper products will set off a whole chain of events, says Riva Litz, grovery manager of Gentle Strength Co-op, a natural foods supermarket in Tempe, Arizona (also found in this book.)

"We're running out of landfill space," Litz says. "The more we recycle, the less goes into a landfill."

And as demand for products made from recycled paper increases, so will the incentive for recycling, she adds.

Perhaps best of all, the price of recycled paper products is competitive. A 450-sheet roll of Charmin (from a nine-roll pack) costs 52¢ at one major grocery store in Tempe. A 500-sheet roll of recycled, unbleached toilet paper costs 51¢ a roll if ordered from Seventh Generation and 55¢ a roll if you grab it off the shelf at Gentle Strength. If you order in bulk at Gentle Strength, you get an additional 10% discount—dropping the price to 49 1/2¢ a roll. Additional discounts for joining—and working in—the co-op drop the price even more.

While the cost of "green" paper products is competitive with their main-stream, brand-name counterparts, more environment-friendly cleaning products are not.

A non-toxic, phosphate-free automatic dishwasher soap costs 22¢ an ounce at Gentle Strength and 34¢ an ounce at Seventh Generation. A 50-ounce bottle of Cascade was recently priced as $2.89—about 6¢ an ounce.

A regular laundry soap such as Ultra Tide will clean you clothes for about 20¢ a load less than green laundry soaps. Liquid laundry soaps, however, are about the same cost.

Green cleaners are better for the environment, Hollender says, because they don't contain artificial dyes and fragrances, or phosphates. Phosphates are a fertilizer that can cause algae blooms in lakes and rivers, choking life out of the water. Green cleaners also don't use petroleum-based chemicals.

The reasons for the higher cost of green cleaning products, Hollender says, is low volume and higher cost of materials. Most natural cleaning products "are made in small quantities by small companies using materials that in any quantity cost more money," he explains.

Vegetable-based soaps and surfactants (the chemical that lifts dirt from the clothes) cost 25¢ more than the petroleum-based surfactants, Middle East crisis or no Middle East crisis, he says.

But Hollender says he expects prices to drop as demand grows and manufacturers can take advantage of economies of scale.

History seems to support his theory. Sales at Seventh Generation are up 800% in 1990 compared to 1989, Hollender says. And since going into business in August 1988, "almost across the board our prices have gone down over the past two years," he says.

The Turtle Lady and Her Ridley Sea Turtles

★ **The Turtle Lady**

Ila Loetscher:
The Turtle Lady

If you're in the South Padre Island area of Texas, everyone says, "You must see the Turtle Lady." There are no big signs to tell you the way to her place, but everyone knows and is glad to help give directions. When you arrive, you realize that this is her home! Twice a week, she opens the doors to her home to give visitors the chance to see her turtles and to explain her work.

The Turtle Lady is Ila Loetscher, and the turtles are the Atlantic ridley, the world's most endangered sea turtle. After she moved to the south Texas coast from New Jersey in the mid-1960's, she joined efforts that others had begun to save this species.

This senior citizen has rescued many sea turtles that have washed ashore injured, or have been brought to her from fishermen. She nurses them back to health, and whenever possible, returns them to the sea. However, some are not able to return to the ocean, and she lovingly cares for them herself.

Those turtles that she keeps are the center of the "performance" she gives at her home. She jumps right into the pond she has built for the turtles, picks them up, hugs them, and explains her work. The donations she receives from the public help fund her work, which would otherwise be too expensive for her to continue on her own.

Besides turtle nursing, she has joined other rescue efforts. There's a small strip of Mexican coast called Rancho Nuevo. This is a mile-long area that is the exclusive nesting area of the ridleys. Unfortunately, poachers have been raiding the area for the turtle meat and shells. In the 1960's, conservationists thought that perhaps the turtles might return to the area where they were hatched, and decided to transplant eggs to the south Texas coast, hoping that the adult turtles would return there to nest.

For years, Ila and this group brought eggs from Mexico to Texas, with the cooperation of the Mexican authorities. They would bury the eggs in the Texas sand, and two months later the hatchlings appeared. Eventually they scurried off to sea.

In later years, the conservationists decided to bring hatchlings instead of eggs. It's still too early to tell if these efforts will lure the adult ridleys back to the Texas coast at maturity to nest. And even though the turtle's numbers are still decreasing by 3 to 4 percent each year, it's been felt that the decline would be greater without the efforts of the conservationists.

Ila's efforts have brought her national attention. She has been on the Johnny Carson and David Letterman shows. She also received a Special Conservation Achievement Award from the National Wildlife Federation.

But if you've met Ila, you know that she doesn't do this for fame or attention. She does it because she truly loves these turtles.

Seven Things You Can Do To Save The Rainforests

Reprinted by permission of the Rainforest Action Movement,
430 E. University, Ann Arbor MI 48109
(313) 764-2147.

1 **Evaluate your consumption patterns.** Buy only products which are environmentally sustainable. This means goods whose production does not contribute to deforestation or environmental destruction. Every little bit counts: selecting the right toilet paper or timber can prevent forests from being wiped out. Learn to check labels and to check up on the activities of companies whose products you buy.

2 **Reduce, Reuse, Recycle.** Reduce the amount of packaging on products you buy. Farmer Jack's and the food co-ops sell bulk food; no forests destroyed here. Reuse food containers. Reuse boxes; reuse envelopes. Using things twice uses half of the resources. Recycle newspapers, white paper, colored paper, cardboard, tin cans, bottles. Each three feet of newspaper recycled saves more than one tree.

3 **Don't eat processed beef products.** Avoid McDonald's, Burger King, Campbell's beef soups, and canned pet foods. Each year, the U.S. imports over 120 million pounds of beef from Central American countries. Two-thirds of these countries' forests have been cleared to raise cattle, whose meat is exported to profit the U.S. food industry. Because beef is not labeled with its country of origin, there is no way to trace it. Write to the Secretary of Agriculture and ask for a beef labeling law:

> Secretary of Agriculture
> 14th and Independence Ave SW
> Washington DC 20250

4 **Don't Buy:**
Conoco Oil or Gas. Conoco is involved in stripping Ecuadorian rainforest to drill for oil.

 Seven Things You Can Do To Save The Rainforests

Tropical hardwoods such as mahogany, teak, purpleheart, rosewood or ebony, unless sustainably grown. Ask your shopkeeper or do your own research to determine the wood's origin. Other woods to watch out for are redwood, Douglas fir, Sitka spruce, and yellow cedar, which are stripped from our own northwestern rainforests.

Virgin paper products. Each year, the U.S. imports tens of millions of dollars of Brazilian rainforest pulp to product paper. Use recycled paper and keep the forests in Brazil.

5 Do Buy:

Orange juice from non-tropical areas. Forest are cleared for citrus plantations just as they are for cattle ranches. These plantations do little to provide local people with money, and do nothing to provide them with food. Buy Florida orange juice instead, such as Tropicana Pure Premium. Check the label for the country of origin.

Recycled paper products. Ask your copyshop to start carrying recycled paper. Ask your boss or teachers to copy on recycled paper. Buy recycled products from EarthCare Paper and others (listed in this book in "Paper Products" chapter.)

Biodegradable household products. Garbage bags, toilet paper, and towels. These consume fewer resources to produce and are less polluting. Seventh Generation and others carry these products (listed in this book.)

Sustainably grown forest products. These include nuts, spices, medicines, and responsibly harvest woods. Buying these products tells the countries that they can make money in sustainable ways, and that forest destruction is, in the long run, unprofitable. Look for personal care products by the Body Shop and food products by Ben & Jerry's and Community Products (found in this book.)

6 Pick up a pen. Demand that legislators support policies that support forest preservation, and that they stop those causing their destruction.

7 Help protect indigenous peoples who are fighting for their forest homes. Worldwide outcry has helped people protect their forests from Asia to the Americas. Rainforest protection is as much a people issue as it is a trees issue. Contact Cultural Survival (found in this book.)

Seven Things You Can Do To Save The Rainforests

Ben and Jerry's®
Combining Business With a Social Mission

Ben & Jerry's ice cream company of Vermont is not your ordinary $58 million a year type of business. This company operates under a strong philosophical influence and has a defined social mission. Headed by two unconventional business-men, Ben Cohen and Jerry Greenfield, the company works to promote recycling, preserving the rainforest and peace. They believe in what the Buddhists call Right Livelihood—earning your living in a way that brings out the best in you and does some good in the world.

Ben and Jerry have been making ice cream since 1978 after taking a $5 correspondence course from Penn State on ice-cream making. They began with a mere $12,000 investment and starting serving customers their ice cream in a renovated gas station in Burlington, Vermont. By 1980, they began delivery routes to independent stores, using an old Volkswagen. By 1981, they achieved national attention when *Time* magazine said that Ben and Jerry's had "the best ice cream in the world." In 1984, Mark Barnicle of the Boston *Globe* said that "Ben and Jerry's Heath Bar Crunch is the greatest ice cream in America." And in 1987, *Life* magazine featured Ben and Jerry's in a double-page feature.

Growth for the company hasn't always been easy. Haagen-Daz tried to limit their distribution, and Ben & Jerry's has had to file two lawsuits against parent company Pillsbury to keep from becoming stifled. Now Dreyers Grand Ice Cream is the master distributor for Ben and Jerry's for most markets outside the Northeast.

Ben Cohen has continuously been involved with social causes. After a Grateful Dead concert for the rainforest in 1988, he met Jason Clay, director of Cultural Survival, an organization involved with rainforest preservation. One of the things that Clay thought would be lifesaving to the rainforests was to prove that the products they could produce are more beneficial in the long run than having trees slashed and burned for short-term gain. He had samples of Brazil nuts and cashews that had been gently harvested by native people.

Cohen's ever-active imagination started working on a project that he thought would help market these nuts. He founded Community Products, Inc., and experimented with recipes until he produced a buttercrunch treat he called Rainforest Crunch. This delicious concoction was an almost instant success. It was called "sublime" by the *New York Times* and "Conscience Candy" by *Food & Wine* magazine.

"Business and economics have been the root cause of destroying the rainforests," says Cohen. "What we're doing here with Rainforest Crunch is using business and the marketplace to turn things around and help preserve the rainforests."

Community Products buys the nuts from Cultural Survival, then donates 40% of its profits to rainforest preservation groups and environmental projects, and 20% of its profits to "1% for Peace," a nonprofit organization advocating legislation to reallocate 1% of the US Defense budget to fund programs promoting peace through understanding.

Ben and Jerry's Rainforest Crunch Ice Cream, flavored with Rainforest Crunch, was introduced in 1988. Sales of the ice cream indirectly benefit rainforest preservation activities. One of the projects is helping Brazilian people set up a nut-shelling cooperative.

Although the Rainforest Crunch Ice Cream has attracted great national attention, Ben & Jerry's has also been active in other projects. They have collaborated with Greyston Bakery of Yonkers, New York, to produce Ben & Jerry's Chocolate Fudge Brownie Ice Cream.

Greyston Bakery is a member of Greyston Community Network, a group that reinvests profits into programs designed to help the homeless with housing, training and jobs. The Greyston Bakery supplies 30,000 pounds of brownies a month for Ben & Jerry's Chocolate Fudge Brownie Ice Cream, which will increase Greyston's annual income by $750,000. This money will help families start living independent, self-sufficient lives and will help revitalize the Yonkers economy.

Another Ben & Jerry's flavor helps support their social mission. The company buys wild blueberries harvested by the Passamaquoddy Indian tribe in

Ben and Jerry's® Environmental Program

Ben & Jerry's has a Green Team headed by Gail Mayville, the company's Environmental Program Developer. The company's goal is to be 100% involved in recycling, conservation, source reduction and avoiding disposables.

Here are some of the things the company does:

★ They use a Solar Aquatics Waste water treatment program, eliminating the need for chemicals to treat waste water.

★ They recycle their plastic egg yolk pails (100,000 lbs per year).

★ They use biodegradable cleaning products.

★ They recycle corrugated cardboard.

★ Their ice cream shops use recycled napkins.

★ They recycle office paper, magazines and newspapers.

★ Company stationary, computer paper and laserprinter paper is 100% recycled, unbleached paper.

★ Printer ribbons are re-inked.

★ Office pens are refillable.

★ They encourage the use of reusable dishes and flatware in the lunchroom.

★ They have improved lighting for energy conservation.

★ They have installed control devices on plant machinery and utilities for energy conservation.

★ They are converting mobile ice cream sampling trucks to photovoltaic refrigeration.

★ They advocate employee carpools.

★ They participate in Vermont's Green-Up Day, an annual ecology event.

★ Their Green Market Day proceeds go to the Environmental Federation of America.

★ The company donates 7.5% of pre-tax income to environmental and peace organizations through Ben & Jerry's Foundation.

eastern Maine for Ben & Jerry's Wild Maine Blueberry Ice Cream. This employs hundreds of members of the tribe.

"Wild Maine Blueberry is another step in how we're defining what caring capitalism is all about," said Cohen. "Our goal is to integrate concern for the community in every business decision we make."

Ben & Jerry's has made a difference by purchasing ingredients from sources that will help improve that quality of life for people and also by donating to worthy causes. They give 7.5% of pre-tax profits to environmental and peace concerns. They have won prestigious awards for their success at combining business with their social consciences. (See chart of awards.)

Within the company, they are always trying to keep harmony between business and the environment. They have a Green Team that oversees the company's environmental commitment. (See Ben & Jerry's Environmental Program.)

Thank goodness for role models like Ben & Jerry's, and may their continued success show the marketplace that it truly is possible to do good while doing well!

> **Ben & Jerry's**
> **Rt 100, Box 240**
> **Waterbury VT 05676**
> **(802) 244-5641**

Ben and Jerry's® Awards

✓ **1987**—Named by *Esquire* Register to the magazine's "Annual honor roll of men and women whose accomplishments, values and dreams reflect America at its best."

✓ **1988**—Received the Corporate Giving Award from the Council on Economic Priorities, presented by Joanne Woodward at a reception in New York City, for donating 7.5% of pre-tax income to nonprofit organizations through the Ben & Jerry's Foundation.

✓ **1988**—Named US Small Business Persons of the Year by President Reagan in a White House Rose Garden ceremony.

✓ **1989**—Received Columbia University's Lawrence A. Wien Prize for corporate social responsibility.

★ **Ben and Jerry's**

Green Cross Certification System:
Identifying Environmental Excellence

Consumers have long been able to identify certified organic foods because of the various organizations that certify organic producers (Organic Crop Improvement Association, Organic Grapes into Wine Alliance, California Certified Organic Farmers, etc.) But how is a consumer able to identify whether or not a product is certifiably environmentally-sound?

"One of the biggest single problems the consumer has had, from an environmental standpoint, is being able to differentiate truth from fiction and the significance of those claims once they are understood," said Gary Swain, of Webster Industries, a company producing trash bags from 80% recycled plastics.

There have been no certifying agencies for this purpose. As the number of environmental claims grows, so does the confusion surrounding these claims. That's where Green Cross comes in.

The Green Cross Certification Company is a neutral scientific certification organization established to independently verify manufacturer's claims of outstanding environmental achievement. Through their certification program, they assist manufacturers in reassuring consumers and retailers that their products meet top environmental standards. Stanley P. Rhodes, President of Green Cross said:

> The Green Cross program was founded in the belief that the most enduring solutions for the environment will arise out of voluntary industry achievement. Our certification program rewards environmental excellence in the marketplace, answering consumer concerns and reassuring retailers that the products they promote meet significant environmental standards.

The goals of Green Cross are::

1. To support manufacturers in meeting the highest environmental standards in products and packaging.

2. To provide retailers with a means of distinguishing and identifying significant environmental product claims.

3. To provide consumers with added assurance of independent certification of environmental claims.

Green Cross maintains complete financial independence from outside investment, which allows the organization to provide true neutral evaluation. They wish to keep the certification process free from any conflict of interest. All certification work is performed according to strict scientific standards by a professional team of scientists. Green Cross determines state-of-the-art industry standards.

"It's (environmental certification) going to make companies a whole lot more responsible in their claims and in what they produce," said Steve Peterson of Confab Company, which produces paper towels, napkins and facial tissues from 100% recycled material.

There are many measures of environmental achievement. The goal of Green Cross is to identify those achievements under such categories as:

1. Recycled Content Certification (Products of Packaging)—Determines recycled content at state-of-the-art levels with standards that emphasize diverting waste from landfills.

2. Biodegradability Certification (Cleaning Products)—Soaps, detergents and cleansers that demonstrate complete biodegradability under aerobic and nonaerobic conditions, with no evidence of toxic buildup in the environment.

3. Energy Efficient Certification (Light Bulbs, Appliances, etc)—Products manufactured in state-of-the-art manner that result in maximum energy savings during manufacturing as well as in use.

4. Sustainable Resources Certification (Cloth, Wood, etc)—Products or packages manufactured from renewable materials that are produced or harvested in an environmentally sustainable manner.

Certification procedures are very thorough. They inspect the factories, review operations and audit purchase records, including receipts of materials.

"The program helps build a recycling economy," said Sandra Jerebek,

 Green Cross Certification System

S.C.S.
Green Cross
C E R T I F I E D

This Williamette paper grocery bag has been independently certified to be made from at least 40% recycled paper fibers.

Green Cross Logo
This logo is always used with qualifying information.

director of the group Californians Against Waste. "I think that the public needs to realize that if people are not buying recycled-content products, they're not really recycling."

Green Cross performs all services on a straight fee-for-service basis, charging only to cover the costs of the actual services performed in conducting the product claims audit. Fees have ranged from $1,000 to $10,000 depending on the extent of services performed. Once a product has been certified, it may use the Green Cross logo at no additional cost. The logo is always accompanied by a specific certification message. (See example.)

The company provides special Weekly Product Bulletins to all interested retailers to keep them up-to-date on the latest certified products.

Consumers should look for the following products that have earned the Green Cross Certification:

★ Williamette Industries, Willcycle™ paper grocery bags, 40% recycled content.

★ Webster Industries, Renew™ (50% recycled content) and Good Sense™ (80% recycled content) trash, lawn & leaf bags.

★ Green Fields Inc., Fire to Go™ firelogs, 100% recycled content.

★ Clorox Company, Clorox 2 Bleach packaging, 81% recycled content.

Green Cross Certification System

★ Confab Companies, Today's Choice™ paper towels, napkins, bath tissue, facial tissue, all 100% recycled content.

★ Dolco Packaging Company, polystyrene egg carton (non CFC) made of at least 25% recycled content.

★ Foodworks, Inc., GrownRight™ apple juice bottles, 22% recycled content.

★ Orchids Paper Products, HOPE™ and START™ paper towels, napkins, bath tissue and facial tissue, all 100% recycled content.

★ Plasco Press Company, Inc., Bottlesack™ plastic shopping bag, 30% recycled content.

★ Pope & Talbot, Inc., Capri™, Pert™, Nature's Choice™, Surety™, Gentle Touch™ and Sun Glory™ paper towels, napkins, bath tissue and facial tissue, all 100% recycled content.

★ Ball-Incon Glass Company, glass products, recycled content.

Retailers planning to highlight Green Cross labeled products include Ralph's Grocery in southern California, Raley's in northern California, Fred Meyer Inc. of Portland and ABCO Markets of Phoenix.

Green Cross Certification Company
A Division of Scientific Certification Systems, Inc.
1611 Telegraph Avenue, Suite 1111
Oakland, CA 94612-2113
(415) 832-1415
FAX # (415) 832-0359
Toll-free 1-800-829-1416

Chapter One:
Baby & Children's Products

Cloth diapers, toys, books & educational materials are some of the environmentally sensitive products found in this chapter. Longer lists of educational materials, including curriculum, are found in "Educational Materials" chapter.

Baby Bunz & Company, PO Box 1717, Sebastopol CA 95473. (707) 829-5347. Specializes in a full line of natural diapering products, which include the top quality Nikky™ line, as well as their own custom cloth diapers. They also have a carefully selected collection of natural fiber baby-wear and accessories. Examples: Nikky 100% lambswool felt, non-irritating and non-allergenic diapers, $13 each; Nikky all-cotton waterproof diapers, $11.95 each; Nikky training pants, cotton knits and terry, waterproofed, $8.75; Rubber Duckies™ pull on covers, lightweight, waterproof, $4 each; Baby Bjorn™ potty, a one-piece potty, lightweight, good for travel, $12.95; "Little One" doll, cotton velour with wool stuffing, $16.50; much more. Direct mail orders to consumers. Also wholesale prices for stores. Informative, color catalog available to readers for $1.

Bumkins International Inc., 291 North 700 East, Payson UT 84651. (801) 465-3995. (801) 465-9330. Bumkins are waterproof, washable, all-in-one diaper liners. They come in baby and toddler sizes. No pins, no folding, soft and absorbent, environmentally safe. Sample diaper (baby size) $5.95; toddler size $7.95. Brochure available.

Co-op America, 2100 "M" St NW, Suite 403, Washington DC 20063. (202) 872-5307. Toll-free 1-800-424-2667. This is a non-profit, member-controlled, worker-managed association linking socially responsible businesses and consumers in a national network, a new alternative marketplace. Co-op America allows consumers to align buying habits with values. Basic information found in "Organizations" chapter.

Baby items from catalog: cloth diapers, Dovetails™ paper diaper liners, and Nikky's™ water proof diaper covers from pure 100% cotton.

Children's items from their catalog: *365 Ways to Save Our Planet in 1991* page-a-day calendar with a little reminder each day how we can make a difference, $9.95; Hugg-a-Planet toy made of 100% cotton, $18.95; *A Kid's Point of View of the Environment* is songs from Michael Mish based on what kids told him about the environment, audio cassette, $9.95; Arcobaleno (rainbow) is a puzzle and a construction toy in one, ages 3-8, from Learning Materials Workshop, $39.50; "Endangered Species" ($29.50) or "Ocean" ($27.50) are very unique puzzles in layers, ages 3 to adult, by Coyote Collections of Oregon.

Products from the catalog are found in "Recycling," "Energy Conservation," "Books," "Organically Grown," "Household & Personal Care Products," and "Paper Products " chapters.

Country Comfort, PO Box 3, 28537 Nuevo Valley Dr, Nuevo CA 92367. (714) 657-3438. This company makes pure and natural herbal baby powder, baby oil and baby cream. The powder is very absorbent but not abrasive because it contains pure mineral clay bu no talc or fillers. Five herbal powders are combined with scents of orange and lavender oils. All of the products contain no preservatives.

Diap-Air, 3331 Gold Run Rd, Boulder CO 80302. (303) 442-3334. Diaper covers (made with Gore-tex) and cloth diapers.

Earth's Best, PO Box 887, Middlebury VT 05753. 1-800-442-4221. Manufacturer of a complete line of certified organic baby foods (purees, juices and cereals) grown without synthetic pesticides or fertilizer and prepared without any salt, sugar, fillers or preservatives. In addition to requiring certification from the growers, the company sends their representatives to inspect each farm during the growing season. At harvest, each crop is independently lab-tested so they can be sure of the purity.

The Council on Economic Priorities, which publishes *Shopping for a Better World*, recently awarded the company a "Top" rating for its commitment to the environment.

Some of the flavors: carrots, green beans & rice, peas & brown rice, sweet potatoes, apples, bananas, pears, apple juice, pear juice, brown rice cereal & mixed whole grain cereal.

These products are available in the baby food section of supermarkets on the East Coast and the West Coast and in Colorado, and in natural food stores nationwide and by mail order.

Energy Store, PO Box 3507, Santa Cruz CA 95063-3507. (408) 464-1938. Toll-free 1-800-288-1938. This is a mail order business specializing in energy conserving products. Free catalog available by calling toll-free number. Children's toy available: solar speed boat, $20.

★ Chapter One: Baby & Children's Products

More products listed in "Books," "Educational Materials" and "Energy Conservation" chapters.

Gentle Strength Co-op, 234 West University Drive, Tempe AZ 85281. (602) 968-4831. This store handles many environmentally sensitive lines of products. Baby products: cotton diapers and accessories.

More products found in "Household & Personal Care Products," "Organically Grown," "Paper Products," "Books," and "Magazines, Newsletters & Brochures" chapters.

Marvelous Toys Works, 2111 Eastern Ave., Baltimore MD 21231. (301) 276-5130. Their two catalogs offer durable toys made of the finest materials with no sharp edges, splinters, or breakable parts. All materials used are non-toxic. Creativity and imagination are encouraged by the use of these toys. Products include: pine rocking horse, 14" high, 29" long, $30; pine doll cradle, 12" by 24", $24; Limber Jack, a rhythm folk toy that originated in Appalachia, $13; People board, 16 "people" in four different colors sit on a 7" square maple board, unlimited uses, $6.50. Also puzzles, pull toys, lots of unit blocks, more. Satisfaction unconditionally guaranteed. Write for catalog.

Papa Don's Toys, Walker Creek Road, Walton OR 97490. (503) 935-7604. I first found out about Papa Don's Toys while doing our book *Home Business Resource Guide* a couple of years ago.

The Council on Economic Priorities, which publishes *Shopping for a Better World,* recently awarded the Earth's Best company a "Top" rating for its commitment to the environment. Earth's Best is a manufacturer of a complete line of certified organic baby foods.

I was so impressed with this business—and the people who run it—that I profiled them in a special article in that book.

This company makes original hardwood toys that incorporate color, movement, and sound. All paints, oils, and materials are guaranteed to be non-toxic, non-splintering, and safe for teething. Stress points are reinforced. Their 16-page color catalog is full of treasures: roller rattle, $5; crib spinner, $14; pull-whale, $6.50; push rainbow maker (18 balls of six colors blend to create a rainbow when the toy is pushed, plus jingle bells for sound) $18; and everyone's favorite: rolling letters (wooden letters on wheels) $3 each. They guarantee satisfaction. Send for free catalog.

Pets 'N People, Inc., 5312 Ironwood Street, Rancho Palos Verdes CA 90274. (213) 373-1559. Manufacturers of environmentally sensitive cleaning products. Mother's Little Miracle is a non-toxic formula for quickly and

Chapter One: Baby & Children's Products

safely cleaning up baby's messiest messes. Deodorizes and removes stains. More products listed in "Household and Personal Care Products" chapter.

R. Duck Company, 650 Ward Dr, Suite H, Santa Barbara CA 93111. (805) 964-4343. Toll-free orders 1-800-422-DUCK (3825). Concerned about disposable diapers in landfills? This company offers a solution to help with your cloth diapers. They have Rubber Duckies™, a pull-on diaper cover. Comes in various colors and sizes, $4 each. Also has Wrap Ups™ that are pinless diaper covers that close with Velcro®. Also comes in various colors and sizes, $5.50 each.

Real Goods Trading Company, 966 Mazzoni St, Ukiah CA 95482. (707) 468-9214. FAX # (707) 468-0301. Order toll-free 1-800-762-7325. This company has an extensive 106-page catalog full of energy-saving equipment and supplies. Products for the younger generation include: 12-volt baby bottle warmer; solar wooden model kits for airplane, helicopter, windmill; 150 Solar Experiments kit, $39; Solar Educational Kit, $9; solar speed boat, $15; Whole Earth Globe, Nasa version $7, wildlife version, $7; three-dimensional state maps; computer terrain maps; *Ecology Action Workbook & Dictionary* for children, $3. More items listed in "Books," "Energy Conservation," "Household & Personal Care Products," "Clean Air, Clean Water" and "Recycling"

chapters.

RMED International Inc., PO Box 3667, 16770 Johnson Drive, Industry CA 91744. (818) 961-7800. FAX # (818) 333-6647. Toll-free 1-800-344-6379. Manufacturers of TenderCare™ disposable biodegradable, chemical-free diapers and Tushies™ disposable diapers that use 50% less plastic than most brands and do not use any tree, wood or plastic products. If you must use disposable diapers, at least use some that are less impacting on the environment.

Seventh Generation, Colchester VT 05446-1672. (802) 655-3116. FAX toll-free # 1-800-456-1139. Order toll-free 1-800-456-1177. Customer service toll-free 1-800-456-1197.

Seventh Generation is one of the most well-known companies for environmentally safe consumer products. Their 48-page catalog "Products for a Healthy Planet" ($2) contains an extraordinary variety of products. They also practice what they preach. For instance, they recycle their office paper, and reuse cardboard boxes for shipping. They have a 1% fund that goes to environmental organizations.

Products for babies include organic baby food and fruit juice; baby food masher so that you can make your own baby food; gentle baby soap & shampoo; cloth diapers; Bumkins all-in-one diapering system; Nikky's Velcro™ diaper covers; un-petroleum jelly; and dioxin-free baby wipes.

If you must use disposable diapers,

try theirs that are bleached with hydrogen peroxide, not chlorine. Also, the manufacturing process for these disposables uses about half the trees normally associated with the production of disposable diapers.

They have baby products made from "green cotton" which is 100% pure unbleached cotton fiber, fabricated without dyes and without formaldehyde. Items from green cotton are: wash mitt & towel; comforter; comforter cover; and crib sheets.

Children's environmental books include: *The Lorax* by Dr. Seuss is a tale about the deforestation of the Truffula Trees ($11.95); *My First Nature Book*—A life-size guide to discovering the world around you, ages 6 and up ($9.95); *Ecology*—A practical introduction with projects and activities, ages 10 and up ($6.95); *The Usborn Science Encyclopedia,* ages 10 and up ($10.95); *50 Simple Things Kids Can Do to Save the Earth*, ages 8 and up ($6.95); *Snips & Snails & Walnut Whales,* ages 8 and up, nature crafts for kids ($8.95).

Unique toys include: a recycled plastic throwing disc ($2.95); yo-yo made from recycled plastic ($1.95); juggling globes (beanbags that look like the earth) for ages 8 and up ($12.50); The Green Game, a board game that asks questions about the environment ($29.95); solar powered toy ($7.95); and their bestselling toy—the Hugg-a-Planet ($19.95, baby $11.95).

There are so many products in this catalog that additional information can

---

> **The audio cassette tape "All in This Together" by Sisters' Choice won a 1990 Parents' Choice Gold Award.**

be found in these chapters: "Household & Personal Care Products," "Books," "Educational Materials," "Paper Products," "Recycling," "Energy Conservation," and "Organically Grown."

Sisters' Choice, 1450 6th St, Berkeley CA 94710. (415) 524-5804. Cassette tape called *All In This Together* (Candy Forest, Nancy Schimmel and the Singing Rainbows Youth Ensemble, ages 9-15, with special guests Laurie Lewis & Rosie Radiator) is 15 ecology songs for the whole family. The songs are folk, jazz & rock numbers about the disappearing rain forest, pet overpopulation, endangered species, the urban forests and other songs about the environment. Some of the song titles are: "My Sister's a Whale in the Sea," "Must Be Johnny Appleseed," "Eating Up the Forest." This tape was a 1990 Parents' Choice Gold Award Winner. Cassette is $10. The company is in the process of developing and testing a study guide to go along with this tape, so inquire about these if you're interested.

The company also has a book called *Frogs That Sing: An Ecology Songbook* which has the song from *All In This Together* plus other songs on the environment by Malvina Reynolds. Melody lines with guitar chords or

---

Chapter One: Baby & Children's Products

piano arrangements. Available 1991, $10.

See also "Seminars, Speakers & Workshops" chapter.

Snugglups Diapers, PO Box 7BB, St. Francis KY 40062. (502) 865-5501. 1-800-876-0674. Snugglups are a simple, easy-to-use environmentally-friendly alternative to disposable diapers as well as traditional cotton diapers. They are shaped like a disposable diapers. They have gathered elastic leg openings and close with Velcro®. They are made with quality craftsmanship from 100% cotton flannel. Prices start from $35 per dozen. Packaged in recycled cardboard boxes.

Solar Electric Engineering, Inc., 116 4th St, Santa Rosa CA 95401. (707) 542-1990. FAX # (707) 542-4358. This is a publicly owned corporation that has been committed to bringing to the marketplace environmentally sound products at affordable prices to the consumer. They have a 40-page "Environmental Catalog," with these products for children: Nikkys® diaper covers made of terry cloth and a water-proof vinyl middle; Hugg-a-Planet toy, small $10.95, regular, $19.95; solar speedboat, $15.95; solar wooden model kits for helicopter, airplane or windmill, $15.95 each; 150 Solar Experiments kit, $37; special T-shirt that kids can design and then wash out and design again, comes with "Fun "Facts" information and in various styles.

More items listed in "Books," "Recycling," "Paper Products," "Clean Air, Clean Water," "Energy Conservation," and "Magazines, Newsletters & Brochures."

Wildlife Games Inc., PO Box 247, Ivy VA 22945. (804) 972-7016. Producers of The Whale Game™ survival at sea, a board game with an objective of building a whale family and guiding it home. Carefully researched "Whale Facts" on game cards make this educational as well as fun. $19 postpaid.

Chapter Two: Books

There are many great books available on the environment, for both children and adults. This chapter lists many books by publishers and also by catalog companies which carry them as well. At the end of the chapter, for cross reference, there's an alphabetical list of titles with the companies that carry them.

Aatec Publications, PO Box 7119, Ann Arbor MI 48107. (313) 995-1470. Publishers of books on residential photovoltaics (solar electricity). Their titles are : *The New Solar Electric Home: The Photovoltaics How-to Handbook* by Joel Davidson, a full 416 well-illustrated pages of facts, how-to, tools, diagrams, charts, tables, formulas, worksheets, for getting your personal power plant started, $18.95; *RVers Guide to Solar Battery Charging: 12 volt DC—120 volt AC Inverters* by Noel and Barbara Kirkby is a how-to guide for installing your photovoltaic system in your recreational vehicle, $12.95; *Practical Photovoltaics: Electricity from Solar Cells* (2nd Edition) by Dr. Richard J. Komp is an understandable guide to the theory, design, manufacturing future of solar cell technology, *Whole Earth Catalog* said, "Read this and you'll know what you're doing," $16.95.

They also sell other titles on energy conservation: *At Home with Alternative Energy: A Comprehensive Guide to Creating Your Own Systems* by Michael Hackelman examines major alternatives—sun, wind, water, wood and methane—and explores methods needed to create your own alternative energy system, $9.95; *Electric Vehicles: Design and Build Your Own* by Michael Hackelman was called "a no-nonsense look" at this non-polluting type of vehicle by *Mother Earth News*, $9.95; *Resource-Efficient Housing Guide* by Robert Sardinsky with Jon Klusmire is a directory that lists and critiques periodicals, catalogs, books,

schools organizations and agencies that deal with resource-efficient house design, construction, etc, $15. Additional titles in their catalog.

Adirondack Mountain Club, Inc., RR 3 Box 3055, Lake George NY 12845. (518) 523-3441. (518) 668-4447. Books available are guidebooks and histories of the Adirondack region. Maps of the regional also for sale.

Also listed in "Eco-tourism," "Seminars, Speakers & Workshops" and "Organizations" chapters.

Air Chek, Inc., Box 2000, Arden NC 28704. (704) 684-0893. FAX # (704) 684-8498. Toll-free 1-800-247-2435 or 1-800-257-2366. Lab and manufacturer of radon test devices and distributor of other environmental tests. Books about radon: *Radon, The Invisible Threat* is an easy-to-understand book by Michael LaFavore, $11.95; *Radon: A Homeowner's Guide to Detection and Control* tells how to determine if you have a radon problem and how to solve it, $2.95.

Alfred A. Knopf, Inc., 201 E 50 St, New York NY 10022. (212) 751-2600. FAX # (212) 572-2593. Toll-free 1-800-638-6460. Publishers of *Saving the Earth: A Citizen's Guide to Environmental Action* by Will Steger & Jon Bowermaster, 306 pgs, $19.95. Called "an environmental book of hope," this book explains the environmental problems facing us in layman's terms, then offers possible solutions. There are chapters on: global warming, ozone depletion, smog, acid rain, rain forests, garbage, hazardous waste, water pollution, overpopulation, and more. Each chapter examines the causes, effects and solutions of the problem presented, then tells it again with storyboards (cartoons). At the end of each chapter there's sections called "Individual Action," "Government Action," "Reading," and "Organizations to Contact." This book is well organized, easy to understand, and an essential book for anyone who wants to understand the environmental problems facing us.

Amberwood, Rt 1, Box 206, Milner GA 30257. (404) 358-2991. Cruelty-free products for home and personal use. Books include: *Animal Ingredients and Their Alternatives,* a 16-page booklet by Nermin Biuikmihci and Carol Watson, $2.50; *Animal Liberation* by Peter Singer, $4.95; *The Case for Animal Rights* by Tom Regan, $10.95 paperback; *For the Vegetarian in You* by Billy Ray Boyd, $6.95; *The Cookbook for People Who Love Animals* with over 300 recipes, $8.95; and more.

More information in the "Household & Personal Use" chapter.

American Council for an Energy-Efficient Economy, 1001 Connecticut Ave NW, Suite 535, Washington DC 20036. (202) 429-8873. Source for the book *1991 Consumer Guide to Home Energy Savings* by Alex Wilson, from *Home Energy Magazine,* 252 pgs, $6.95. Dennis Hayes, international

director of Earth Day 1990 said that this book "represents the current state of the art for energy-conscious American consumers." This guide provides numerous affordable, practical and easily understandable steps consumers can take to make their homes more energy efficient, cut their utility bills, and avoid harming the environment—all without discomfort or inconvenience. Highly illustrated; lots of informative charts.

American Solar Energy Society, 2400 Central Ave, B-1, Boulder CO 80301. (303) 443-3130. A national society for professionals and others involved in the fields of solar energy. Books available from their publication list: *The New Solar Home Book* is a comprehensive guide to the fundamentals of solar energy, $16.95; *The Greenhouse Trap: What We're Doing to the Atmosphere and How We Can Slow Global Warming* provides the essential background that citizens need to know, $9.95; *Solar Resources* describes the evolution of theoretical models, algorithms and equipment for measuring, analyzing and predicting the quantity and composition of solar radiation, $45; *Affordable Passive Solar Homes* shows over 40 projects of various sizes, $20; *Natural Lighting: How to Use Daylight,* $7; *Heat Saving Home Insulation* answers questions about using cellulose, masonry walls, fiberglass batts, more, $7; *How to Design and Build a Solar Swimming Pool Heater,* $5. More titles available.

The Athene Series/Pergamon Press,

Inc., Maxwell House, Fairview Park, Elmsford NY 10523. (914) 592-7700. Toll-free for orders only 1-800-257-5755. Telex: 13-7328. Publishers of *The Recurring Silent Spring* by H. Patricia Hynes, 225 pgs. This book discusses the life and work of Rachel Carson, who was the author of *Silent Spring,* the book that launched a campaign against pesticides. Hynes' book shows how Carson aroused the world into environmental concern and its effects on the Environmental Protection Agency. Softcover, $12.95; hardcover $27.50.

Avon Books, 105 Madison Ave, New York NY 10016. (212) 481-5600. FAX # (212) 532-2172. Toll-free 1-800-238-0658. Telex: 88-0261. Publishers of *A Kid's Guide to How to Save the Planet* by Billy Goodman, 137 pgs, $2.95. This illustrated book tells kids what's wrong with the planet and how they can help. It tells them about recycling, extinction, overpopulation, the greenhouse effect, acid rain, energy conservation, desertification, pesticides, tropical rain forests, incineration, and more.

Ballantine/ Del Rey/ Fawcett/ Ivy Books, Division of Random House, Inc., 201 E 50th St, New York NY 10022. (212) 751-2600. Toll-free 1-800-638-6460. Ivy Books imprint published *1001 Ways to Save the Planet* by Bernadette Vallely, 285 pgs, $4.95. This book contains "green" tips for your home, your personal grooming, your children, your shopping

habits, your workplace, your travel habits, and for your community.

Basil Blackwell, Inc., 64 Depot Road, Colchester VT 05466 (order address). Toll-free order number 1-800-445-6638. Customer Service FAX # (802)878-1102.*United Nation Environment Programme: Environmental Data Report* (Second Edition, 1989-1990). International data on: environmental pollution; climate; natural resources; population; human health; energy; transportation; waste disposal; natural disasters; and international cooperation. Very precise scientific information. $44.95. *The Green Machine: Ecology & the Balance of Nature* by Wallace Arthur. This book is aimed at understanding the balance of nature (the ecosystem), how that balance is maintained, and how that balance is now threatened by human activities. A basic principles of ecology book. $19.95. *Greening Business* by John Davis. This book provides 9 practical change strategies with which to respond to the most important challenge now facing today's business leaders. It gives workable ideas for sustainable development. $24.95.

Baubiologie Hardware, 207 16th St, Unit B, Pacific Grove CA 93950. (408) 372-8626. Books about the electromagnetic pollution are: *Current Switch: How to reduce or eliminate electromagnetic pollution in the home & office* by John Banta, easy simple and understandable guidelines, $49.95; *Currents of Death: Power Lines, Computer Terminals, and the Attempt to Cover Up Their Threat to Your Health* by Paul Brodeur, $19.95; *Cross Currents: The Perils of Electropollution; The Promise of Electromedicine* by Dr. Robert O. Becker, $19.95.

Other books include: *Nontoxic & Natural: A Guide for Consumers* by Debra Lynn Dadd, $10.95; *The Nontoxic Home: Protecting Yourself and Your Family from Everyday Toxics and Health Hazards* by Debra Lynn Dadd, $9.95; *Radon: The Invisible Threat* by Michael Lafavore, $12.95; *The Smart Kitchen* by David Goldbeck that shows how to make kitchens environmentally friendly, $15.95; *Healing Environments* by Carol Venolia teachers you how buildings can influence your mental, physical and emotional well-being, $8.95; *Shepherd's Purse: Organic Pest Control Handbook* $5.95.

More information found in "Household & Personal Care Products," "Energy Conservation," "Clean Air, Clean Water," and "Educational Materials" chapters.

Beacon Press, 25 Beacon St, Boston MA 02108. (617) 742-2110. FAX # (617) 367-3237. Publishers of *The Global Ecology Handbook: What You Can Do About the Environmental Crisis* by the Global Tomorrow Coalition, 414 pgs, $16.95. This enormous book has current information on: air; water; climate change; energy; toxic waste; tropical forests; population; garbage; global warming; biological diversity; and more. This is a practical supplement to the PBS series *Race to Save the Planet.*

Cambridge University Press, 110 Midland Avenue, Port Chester NY 10573. (212) 924-3900. Toll-free order number 1-800-872-7423 outside New York State. For New York state toll-free orders 1-800-227-0247. FAX # (914) 937-4712. *Air in Danger: Ecological Perspectives of the Atmosphere* by Georg Breuer. Discusses the problems of maintaining a healthful atmosphere. $12.95. *The New Environmental Age* by Max Nicholson. This book explains the emergence of ecology and conservation from obscurity to how it is becoming a major force in the modern world. Could be called the history book of ecology. Out-of-print, but available in many libraries.

This publishing company has many scholarly and scientific titles in the field

Chapter Two: Books

of ecology. Examples: *Ecology, Recreation and Tourism; The Living Tundra; Ecological Studies in Tropical Fish Communities; New Direction in Ecological Physiology;* etc. For a complete list, send for catalog.

Celestial Arts, PO Box 7327, Berkeley CA 94707. (415) 524-1801. FAX # (415) 524-1052. Publishers of *Healing Environments* by Carol Venolia, a designer with an interest in the relationship between life and buildings. The book shows principles that readers can apply to their homes, schools, and workplaces by covering such topics as light, color, temperature, noise, air quality, plants, and design elements. The places we inhabit should bring us into greater harmony with life. $9.95, 225 pgs.

Center for Science in the Public Interest, 1875 Connecticut Ave NW #300, Washington DC 20009. (202) 332-9110. FAX # (202) 265-4954. The issues they are presently working on are organic and sustainable agriculture, food additives, nutrition and ingredient labeling, deceptive food and beverage advertising, fast food, and they serve as a watchdog of government and industry.

Books available are: *Eat, Think & Be Healthy* ($8.95) for kids with 56 activities; *Creative Food Experience for Children* ($7.95) has practical games, recipes and activities for children, 256 pgs; *Fast Food: An Eater's Guide* ($5.95) has complete nutrient breakdowns of virtually all food items of-

fered by more than one dozen chains; *Supermarket Savvy* ($29.95) teaches product by product how to read the fine print and not be misled; *Eater's Choice: The Food Lover's Guide to Lower Cholesterol* ($12.95) contains more than 200 recipes low in saturated fat and teaches how to calculate exactly how much saturated fat it's OK to eat; *Fast Vegetarian Feasts* ($12.95) is a revised edition of the book that won a "Tastemaker Award"; more.

More information in "Organizations" and "Educational Materials" chapters.

The Compassionate Consumer, PO Box 27, Jericho NY 11753. (718) 445-4134. Cruelty-free products for the home. (See "Household & Personal Care" chapter.) Books also available, such as *Fifty Simple Things You Can Do to Save the Earth,* $4.95; *Vegetarian Sourcebook,* $9.95; *Cookbook for People Who Love Animals,* $9.95; *Slaughter of the Innocent,* $3.95; *The Struggle for Animal Rights,* $5.95, and more. Catalogs are $1.

Conari Press, 1339 61st St, Emeryville CA 94608. (415) 596-4040. FAX # (415) 428-2861. Publishers of *EarthCards: Postcards You Can Sign and Send to Save the Earth,* ($6.95 trade paperback on recycled paper, 64 pages) which has an unusual format. It has 32 postcards on perforated pages, each dealing with an environmental crisis and addressed to the corporate executive or politician who has the power to change it. The book says,

"Just sign 'em, stamp 'em and send 'em." What a great idea!!!

Co-op America, 2100 "M" St NW, Suite 403, Washington DC 20063. (202) 872-5307. Toll-free 1-800-424-2667. This is a non-profit, member-controlled, worker-managed association linking socially responsible businesses and consumers in a national network, a new alternative marketplace. Co-op America allows consumers to align buying habits with values. Basic information found in "Organizations" chapter.

Books from catalog: *The Green Consumer* book and newsletter subscription, $27; *Real Goods Alternative Energy Sourcebook* is not just a catalog but 332 pages of energy saving ideas and diagrams, $10; *Nontoxic, Natural and Earthwise* is a very popular book on in-depth product information, $10.95; *The Essential Whole Earth Catalog,* $20.

Products from the catalog are found in "Recycling," "Energy Conservation," "Organically Grown," "Household & Personal Care Products," "Paper Products, " and "Baby & Children's Products" chapters.

Council of State Governments, Iron Works Pike, PO Box 11910, Lexington KY 40578-9989. (606) 252-2291. Toll-free order line 1-800-800-1910. *Resource Guide to State Environmental Management,* by R. Steven Brown & L. Edward Garner. Very comprehensive book of state environmental organization charts (who's the director of what); state environmental expenditures; and names of state environmental agencies with full address and phone numbers. 1988 edition, $40.

Council on Economic Priorities, 30 Irving Place, New York NY 10003. (212) 420-1133. Toll-free 1-800-822-6435. Their highly acclaimed book *Shopping for a Better World* has been adopted by many other nonprofit organizations and is available from CEP or other environmentally-responsible catalog companies. This book is a handy pocket size so that you can carry it shopping. This guide is great! It has chapters for shopping to end animal testing, shopping for energy alternatives, shopping to end apartheid, shopping for equal opportunity, shopping for a cleaner world, and more!! They even rate gas & oil companies. There's a form at the end of the book so you can request ratings of companies from which you generally buy products.

Chapter Two: Books ★

More in "Organizations" chapter.

Cultural Survival, Inc., 53 Church St, Cambridge MA 02138. (617) 495-2562. Order address is: Cultural Survival, 11 Divinity Ave, Cambridge MA 02138. The organization has a catalog containing many book titles, including: *Indigenous Survival Among the Bari and Arhuaco,* 77 pgs, 1987, $6.80; *Aborigines Today: Land & Justice,* 1988, $6; *The Indigenous Voice: Visions & Realities,* volume I, 432 pgs, $25.95; volume II, 329 pgs, $19.95; *Tourism: Manufacturing the Exotic,* 193 pgs, $13; and many more titles about indigenous people and their right to survive.

More information in "Magazines, Newsletters & Brochures" and "Organizations" chapters.

Dell Publishing Company, 666 Fifth Ave, New York NY 10103. (212) 765-6500. FAX # (212) 492-9698. Toll-free 1-800-223-6834. Telex: 23-8781 DELL UR. Publishers of *Save Our Planet: 750 Everyday Ways You Can Help Clean Up the Earth* by Diane MacEachern, 210 pgs, $9.95. This attractive book gives practical hints on how to make a difference by practices in your home, your garden, while shopping, at school, at the office, in the community, on vacations, and more. This book gives educational information about environmental problems at the same time it gives helpful hints for changing habits to make a difference. There's an appendix of resources and a chart about environmental organizations.

The Earthwise Consumer, PO Box 279, Forest Knolls, CA 94933. (415) 488-6614. *Nontoxic, Natural & Earthwise: How to Protect Yourself and Your Family from Harmful Products and Live in Harmony with the Earth* ($12.95, Jeremy P. Tarcher) by Debra Lynn Dadd, the editor/publisher of *The Earthwise Consumer* newsletter (more information in "Magazines, Newletters, & Brochures" chapter.) This book is billed as "the most complete guide yet assembled on products that are both good for the environment and your own personal health." Lists more than 2000 brand names, 600 mail order catalogs and 400 inexpensive do-it-yourself formulas. *The Nontoxic Home* ($9.95, Jeremy P. Tarcher) by Debra Lynn Dadd. A basic primer that identifies toxic chemicals and other health hazards in your home. Gives helpful tips.

Other books are also available from them. You can get *The Natural House* ($17.95, Simon & Schuster) by David Pearson which gives ideas for creating an ecologically-sound home environment. Also *Clean & Green* ($8.95, Ceres Press) that contains over 500 simple, natural formulas for every cleaning need. Send for the book brochure for complete list of titles available.

Earthworks Press, Box 25, 1400 Shattuck Ave, Berkeley CA 94709. (415) 841-5866. Publishers of the popular #1 bestseller *50 Simple Things You Can*

These are all excellent environmental books.

Do To Save The Earth, 50 pgs, $4.95. Each "green" tip is accompanied with appropriate information, like why it's necessary and what environmental effect the practice will have. There's a similar book for children: *50 Simple Things Kids Can Do To Save The Earth,* $6.95. Two great books that should be in every household!

Eco Source™, 9051 Mill Station Road Bldg #E, Sebastopol CA 95472. (717) 829-7957 or (707) 829-8345. Catalog of products for a cleaner, safer world. Includes many books, including *Earth Book for Kids* from the Learning Works, $9.95; *Building a Healthy Lawn,* $9.95; *The Secret Life of Plants* by Peter Tompkins and Christopher Bird for pesticide-free high-yield growing; *Non-toxic, Natural and Earthwise,* $12.95; *The Peace Catalog* by Duane Sweeney, which contains a directory of over 1000 peace organizations across the US, $14.95; *Earthright: Every Citizen's Guide,* $12.95; *50 Simple Things You Can Do to Save the Earth,* $4.95; *Shopping for a Better World,* $4.95; *Save Our Planet: 750 Everyday Ways You Can Help Clean Up The Earth* by Diane MacEachern, $9.95; and more.

Many more products in this catalog. See "Household and Personal Care," "Recycling," "Clean Air, Clean Water," "Energy Conservation" and "Educational Materials" chapters.

E. L. Foust Company, Inc., Box 105, Elmhurst IL 60126. (708) 834-4952. 1-800-225-9549. Books available

from this company are: *Nontoxic and Natural* by Debra Lynn Dadd, $9.95; *The Nontoxic Home* by Debra Lynn Dadd, $9.95; *Allergies and the Hyperactive Child* by Dr. Doris Rapp on how to alleviate hyperactivity in allergic children, $9.95; *The Impossible Child* by Dr. Doris Rapp shows you how to recognize which children have allergies and how to help them, $9.95; *Environmental Medicine* by Golos, O'Shea, Waickman & Golbitz shows how to diagnose and manage allergies, $14.95; *Why Your House May Endanger Your Health* by Dr. Alfred Zamm, $7.95; *Coping with Your Allergies* by Natalie Golos is a self-help guide to dealing with allergies, $10.95; *Your Home, Your Health & Well-Being* by David Rousseau, Dr. William Rea & Jean Enwright shows what you can do to design or renovate your house or apartment to be free of outdoor and indoor pollution, $19.95.

The main products available from this company are air purifiers. See the "Clean Air, Clean Water" chapter.

Energy Store, PO Box 3507, Santa Cruz CA 95063-3507. (408) 464-1938. Toll-free 1-800-288-1938. This is a mail order business specializing in energy conserving products. Free catalog available by calling toll-free number. Books available in catalog: *The New Solar Electric Home,* $18.95; *The Bicycle Commuting Book,* $7.95; *The Chemical-Free Lawn,* $14.95; *Cut Your Electric Bills in Half,* $9.95; *The Energy Savers Handbook,* $9.95; *The*

Healthy Home, $21.95; *Your Afford-able Solar Home,* $7.95; *The Solar Cat Book,* for humor and information, $4.95; *The Solar Boat Book,* $8.95.

More products listed in "Baby & Children's Products," "Educational Materials" and "Energy Conservation" chapters.

Environmental Economics, 1026 Irving Street, Philadelphia PA 19107. (215) 925-7168. Publishers of the third annual *Directory of Environmental Investing,* 1990. This directory helps investors know about the health of environmental services industry—an area in which the profit picture improved in 1989 and early 1990. This industry is showing remarkable strength in an otherwise sluggish economic. Along with material about the environmental industry, the directory looks at how the environmental restructuring of the economy is affecting operations in key industries such as petro-chemicals, banking, real estate, health care, agriculture, and utilities. Michael Silverstein, the author of the book, is also the author of *The Environmental Factor.* He writes a daily Environmental Report the the UPI and does regular "Green Economics" columns for several business publications. The book is 150 pages, $60.

Fowler Solar Electric Inc, PO Box 435, 13 Bashan Hill Road, Worthington MA 01098. (413) 238-5974. Publishers of *The Solar Electric Independent Home* book, by Paul Jeffrey Fowler, written specifically for the PV (photovoltaic)

home owner or the potential PV home owner. Extensive diagrams and photographs aid the reader in the assimilation of new information. *Real Goods Alternative Energy Sourcebook 1990* said, "This is probably the best all around book on writing your 12V system. Lots of good diagrams, and a good glossary and appendix." 184 pages, $15.95. New edition.

See also "Energy Conservation" and "Seminars, Speakers & Workshops" chapter.

Gaia™, 1400 Shattuck Ave #15, Berkeley CA 94709. (415) 548-4172. Gaia™ is a store and mail order source that calls itself a center for "global, ecological & spiritual resources." It is primarily New Age oriented, with an emphasis on Gaia, the earth goddess. However, it also carries environmental books, such as: *50 Simple Things You Can Do to Save the Earth,* $4.95; *50 Simple Things Kids Can Do to Save the Earth,* $7.95; *The Green Consumer,* $8.95; *Healing Environments* tells how to create a natural home and work environment, $9.95; *Save Our Planet,* $9.95.

Gentle Strength Co-op, 234 West University Drive, Tempe AZ 85281. (602) 968-4831. This store handles many environmentally sensitive lines of products. Books: Debra Dadd's books on creating a non-toxic home and more.

More products found in "Household & Personal Care Products," "Organically Grown," "Paper Products," "Baby & Children's Products," and "Magazines, Newsletters & Brochures" chapters.

Harmony Farm Supply & Nursery, 3244 Gravenstein Hwy North, Sebastopol CA 95472. Mail address: PO Box 460, Graton CA 95444. (707) 823-9125. FAX (707) 823-1734. Books available in their organic supply catalog ($2): *Biodynamic Agriculture* includes information on soils and fertilization, animal husbandry, and theory and practice of using biodynamic preparations, $20; *The Biodynamic Farm* with an emphasis on composts, animal and crop production, $20; *Earth Manual: How to Work on Wild Land Without Taming It,* $12.95; *Feed the Soil* is an excellent reference on all types of cover crops, $12.95; *Handbook of Plants with Pest Control Properties* reviews about 2400 plant species, $46.95; *The Home Water Supply: How to Find, Filter, Store and Conserve It,* $14.95; a line of integrated pest management manuals from the University of California; *The Natural Way of Farming,* $17.95; *The New Organic Grower,* $19.95; many more titles.

More information in "Organically Grown" and "Workshops, Seminars & Speakers" chapter.

Harper & Row, Publishers, 10 E 53rd St, New York NY 10022. (212) 207-7000. Toll-free 1-800-242-7737. In Pennsylvania toll-free 1-800-982-4377. Telex 12-5741 (US); Telex 6-2501 (International). Publishers of *2 Minutes a Day for a Greener Planet* by Marjorie Lamb, 243 pgs, $7.95. Helpful "green" tips for: saving water; saving paper; non-toxic cleaning; packaging; energy conservation; gardening; holidays; shopping; writing your congressman; and more.

Houghton Mifflin Company, One Beacon St, Boston MA 02108. (617) 725-5000. FAX # (617) 227-5409. Telex: 4430255. Publishers of *Silent Spring* by Rachel Carson, 368 pgs, $7.95; now in its 25th anniversary edition. This is a landmark book of the 20th century. It called attention to the threat of pesticides and it was instrumental in launching the environmental movement. The book is still as pertinent today as it was 25 years ago.

Household Hazardous Waste Project, 901 South National Ave, Box 108, Springfield MO 65804. (417) 836-5777. Their book *Guide to Hazardous Products Around the Home* has been recognized and used throughout the United States and by the United Nations Environment Programme. It has also been endorsed by Greenpeace, The Cousteau Society, Seventh Generation and *McCall's* Magazine. This manual helps you understand product labels, helps you select safer products before bringing toxic chemicals into your home, helps minimize waste leaving your home, and helps you located recycling options in your community for some types of hazardous waste. $9.95, 178 pages.

Additional listings in "Educational Materials," "Organizations," "Magazines, Newsletters & Brochures" chapters.

INFORM, 381 Park Avenue South, New York NY 10016. (212) 689-4040. Books: *Cutting Chemical Wastes: What 29 Organic Chemical Plants are Doing to Reduce Hazardous Wastes,* 548 pgs, in-depth study, $47.50; *Drive for Clean Air: Natural Gas & Methanol Vehicles,* 252 pgs, shows the obstacles standing in the way of developing these forms of transportation as well as the potential for reducing air pollution, $65. More information in "Organizations" chapter and brochures listed in "Magazines, Newsletters & Brochures" chapter.

Institute for Local Self-Reliance, 2425 18th St NW, Washington DC 20009. (202) 232-4108. FAX # (202) 332-0463. Publications available include *Beyond 40%: Record-Setting Recycling and Composting Programs,* a book that proves that recycling and composting can be a primary solid waste management strategy. The book documents 17 communities with the highest materials recovery levels in the country. All are recovering above 30% and 14 recover at or above 40%, letting the rest of the country know that this is, indeed, possible. Book is $50 to individuals, $25 to nonprofit, community groups.

Other books: *Salvaging the Future: Waste-Based Production* that shows the value of raw materials in garbage, $50; *Proven Profits from Pollution Preventions: Case Studies in Resource Conservation & Waste Reduction,* Volumes I ($25) and II ($20) shows how companies have increased profits by incorporating changes to reduce wastes and promote resource conservation; *Worms Eat My Garbage,* descriptions for setting up and maintaining small scale vermicomposting operations, ideal for school project, $6.95; *Self-Reliant Cities* (Sierra Club Books, $8.95) describes cities that finance and regulate decentralized, renewable energy systems; *Be Your Own Power Company* (Rodale Press, $9.95) shows how to sell electricity to local utilities and what technology to use.

More information in "Organizations" chapter.

IPM Laboratories, Inc., Main St, Locke NY 13092-0099. (315) 497-3129. Useful literature available from them includes: *Biological Pest Management for Interior Plantscapes,* 2nd edition, by Marilyn Y. Steiner & Don P. Elliot, 32 pgs, $5; *Insect Pests of Farm, Garden & Orchard,* 7th edition by Ralph H. Davison & William F. Lyon, comprehensive coverage of crop pests throughout the US, their life cycles and control practices, 596 pgs, $42.50; *Insects That Feed on Trees and Shrubs,* 2nd edition by Warren T. Johnson & Howard H. Lyon, provides quick visual identification of most pests and the damage they cause including 241 full-color plates, 556 pages, $49.95.

See also "Organically Grown" chapter.

Island Press, PO Box 7, Covelo CA 95428. Toll-free order number 1-800-828-1302. FAX # (707) 983-6414. *Crossroads: Environmental Priorities for the Future*, edited by Peter Borrelli, 1988. This book examines the environmental policy changes that have taken place since the first Earth Day twenty years ago, identifies current trends, and looks at perspectives of interest to environmentalists. The book is a compilation of the views of numerous environmentalists, including Peter A. A. Berle of the National Audubon Society, Janet Welsh Brown from the World Resources Institute, Lois Marie Gibbs from the Citizen's Clearinghouse for Hazardous Wastes, Jay D. Hair from the National Wildlife Federation, Cynthia Wilson from Friends of the Earth, and many more nationally recognized environmentalists. The editor is Peter Borrelli from the National Resources Defense Council. Excellent book for across-the-board perspective. Hardcover $29.95, paperback $17.95.

Plastics: America's Packaging Dilemma by Ellen Feldman of the Environmental Action Coalition. This book shows how plastics strain already over-loaded disposal systems and examines better ways to recover these plastic wastes. This book separates myth from fact in the controversies of "degradability" and "recyclability." Cloth, $19.95. Paper $12.95.

Recycling & Incineration: Evaluating the Choices by Richard A. Denison & John Ruston of the Environmental Defense Fund. Provides current information on managing the solid waste crisis. Designed to help policy makers, waste management professionals, and concerned citizens determine the most appropriate ways to handle waste. Includes the basics of waste reduction, recycling, and incineration methods; cost comparisons of the methods; and an evaluation of the health impacts of incineration. Cloth, $34.95. Paper, $19.95.

Island Press has an entire catalog devoted to environmental books, including such titles as: *Resolving Environmental Disputes; Balancing on the Brink of Extinction; The Complete Guide to Environmental Careers; Fighting Toxics; The Challenge of Global Warming;* and many more.

Karen's Nontoxic Products, 1839 Dr. Jack Road, Conowingo MD 21918. (301) 378-4621. 1-800-KARENS-4. Write or call toll-free number for the free catalog of non-toxic, cruelty-free, organic and natural products. Books offered in the catalog include Debra Dadd's *Nontoxic and Natural* ($9.95) and *Nontoxic Home* ($9.95); *Shepherd's Purse Organic Pest Control* (Pest Publications, $5.95); *Keep Pets Healthy the Natural Way* by Pat Lazarus, $2.50; and others on holistic health and natural childbirth.

Many more products included in this catalog. See "Household and Personal Care Products" chapter.

Land Stewardship Project, 14758 Ostlund Trail North, Marine on St. Croix MN 55047. (612) 433-2770. FAX # (612) 433-2704. Offers titles on land stewardship ethics and sustainable agricultural practices. *Soil and Survival* ($11) is a look at the values that shape American agriculture and what we can do to improve the care of our farmland; *Excellence in Agriculture* ($10) contains interviews with 10 Minnesota farm families who are stewards of the land; *Reshaping the Bottom Line* ($10) is a collection of practical ideas being tried on working farms that make farming more economically and environmentally sustainable; *Sowing a Future for the Land* ($6) is a summary of the Land Stewardship Project's 3-year Winona Model Country Program.

More information in "Organizations" and "Educational Materials" chapters.

MasterMedia Ltd., 215 Park Ave South,, Suite 1601, New York, NY 10003. (212) 260-5600. Toll-free 1-800-334-8232. Publishers of *The Solution to Pollution: 101 Things You Can Do To Clean Up Your Environment* by Laurence Sombke, 116 pgs, $7.95. This book explains how to conserve more energy; how to start a recycling center; how to proceed with individual clean-up projects; and how to be a environmentally sensitive consumer. There's a resource chapter for finding government agencies state by state.

Mountain Ark, 120 South East Ave, Fayetteville AR 72701. 1-800-643-8909. Free catalog of organic and macrobiotic foods. Also gourmet cookware, books, water purifiers and

more.

Natural Resource Defense Council, 40 West 20th St, New York NY 10011. (212) 727-2700. Membership department, zip 10114-0466. The NRDC has a "Rainforest Rescue Catalog" which features *The Rainforest Book: How You Can Save the World's Rainforests* for people who want to translate their concern into action ($5.95).

More information in "Organizations" chapter.

The Nature Company, PO Box 2310, Berkeley CA 94702. 1-800-227-1114. FAX (415) 849-0465. Beautiful full-color catalog full of interesting items for people who love nature. Books offered include: *50 Simple Things You Can Do to Save the Earth*, $4.95; *50 Things Kids Can Do to Save the Earth*, $6.95; *The Next Step: 50 More Things You Can Do to Save the Earth*, $6.95; *The Simple Act of Planting a Tree* shows how to organize tree planting programs in your community, $12.95; *Rachel Carson's The Sense of Wonder*, first published in 1956, still marvelous today, describes a sense of wonder felt about nature, $19.95; *Earth Facts* a pocket-sized reference book which illustrates and explains many things about the environment, such as what is the greenhouse effect, etc, $15.95; *The Man Who Planted Trees*, book by Jean Giono and cassette tape with music by Paul Winter, $19.95.

Other items in the catalog described in "Recycling," "Household & Personal Care Products," and "Educational Materials" chapters.

Nitron Industries, Inc., PO Box 1447, 4605 Johnson Road, Fayetteville AR 72702. (501) 750-1777. 1-800-835-0123. Manufacturer and distributor of natural fertilizers and soil conditioners. Other services include books on farming and gardening, an annual organic growing seminar, composting information, and other technical information for organic growers. FREE catalog by calling toll-free number.

More information in "Organically Grown" chapter.

Northeast Publishing, Inc., PO Box 571, Emmaus PA 18049. Source for the book *Water Treatment Handbook: A Homeowners Guide to Safer Drinking Water,* 45 pgs, $9.95 postpaid. This guide gives test analysis of water treatment devices: activated carbon filters, distillers, and reverse osmosis systems. You might call is the "Consumer Report" of water treatment systems.

Pan North America Regional Center, 965 Mission St #514, San Francisco CA 94103. (415) 541-9140. FAX # (415) 541-9253. Telex: 15683472 PANNA. Econet: PANNA.

Books from this organization are: *Biotechnology's Bitter Harvest: Herbicide-Tolerant Crops and the Threat to Sustainable Agriculture,* 1990, 73 pgs, $5; *Problem Pesticides, Pesticide Problems,* 1989, 183 pgs, $15; *Monitoring the International Code of Conduct on the Distribution and Use of Pesticides in North America,* 25 pgs, $5; *Escape from the Pesticide Treadmill: Alternatives to Pesticides in Developing Countries,* detailed case studies, 185 pgs, $12; Breaking the Pesticide Habit: *Alternatives to 12 Hazardous Pesticides,* 372 pgs, history of pest control strategies plus a comprehensive guide to sustainable alternatives, $20.

More about the organization in "Organizations" chapter.

Penguin USA, 1633 Broadway, New York NY 10019. (212) 397-8000. FAX # (212) 397-8273. Telex: 23-6109. Publishers of *The Green Consumer* by John Elkington, Julia Hailes, & Joel Makower, 342 pgs. This book shows how you can shop for a better environment for your home, for cleaning products, for your car, for your garden, for gifts, for travel, and for personal care products. There's also ideas for energy conservation and environmentally safe household paints and other home improvement products. A section of the book is devoted to telling how to get involved locally, nationally and economically.

This company (Puffin imprint) also publishes *Going Green: A Kid's Handbook to Saving the Planet* by John Elkington, Julia Hailes, Douglas Hill and Joel Makower, 112 pgs, $8.95. This is the children's version of *The Green Consumer.* This very attractive (four-color humorous illustrations by Tony Ross throughout) book is sure to educate kids about the environment without frightening them. First there's information about: the greenhouse ef-

You can buy products that don't cost the earth

THE GREEN CONSUMER

- Baby products • Groceries • Appliances
- Cosmetics • Gardening supplies
- Gifts • Much more!

JOHN ELKINGTON, JULIA HAILES, AND JOEL MAKOWER

Foreword by Ben Cohen, Ben & Jerry's Homemade

GOING GREEN

A Kid's Handbook to Saving the Planet

John Elkington, Julia Hailes, Douglas Hill, and Joel Makower

Illustrated by Tony Ross

fect; the ozone holes; acid rain; water pollution and other environmental problems. Then the kids are given practical solutions on their level. An A-Z list shows things they can do. This incredible publication should be a "must" for kids.

Planet Drum Foundation, Box 31251, San Francisco CA 94131. (415) 285-6556. The organization's publications include *A Green City Program for San Francisco Bay Area Cities and Towns* by Peter Berg, Beryl Magilavy and Seth Zuckerman, $5.95. This book provides agendas for short- and long-range changes, and visions of what a green city would be like. Their book *Reinhabiting a Separate Country: A Bioregional Anthology of Northern California* by Peter Berg, $7, is a collection of essays, natural history, biography, poems and stories revealing Northern California as a distinct bioregion. The organization's newsletter is *Raise the Stakes,* with back issues available. More information in the "Organizations" chapter.

Prentice Hall Press, 15 Columbus Circle, New York NY 10023. (212) 373-8500. Publishers of *Ecologue: The Environmental Catalogue and Consumer's Guide for a Safe Earth* edited by Bruce N. Anderson, 255 pgs, $18.95. This incredibly informative and attractive book tells what products to buy (and which to avoid), earth-mending practices, recycling tips, and energy conservation hints. This book reviews over 600 products including:

Chapter Two: Books ★

personal care; baby; cleaners; energy savers; gardening; recycling equipment; solar energy; cruelty-free cosmetics; and more. The editor, Bruce Anderson, has written 5 books on solar energy; was on the International Policy Board for Earth Day 1990; was a principal organizer for New Hampshire's Earth Day 1990; and is the president of International Environment Group.

Prima Publishing & Communications, PO Box 1260PH, Rocklin CA 95677. (916) 624-5718. *Earth Right: Every Citizen's Guide* by H. Patricia Hynes. A guide to what an individual can do in the home, the workplace, and in the environment to save the environment. The issues discussed are pesticides, solid waste, drinking water, the ozone layer, and global warming. Each issue is defined, the problem clearly explained in layman's terms, and then suggestions are given what actions can be taken by an individual. The book was written by H. Patricia Hynes, director of the Institute on Women and Technology. Hardcover, $24.95. Paperback $12.95. Shipping and handling add $3.

The Putnam Berkeley Group Inc., (Perigee Books), 200 Madison Avenue, New York NY 10016. (212) 951-8400. FAX # (212) 213-6706. Toll-free 1-800-631-8571. Telex: 42-2386. Publishers of *Heloise Hints for a Healthy Planet,* 160 pgs, $7.95. For over thirty years, the "Hints from Heloise" column has given helpful advice to homemakers. Now Heloise gives

hundreds of "green" tips for the home, garden, office, entertainment, pets, children, travel and more.

Rainforest Action Network, 301 Broadway, Suite A, San Francisco CA 94133. (415) 398-4404. FAX # (415) 398-2732. Books from this organization include: *The Primary Source,* an account of the crisis that will develop if exploitation of the rainforests continues, $10.95; *Stranger in the Forest,* a plea for the survival of the rainforest's people, $7.95; *In the Rainforest, Report from a Strange Beautiful Imperiled World,* $10.95. They also have a list of resources you can obtain from other sources. More information in "Organizations" chapter.

Random House, 201 E 50 St, New York NY 10022. (212) 751-2600. FAX # (212) 872-8026. Toll-free 1-800-638-6460. Telex: 12-6575. Publishers of *The Green Pages* from the Bennet Information Group, 237 pages, $8.95. This book has tables of information on products that you can buy at the market or through mail order for the home, for your children, for your pets, for your yard, and for your car. There are helpful hints on what to look for in "green" products and what to avoid. There's also a helpful table of common substances, their use, and their known environmental or health effect.

Real Goods Trading Company, 966 Mazzoni St, Ukiah CA 95482. (707) 468-9214. FAX # (707) 468-0301. Order toll-free 1-800-762-7325. This company has an extensive 106-page catalog full of energy-saving equipment and supplies. Books include: their very own *1990 Real Goods Alternative Energy Sourcebook* that is more than a catalog, it's also information, charts, graphics, stores, and instructions for setting up systems, 332 pages, $10 refundable with first order; *Electric Vehicles,* $10.95; *Electric Vehicle Directory* shows 5 different vehicles on the market today complete with specifications and suppliers, 14 pgs, $5; *At Home With Alternative Energy,* $10.95; *The New Solar Electric Home* is probably the best all-around book for getting started with alternative energy, 408 pages, $18.95; *Living on 12 Volts with Ample Power,* $25; *Planning for an Individual Water System,* $17.95; *The Solar Electric House,* $12.95; *RV'ers Guide to Solar Battery Charging,* $12.95; *Heaven's Flame Solar Cookers,* $7; *50 Simple Things You Can Do to Save the Earth,* $4.95; *Treating the Earth as if We Plan to Stay,* $3.50; *Good Planets are Hard to Find,* $3.50; *Ecology Action Workbook & Dictionary* for children, $3; *Resource-Efficient Housing Guide,* $16.95.

More items listed in "Baby & Children's Products," "Energy Conservation," "Household & Personal Care Products," "Clean Air, Clean Water" and "Recycling" chapters.

Seventh Generation, Colchester VT 05446-1672. (802) 655-3116. FAX toll-free # 1-800-456-1139. Order toll-free 1-800-456-1177. Customer service toll-free 1-800-456-1197.

Seventh Generation is one of the most well-known companies for environmentally safe consumer products. Their 48-page catalog "Products for a Healthy Planet" ($2) contains an extraordinary variety of products. They also practice what they preach. For instance, they recycle their office paper, and reuse cardboard boxes for shipping. They have a 1% fund that goes to environmental organizations.

Their environmental bookshelf includes some very popular titles: *How to Make the World a Better Place* ($9.95, autographed $11.95); *50 Simple Things You Can Do To Save The Earth* ($4.95); *The Green Consumer* ($8.95); *Nontoxic, Natural & Earthwise* ($10.95); *Silent Spring* ($8.95); *Shopping for a Better World* ($4.95); *Green Limericks* ($5.95); *The Complete Guide to Environmental Careers* ($14.95); *The Seventh Generation Consumer Letter* (newsletter, 12 issues, 1 year, $27.)

Children's books listed in "Baby & Children's Products" chapter.

There are so many products in this catalog that additional information can be found in these chapters: "Baby and Children's Products," "Household & Personal Care Products," "Educational Materials," "Paper Products," "Recycling," "Energy Conservation," and "Organically Grown."

Sierra Club, 730 Polk Street, San Francisco CA 94109. (415) 776-2211. Sierra Club Books provides education through nearly 350 titles. The Sierra Club Books address is: 100 Bush St.,

Chapter Two: Books ★

13th Floor, San Francisco CA 94104. (415) 291-1600.

More information about Sierra Club included in the "Organizations" chapter.

Solar Electric Engineering, Inc., 116 4th St, Santa Rosa CA 95401. (707) 542-1990. FAX # (707) 542-4358. This is a publicly owned corporation that has been committed to bringing to the marketplace environmentally sound products at affordable prices to the consumer. They have a 40-page "Environmental Catalog," with books, including: *The Solar Electric Book,* $11.95; *Shopping for a Better World,* $4.95; *The Green Consumer,* $8.95; *50 Simple Things You Can Do to Save the Earth,* $4.95; *Cut Your Electric Bills in Half,* $14.95.

More items listed in "Energy Conservation," "Recycling," "Paper Products," "Clean Air, Clean Water," "Baby & Children's Products," and "Magazines, Newsletters & Brochures."

Solar Survival, PO Box 250, Cherry Hill Rd, Harrisville NH 03450. (603) 827-3811. *The Solar Greenhouse Book* (Rodale, $10.95);*Home Food Hydration,* $3.50; *How to Dry Food,* $10.50. For much more information about this company and their wonderful solar designs and products, see the "Energy Conservation" chapter.

Sprout House, 40 Railroad St, Great Barrington MA 01230 (413) 528-5200. Books available: *Recipes from the Sproutman* ($7.95) with recipes for spout breads, cookies, crackers, soups, dressing, dips, more; *Juice Fasting* ($7.95) about types of fasts, pre-fasting diet, how and when to fast, liver flushes, and menus; *Growing Vegetables Indoors* ($6.95) that is a training course for growing miniature vegetables indoors—all without soil; *Making Sprout Bread* ($4.95) with step-by-step preparation and advantages of sprout bread; and more titles. More information in "Organically Grown" chapter.

Sunnyside Solar, RD 4 Box 808, Green River Road, Brattleboro CT 05301. (802) 257-1482 (in Vermont). 1-800-346-3230. Books on photovoltaics: *The New Solar Electric Home* a how-to handbook by Joel Davidson & Richard Komp, $18.95; *RVer's Guide to Solar Battery Charging* by Noel and Barbara Kirkby, $13.95; *The Solar Electric House: A Design Manual for Home Scale PV Power Systems* by Steven J. Strong, $19.95; *Guide to the Photovoltaic Revolution* by Paul D. Maycock & Edward N. Stirwalt, $9.95; *Photovoltaics: A Manual for Design & Installation of Stand-Alone Photovoltaic Systems* by McCarney, Olsen & Weiss, $35; *Solar Electricity for the Remote Home Site* by Paul J. Fowler, $15; *Electricity from Sunlight* by Chris Flavin, $4.

More information found in "Energy Conservation" and "Seminars" chapters.

SunWatt®, RFD Box 751, Addison ME 04606. (207) 497-2204. Books available: *Practical Photovoltaics,* 216 pgs, $16.95; *RVers' Guide to Solar Battery Charging,* $12.95; *Solar Census,* a comprehensive sourcebook, 1984, 208 pgs, $14.95. Also listed in "Energy Conservation" chapter.

Union of Concerned Scientists, 26 Church St, Cambridge MA 02238. (617) 547-5552. *Cool Energy: The Renewable Solution to Global Warming* (1990, 89 pgs, $4.95) is a report that discusses the status of various renewable-energy technologies and their roles in slowing global warming; *Safety Second: The NRC and America's Nuclear Power Plants* (1987, 194 pgs, $22.50) examines the performance of the Nuclear Regulatory Commission and makes recommendations for improving the regulation of nuclear power. More information in "Organizations," "Educational Materials," and "Magazines, Newsletters & Brochures" chapter.

University of California Press, 2120 Berkeley Way, Berkeley CA 94720. (415) 642-4247. *Acceptable Risk? Making Decisions in a Toxic Environment* by Lee Clarke. This book examines the decision-making levels of major organizations, and how these processes influence our environment. It is in the boardroom that some risks are defined as acceptable and others not. Lee Clarke gives case studies of the internal workings of organizations that have affected the environment, and how these organizations did or did not go about solving these problems within the decision-making process.

U. S. Environmental Directories, PO Box 65156, St. Paul MN 55165. The *Directory of National Environmental Organizations,* Third Edition, $35 postpaid, is a compilation of the most comprehensive listing of environmental groups in the country. It lists addresses and descriptions of over 375 non-governmental environmental and conservation organizations in alphabetical order. Most of the organizations are national in scope, a few are regional but have national significance. There's a subject index with over 40 major environmental subject areas.

Wildlife Information Center, Inc., 629 Green St., Allentown PA 18102. (215) 434-1637. Books available are: *The Migrations of Hawks* by Donald S. Heintzelman, 369 pgs, $35; *A Guide to Hawk Watching in North America* by Donald S. Heintzelman, 284 pgs, $10; *A Manual for Bird Watching in the Americas* by Donald S. Heintzelman, 255 pgs, $8.

More information in "Organizations" chapter.

William Morrow & Company, Inc., (imprint Quill), 105 Madison Ave, New York NY 10016. (212) 889-3050. FAX # (212) 689-9139. Toll-free 1-800-843-9389. Telex: 22-4063 WILMOR. Publishers of *How to Make the World a Better Place: A Guide to Doing Good* by Jeffrey Hollender, 303 pgs, $9.95. This book presents specific actions that the individual can take that will make a difference in the areas of the environment, hunger, peace, investing, travel, responsible shopping, and more. This is an excellent resource because the author tells you exactly what to do, who to write to, and how it will make a difference.

Xerces Society, 10 SW Ash St, Portland OR 97204. (503) 222-2788. Dedicated to the preservation of invertebrate species, especially butterflies. Books: *Butterfly Gardening: Creating Summer Magic in Your Garden,* $17.45 ppd; *The Common Names of North American Butterflies,* $8.95 ppd. More information in "Educational Materials" and "Organizations" chapters.

Alphabetical listing of books in this chapter
Source for the book follows for easy cross-reference
*** Indicates author's favorite titles

Aborigines Today: Land & Justice (Cultural Survival)

Acceptable Risk? Making Decisions in a Toxic Environment (University of California Press)

Affordable Passive Solar Homes (American Solar Energy Society)

Air in Danger: Ecological Perspectives of the Atmosphere (Cambridge University Press)

***A Kids' Guide to How to Save the Planet (Avon Books)

Allergies and the Hyperactive Child (E.L. Foust Company)

Alternatives to 12 Hazardous Pesticides (Pan North American Regional Center)

Animal Ingredients and Their Alternatives (Amberwood)

Animal Liberation (Amberwood)

At Home with Alternative Energy: A Comprehensive Guide to Creating Your Own Systems (Aatec Publications, Real Goods Trading Company)

Balancing on the Brink of Extinction (Island Press)

Beyond 40%: Record-Setting Recycling & Composting Programs (Institute for Local Self-Reliance)

Be Your Own Power Company (Institute for Local Self-Reliance)

The Bicycle Commuting Book (Energy Store)

Biodynamic Agriculture (Harmony Farm Supply & Nursery)

The Biodynamic Farm (Harmony Farm Supply & Nursery)

Biological Pest Management for Interior Plantscapes (IPM Laboratories Inc.)

Biotechnology's Bitter Harvest: Herbicides-Tolerant Crops and the Threat to Sustainable Agriculture (Pan North American Regional Center)

Building a Healthy Lawn (Eco Source)

Butterfly Gardening: Creating Summer Magic in Your Garden

(Xerces Society)

The Case for Animal Rights (Amberwood)

The Chemical-Free Lawn (Energy Store)

Clean & Green (The Earthwise Consumer)

The Complete Guide to Environmental Careers (Island Press, Seventh Generation)

The Common Names of North American Butterflies (Xerces Society)

The Cookbook for People Who Love Animals (Amberwood, The Compassionate Consumer)

Cool Energy: The Renewable Solution to Global Warming (Union of Concerned Scientists)

Coping With Your Allergies (E.L. Foust Company)

Creative Food Experience for Children (Center for Science in the Public Interest)

Cross Currents: The Perils of Electropollution; The Promise of Electromedicine (Baubiologie Hardware)

Currents of Death: Power Lines, Computer Terminals, and the At-tempt to Cover Up Their Threat to Your Health (Baubiologie Hardware)

Current Switch: How to reduce or eliminate electromagnetic pollution in the home and office (Baubiologie Hardware)

Cutting Chemical Wastes: What 29 Organic Chemical Plants are Doing to Reduce Hazardous Wastes (INFORM)

Cut Your Electric Bills in Half (Energy Store, Solar Electric Engineering Inc.)

Directory of Environmental Investing (Energy Store)

Directory of National Environmental Organizations (U.S. Environmental Directories)

Drive for Clean Air: Natural Gas & Methanol Vehicles (INFORM)

***Earth Book for Kids (Eco Source)

***Earthcards: Postcards You Can Sign and Send to Save the Earth (Conari Press)

Earth Manual: How to Work on Wild Land Without Taming It (Harmony Farm Supply & Nursery)

***Earthright: Every Citizen's

Guide (Prima Publishing & Communications, Eco Source)

Eater's Choice: The Food Lover's Guide to Lower Cholesterol (Center for Science in the Public Interest)

Eat, Think & Be Healthy (Center for Science in the Public Interest)

Ecological Studies in Tropical Fish Communities (Cambridge University Press)

***Ecologue: The Environmental Catalogue and Consumer's Guide for a Safe Earth (Prentice Hall Press)

Ecology Action Workbook & Dictionary (Real Goods Trading Company)

Ecology, Recreation & Tourism (Cambridge University Press)

Electricity From Sunlight (Sunnyside Solar)

Electric Vehicle Directory (Real Goods Trading Company)

Electric Vehicles (Real Goods Trading Company)

Electric Vehicles: Design and Build Your Own (Aatec Publications)

The Energy Savers Handbook (Energy Store)

Environmental Medicine (E.L. Foust Company)

***Environmental Priorities for the Future (Island Press)

Escape from the Pesticide Treadmill: Alternatives to Pesticides in Developing Countries (Pan North American Regional Center)

The Essential Whole Earth Catalog (Co-op America)

Excellence in Agriculture (Land Stewardship Project)

Fast Food: An Eater's Guide (Center for Science in the Public Interest)

Fast Vegetarian Feasts (Center for Science in the Public Interest)

Feed the Soil (Harmony Farm Supply & Nursery)

***50 Simple Things Kids Can Do To Save The Earth (Earthworks Press, Gaia, The Nature Company)

***50 Simple Things You Can Do To Save The Earth (Earthworks Press, The Compassionate Consumer, Eco Source, Gaia, The Nature Company, Real Goods Trading Company, Seventh Generation, Solar Electric Engineering Inc)

Fighting Toxics: The Challenge of

Global Warming (Island Press)

For the Vegetarian in You (Amberwood)

The Global Ecology Handbook: What You Can Do About the Environmental Crisis (Beacon Press)

***Going Green: A Kid's Handbook to Saving the Planet (Penguin USA)

Good Planets are Hard to Find (Real Goods Trading Company)

A Green City Program for San Francisco Bay Area Cities and Towns (Planet Drum Foundation)

***The Green Consumer (Penguin USA, Co-op America, Gaia, Seventh Generation, Solar Electric Engineering Inc.)

The Greenhouse Trap: What We're Doing to the Atmosphere and How We Can Slow Global Warming (American Solar Energy Society)

Greening Business (Basil Blackwell, Inc.)

Green Limericks (Seventh Generation)

***The Green Machine: Ecology & the Balance of Nature (Basil Blackwell, Inc.)

***The Green Pages (Random House)

Growing Vegetables Indoors (Sprout House)

A Guide to Hawk-Watching in North America (Wildlife Information Center Inc.)

***Guide to Hazardous Products Around the House (Household Hazardous Waste Project)

Guide to the Photovoltaic Revolution (Sunnyside Solar)

Handbook of Plants with Pest Control Properties (Harmony Farm Supply & Nursery)

***Healing Environments (Celestial Arts, Baubiologie Hardware, Gaia)

The Healthy Home (Energy Store)

Heat Saving Home Insulation (American Solar Energy Society)

Heaven's Flame Solar Cookers (Real Goods Trading Company)

***Heloise's Hints for a Healthy Planet (The Putnam Berkeley Group Inc.)

Home Food Hydration (Solar Survival)

The Home Water Supply: How to Find, Filter, Store and Conserve It

(Harmony Farm Supply & Nursery)

How to Design and Build a Solar Swimming Pool Heater (American Solar Energy Society)

How to Dry Food (Solar Survival)

***How to Make the World a Better Place (William Morrow & Company, Seventh Generation)

The Impossible Child (E.L. Foust Company)

Indigenous Survival Among the Bari and Arhuaco (Cultural Survival)

The Indigenous Voice: Visions & Realities (Cultural Survival)

Insect Pests of Farm, Garden & Orchard (IPM Laboratories Inc.)

Insects That Feed on Trees & Shrubs (IPM Laboratories Inc.)

In The Rainforest, Report from a Strange Beautiful Imperiled World (Rainforest Action Network)

Juice Fasting (Sprout House)

Keep Pets Healthy the Natural Way (Karen's Nontoxic Products)

Living on 12 Volts with Ample Power (Real Goods Trading Company)

The Living Tundra (Cambridge University Press)

Making Sprout Bread (Sprout House)

A Manual for Bird Watching in the Americas (Wildlife Information Center Inc.)

The Man Who Planted Trees (The Nature Company)

The Migration of Hawks (Wildlife Information Center Inc.)

Monitoring the International Code of Conduct on the Distribution and Use of Pesticides in North America (Pan North American Regional Center)

The Natural House (The Earthwise Consumer)

Natural Lighting: How to Use Daylight (American Solar Energy Society)

The Natural Way of Farming (Harmony Farm Supply & Nursery)

New Direction in Ecological Physiology (Cambridge University Press)

The New Environmental Age (Cambridge University Press)

The New Organic Grower (Harmony Farm Supply & Nursery)

The New Solar Electric Home: The Photovoltaics How-to Handbook (Aatec Publications, Energy Store, Real Goods Trading Company, Sunnyside Solar)

The New Solar Home Book (American Solar Energy Society)

The New Solar Electric House: A Design Manual for Home Scale PV Power Systems (Sunnyside Solar)

The Next Step: 50 More Things You Can Do to Save the Earth (The Nature Company)

1990 Real Goods Alternative Energy Sourcebook (Real Goods Trading Company)

1991 Consumer Guide to Home Energy Savings (American Council for an Energy-Efficient Economy)

Nontoxic & Natural: A Guide for Consumers (Baubiologie Hardware, E.L. Foust Company, Karen's Nontoxic Products)

***The Nontoxic Home: Protecting Yourself and Your Family from Everyday Toxics and Health Hazards (Jeremy P. Tarcher, The Earthwise Consumer, Baubiologie Hardware, E.L. Foust Company, Karen's Nontoxic Products)

***Nontoxic, Natural & Earthwise (Jeremy P. Tarcher, The Earthwise Consumer, Co-op America, Seventh Generation)

***1001 Ways to Save the Planet (Ballantine)

The Peace Catalog (Eco Source)

Photovoltaics: A Manual for Design & Installation of Stand-Alone Photovoltaic Systems (Sunnyside Solar)

Planning for an Individual Water System (Real Goods Trading Company)

***Plastics: America's Packaging Dilemma (Island Press)

Practical Photovoltaics: Electricity From Solar Cells (Aatec Publications, SunWatt)

The Primary Source (Rainforest Action Network)

Problem Pesticides, Pesticide Problems (Pan North American Regional Center)

Proven Profits from Pollution Preventions: Case Studies in Resource Conservation & Waste Reduction (Institute for Local Self-Reliance)

Rachel Carson's Sense of Wonder (The Nature Company)

Radon: A Homeowner's Guide to Detection and Control (Air Chek, Inc.)

Radon, the Invisible Threat (Air Chek, Inc., Baubiologie Hardware)

The Rainforest Book: How You Can Save the World's Rainforests (Natural Resource Defense Council)

Real Goods Alternative Energy Sourcebook (Real Goods Trading Company, Co-op America)

Recipes from the Sproutman (Sprout House)

The Recurring Silent Spring (The Athene Series/ Pergamon Press, Inc.)

Recycling & Incineration: Evaluating the Choices (Island Press)

Reinhabiting a Separate Country: A Bioregional Anthology of Northern California (Planet Drum Foundation)

Reshaping the Bottom Line (Land Stewardship Project)

Resolving Environmental Disputes (Island Press)

Resource-Efficient Housing (Aatec Publications, Real Goods Trading Company)

Resource Guide to State Environmental Management (Council of State Governments)

RVers Guide to Solar Battery Charging: 12 Volt DC—120 Volt AC Inverters (Aatec Publications, Real Goods Trading Company, Sunnyside Solar, SunWatt)

Safety Second: The NRC and America's Nuclear Power Plants (Union of Concerned Scientists)

Salvaging the Future: Waste-Based Production (Institute for Local Self-Reliance)

***Save Our Planet: 750 Everyday Ways You Can Help Clean Up the Earth (Dell Publishing Company, Eco Source, Gaia)

***Saving the Earth: A Citizen's Guide to Environmental Action (Alfred A. Knopf, Inc.)

The Secret Life of Plants (Eco Source)

Self-Reliant Cities (Sierra Club Books, Institute for Local Self-Reliance)

Shepherd's Purse: Organic Pest Control Handbook (Baubiologie Hardware, Karen's Nontoxic Products)

***Shopping for a Better World

Chapter Two: Books

(Council on Economic Priorities, Eco Source, Seventh Generation, Solar Electric Engineering Inc.)

***Silent Spring (Houghton Mifflin, Seventh Generation)

The Simple Act of Planting a Trees (The Nature Company)

Slaughter of the Innocent (The Compassionate Consumer)

The Smart Kitchen (Baubiologie Hardware)

Soil & Survival (Land Stewardship Project)

The Solar Boat Book (Energy Store)

The Solar Cat Book (Energy Store)

Solar Census (SunWatt)

The Solar Electric Book (Solar Electric Engineering Inc.)

The Solar Electric Independent Home (Energy Store)

Solar Electricity for the Remote Home Site (Sunnyside Solar)

The Solar Greenhouse Book (Solar Survival)

Solar Resources (American Solar Energy Society)

***The Solution to Pollution: 101 Things You Can Do To Clean Up Your Environment (MasterMedia Ltd)

Sowing a Future for the Land (Land Stewardship Project)

Stranger in the Forest (Rainforest Action Network)

Struggle for Animal Rights (The Compassionate Consumer)

Supermarket Savvy (Center for Science in the Public Interest)

Tourism: Manufacturing the Exotic (Cultural Survival)

Treating the Earth as if We Plan to Stay (Real Goods Trading Company)

***2 Minutes a Day for a Greener Planet (Harper & Row)

United Nation Environmental Data Report (Basil Blackwell, Inc.)

Vegetarian Sourcebook (The Compassionate Consumer)

Water Treatment Handbook: A Homeowners Guide to Safer Drinking Water (Northeast Publishing Inc.)

Why Your House May Endanger Your Health (E.L. Foust Company)

Worms Eat My Garbage (Institute for Local Self-Reliance)

Your Affordable Solar Home (Energy Store)

Your Home, Your Health & Well-Being (E.L. Foust Company)

If we are blind to the environmental problems, and if we each do not speak out, then what right do we have to blame someone else?

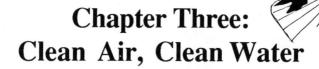

Chapter Three:
Clean Air, Clean Water

This chapter contains products for air purification, water purification, testing kits and other products that will assure you that your home is free from harmful substances in your air or water.

Abbeon Cal Inc., 123 Gray Ave, Santa Barbara CA 93101. (805) 966-0810. FAX # (805) 966-7659. Offers an electronic air-cleaner that cleans 7800 cubic feet per hour. Removes particles to .01 micron (pollen, line & dust are generally larger than 5 microns). Removes smoke, dust, pollen, odors and gasses. Washable electronic filter cell. Replaceable mechanic filter (2-3 months). Air cleaner is $197 ppd; filters are $16 each ppd.

Air Chek, Inc., Box 2000, Arden NC 28704. (704) 684-0893. FAX # (704) 684-8498. Toll-free 1-800-247-2435 or 1-800-257-2366. Lab and manufacturer or radon test devices and distributor of other environmental tests. Products: activated charcoal samplers, alpha track monitors, waterborn radon tests, lead in water tests, lead check swabs,

formaldehyde monitors.

Books about radon: *Radon, The Invisible Threat* is an easy-to-understand book by Michael LaFavore, $11.95; *Radon: A Homeowner's Guide to Detection and Control* tells how to determine if you have a radon problem and how to solve it, $2.95.

Amway Corporation, 7575 Fulton Street East, Ada MI 49355-0001. (616) 676-6000. FAX #(616) 676-8140. 1-800-544-7167. Amway® Water Treatment System can reduce lead in drinking water to levels below those established by the EPA. This system uses a pressed carbon filter to effectively remove more than 100 EPA priority pollutants including organic contaminants such as pesticides and trihalomethanes. It also effectively removes asbestos, sediments, dirt,

Photo: Ed Carlin/ THE PICTURE CUBE

Pure water is something we should not take for granted.

Chapter Three: Clean Air, Clean Water ★

scale, and chlorine.

The company also offers the Pure-flow® Air Treatment System that reduces many unwanted contaminants from indoor air. This system uses 5 filters—more than any comparable system on the market today. It removes 99.9% dust, 99.7% pollen, 95.8% asbestos, and 94.1% smoke from the air in a single pass through the unit!

Amway is the exclusive distributor of Freedom Fuel Additive, which is a product that improves fuel economy, reduces hydrocarbon emissions, reduces engine knock, and fights valve recession when unleaded gas is used in engines built to run on leaded fuel.

More information about Amway products and their corporate environmental policy and activities found in "Household & Personal Care Products" chapter.

Baubiologie Hardware, 207 16th St, Unit B, Pacific Grove CA 93950. (408) 372-8626.The catalog includes environmental test kits, such as the Comprehensive Environmental Test Kit, $159.95; Water Analysis Kit, $150 basic kit; Watercheck water test, $150; LeadCheck Swabs for checking lead in your plumbing, house paint, ceramic dishes, toys, furniture, 12 for $24.95; Verify Water Test, $9.95; Carbon Monoxide Tester, $19.95; Mold Testing Kit, $25; Formaldehyde Tester, $56; Radon Gas Detector, $25.

Other clean air products include: the AutoAire filter for your car that removes exhaust, chemical odors, dusts, pollens, mold spores, $199; the

Martinaire VH300 for the home has a patented five filter design, $499; the Airstar 5C with four separate methods of filtration, $323; the permastatic furnace filter for filtering contaminants coming through your heating system, $89.

More information found in "Books," "Energy Conservation," "Household & Personal Care Products" and "Educational Materials" chapters.

Clean Water Tech, PO Box 15330, San Luis Obispo CA 93406. Manufacturer of Ozone™ PR-1300, an ozone generator by Clean Water Tech. This product generates ozone, which is a powerful oxidizing agent. When ozone is injected into spa water, it kills many bacteria, viruses or mold spores. Ozone reverts back to pure oxygen with a half life of approximately 20 minutes. If the spa is run daily, four separate one-hour cycles per day will generate a sufficient amount of ozone to keep the spa free of biological contamination. Rates up to 1,000 gallon spa or 2,000 gallon pool. Average lamp life: 9,000 hours. Size: 20 x 9 x 4. Weight: 22 pounds.

Conscious Connection Magazine, 432 Altair Place, Venice CA 90291. (213) 392-9661. FAX #(213) 392-7420. Distributors of the Rainshow'r™ natural shower alternative. This is an effective, trouble free, economical shower filter that protects against contaminants such as chlorine, lead, mercury, iron phosphates, magnesium, calcium, sulphur and other organic and inorganic compounds. There are no carbon filters to replace. Easy to install. Can be taken along when traveling. $69 postpaid. Distributor of the Vitalizer™, a revolutionary device that, when installed on the fuel line of your car, will allow the engine to burn more efficiently. The result are: more miles per gallon; more power; cleaner engine; and thus less pollution. Also distributor of Ozone™ PR-1300, an ozone generator by Clean Water Tech. This product generates ozone, which is a powerful oxidizing agent. When ozone is injected into spa water, it kills many bacteria, viruses or mold spores. Ozone reverts back to pure oxygen with a half life of approximately 20 minutes.

Eco Source™, 9051 Mill Station Road Bldg #E, Sebastopol CA 95472. (717) 829-7957 or (707) 829-8345. Catalog of products for a cleaner, safer world. Includes clean air products such as: CRSI 600H air filtration system that is highly recommended by allergists, removes all known airborne organisms and allergens, $989; portable filtration system, a mini-version of the 600H that comes with two wheels and a handle, $625; Vornado air circulation systems on shortstand ($119) and on longstand ($149); Fresh-Aire purification systems, model FMC 330 ($495) and model FMC 440 ($995).

Clean water and water conservation products in the catalog include: Care Free water conditioner that prevents hard water scale and corrosion problems without removing minerals or adding salt or chemicals, 1/2 inch $725 or 3/4 inch $988; Rainshower filter removes chlorine conserves water, $68.95; garden de-chlorinator, $68.95; Multi-Pure™ water filter systems, starting from $209.95 for a counter-top model; low-flow showerheads of various styles; toilet dams, save 10,000 gallons of water a year, fits standard toilet, 2 for $11.50; faucet aerators to conserve up to 3,300 gallons per year, from $5.95 to $6.95 each.

More products found in "Books," "Recycling," "Household & Personal Care," "Energy Conservation" and "Educational Materials" chapters.

E. L. Foust Company, Inc., Box 105, Elmhurst IL 60126. (708) 834-4952. 1-800-225-9549. Activated carbon purifiers, whole-house central purification, face masks, foil vapor barrier, hepa filters, and water filters. Constructed according to high standards of environmental integrity—no plastics, no ozone. Their model Series 400 removes a wide range of pollutants such as formaldehyde, phenol, ozone, cigarette smoke, paint fumes, perfumes, ethanol. This model also controls particulate pollutants into submicron range: pollens, plant spores, tobacco smoke, molds, bacteria, viruses. This machine was reported as an expert's choice in a *New York Times* article by Deborah Blumenthal entitled "Out With the Bad Air: Dirt and Noise Fighters." The author noted that small table top air filters were virtually "worthless," and that the Foust Series 400 filter is the kind of purifier that

Chapter Three: Clean Air, Clean Water

combines activated carbon filters and top-of-the-line HEPA filter for maximum control of chemicals and particles. Price is $499 for particle control only; $549 for chemical and particle control.

Other air purifiers manufactured by them are: 160A Auto Air Purifier that plugs into your cigarette lights; the 160DT Desktop Air Purifier for offices; the 160R2 Room Air Purifier for up to 400 square feet of living space; and the C2 Converter for using your auto air purifier in a motel room.

Other pure air products include the 3M Dust/ Mist Respirator, 2 for $5.75; a cotton/ carbon fact mask with ties, $10.

Books on clean air and allergies are available from this company. See "Books" chapter.

Environmental Purification Systems, PO Box 191, Concord CA 94522-9964. (415) 284-2129. 1-800-829-2129. Shower filter, reverse osmosis drinking water system, whole house water filter, whole house HEPA air filter.

Everpure, Inc., 660 Blackhawk Dr, Westmont IL 60559-9005. (708) 654-4000. Everpure® Drinking Water Systems are a compact alternative to the expense and inconvenience of bottled water or complex treatment devices. The installation is simple and the cartridge needs only annual changing. There are several models to choose from and also a Monitor™ Faucet Kit that you can use to separate drinking

water from regular water.

Jade Mountain, PO Box 4616, Boulder CO 80306. (303) 449-6601. FAX # (303) 449-8266. Toll-free 1-800-442-1972. Large selection of energy saving and appropriate technology products. Clean air products: Enviracaire Portable AirCleaner, completely recirculates and cleans the air in a 16' x 20' room 6 times an hour, $250; Non-Scents Household Clean Air System, a natural mineral that takes odors out of the air, no coverup, no fragrance, 1 lb, $10.95; CleanRoom Air Filters that just peel and stick to the exhaust air vents of your heating system, $12.75.

Water purification products: Life Support Systems household water filter is a double cartridge system, $239; Life Support Systems reverse osmosis filter system, $598; AC/DC ultraviolet water filter; Shower Master water saving showerhead dechlorinator, $55; Survivor hand-operated watermaker for making pure water wherever you travel.

Newsletter/ catalog (80-page) subscription, $3 for one year. Also listed in "Paper Products," "Household & Personal Care Products," "Energy Conservation" chapters.

Mountain Ark, 120 South East Ave, Fayetteville AR 72701. 1-800-643-8909. Free catalog of organic and macrobiotic foods. Also gourmet cookware, books, water purifiers and more.

National Ecological & Environmental

 Chapter Three: Clean Air, Clean Water

Delivery System (N.E.E.D.S.), 527 Charles Ave., Syracuse NY 13209. 1-800-634-1380. Catalog of air purifiers, water purifiers, sealants, and more.

Nigra Enterprises, 5699 Kanan Road, Agoura CA 91301-3358. (818) 889-6877. Jim Nigra has helped thousands of people improve the quality of their air and water. He specializes in satisfying the environmental needs of those with chemical sensitivities and traditional allergies. In addition to improving home and office environments, Jim has also been involved in designing systems for a wide variety of other applications, including studios, pet stores, doctors' offices, and music schools.

Jim acts as an independent agent offering personalized service (starting with a free telephone consultation); a variety of state-of-the-art equipment shipped direct to you from the manufacturer in most cases; discount prices because of low overhead; and return privileges.

He specializes in air and water purification systems, but also can provide a variety of other products: vacuums; face masks; lighting & fixtures; paints; sealants; wood stains; spackle; caulk; waxes; adhesive; cleansers; etc.

See also "Seminars, Workshops & Speakers" chapter.

The Pure Water Place, Inc., PO Box 6715, Longmont CO 80501. (303) 776-0056. Specializes in systems for the removal of toxic chemicals from drinking water. Provides personalized systems to meet individual needs.

Real Goods Trading Company, 966 Mazzoni St, Ukiah CA 95482. (707) 468-9214. FAX # (707) 468-0301. Order toll-free 1-800-762-7325. This company has an extensive 106-page catalog full of energy-saving equipment and supplies. Products for clean air & clean water include: reverse osmosis filtration systems; Rain-shower shower filter; hand water purifier; ozone water purifiers; Blue Springs Air Life air purification systems. More items listed in "Books," "Energy Conservation," "Household & Personal Care Products," "Baby & Children's Products" and "Recycling" chapters.

Simmons Handcrafts, 42295 Hwy 36, Bridgeville CA 95526. (707) 777-3280, ext 6074 (radio phone). Their catalog contains the Multi-Pure water purifier, model 400 and model 500. The Multi-Pure housings are warranted for ten years. These water purifiers are designed to be highly economical and to operate up to and over 1 year with low cost replacement element. More items from Simmons Handcrafts are listed in the "Household and Personal Care Products" chapter.

Solar Electric Engineering, Inc., 116 4th St, Santa Rosa CA 95401. (707) 542-1990. FAX # (707) 542-4358. This is a publicly owned corporation that has been committed to bringing to the marketplace environmentally sound products at affordable prices to the consumer. They have a 40-page

"Environmental Catalog," with clean air and water products, including: MultiPure drinking water systems; The Rainshower filter to remove chlorine and other pollutants from your water; Instapure® water filter; PowerSurvivor™ to make fresh water from the sea; room, desktop or auto air purifiers; and charcoal stacker to start your grill so that you don't need to use lighter fluid.

More items listed in "Energy Conservation," "Recycling," "Paper Products," "Clean Air, Clean Water," "Baby & Children's Products," and "Magazines, Newsletters & Brochures."

ThermaFlo, 3640 Main St, Springfield MA 01107. (413) 733-4433. FAX #(413) 733-9267. 1-800-8484-CFC. Manufacturer of Therma-Flo OZ Saver™, a CFC Recovery & Charging Station. This product can recover and charge CFCs from any refrigeration system running on R-12, R-22, R-500 and R-502. The patented design emphasizes safety, portability, superior evacuation rates and exceptional recovery and charging speeds. This product is used in conjunction with ThermaFlo's locally owned and operated central purification sites and completes the loop in their "total solution" approach to CFC's recovery and reclamation. Works on 115 volts; weighs 79 pounds. Full 1-year warranty on all parts and labor on this OZ Saver.

Please! I <u>promise</u> I'll never throw away another aluminum can!

 Chapter Three: Clean Air, Clean Water

Chapter Four:
Eco-Tourism

Eco-tourism is travel, whether it be hiking, camping, and safaris, with minimum impact on the environment. The eco-tourism philosophy also encompasses and minimum impact on the cultures that are visited. Some eco-tours include visits to areas of great natural resources, such as the Galapagos Islands or the rainforest.

ABEC's Alaska Adventures, 1304 Westwick Drive, Fairbanks AK 99712. (907) 457-8907. Their tours are committed to minimum impact camping techniques. Every effort is made to minimize the signs of their passing as they travel through a wilderness area. Group size is limited in order to provide this experience. This company offers various wilderness Alaska tours, such as: Caribou Migration Backpack (12 days); Kongakut River (10 days); Backpack/ River (12 days); Hulahula River (13 days); Artic Refuge Backpack (11 days); Arctic Ocean Backpack (12 days); Gates of the Artic Backpack (8 days); Alatna River (7 days); Noatak River (12 days). Provides personal references of people who have taken the trips.

Adirondack Mountain Club, Inc., RR 3 Box 3055, Lake George NY 12845. (518) 523-3441. (518) 668-4447. A non-profit membership organization with chapters throughout New York, New Jersey, and Pennsylvania, dedicated to broadening public appreciation for the New York State Forest Preserve, to providing opportunities for environmentally-responsible outdoor recreation, and for retaining the wilderness by working on conservation issues.

Countless outdoor activities are provided all year long, such as backpacking and day trips. The club provides guidebooks that are a recognized source of information for the Adirondacks. Volunteer activities also available, such as trial maintenance, out-

East Africa
Australia
Alaska
Galapagos
Costa Rica

Cheesemans' Ecology Safaris
Wildlife Tours; Daytrips in Monterey Bay in January
20800 Kittredge Road • Saratoga, CA 95070
(408) 741-5330 or 867-1371

house installation, erosion control, relocation & revegetation. Several lodges open to the public are located in the Adirondacks.

Also listed in "Books," "Seminars, Speakers & Workshops" and "Organizations" chapters.

Adventure Center, 1311 63rd St, Suite 200, Emeryville CA 94608. (415) 654-1879. FAX # (415) 654-4200. Telex 275963. Toll-free 1-800-227-8747. This company's philosophy has been to maintain low-impact travel, thereby ensuring closer interaction with local cultures, support for local economies and respect for the environment being visited. They inform their trip participants on how to be conservation-oriented travelers. They support non-profit environmental organizations such as Earth Island Institute.

Many tours are available, some of which are: Subantarctic islands of Australia & New Zealand sailing on tall ship for 11-31 days, you will see sea lions, fur seals, penguins and mollymawks, albatross, elephant seals; Himalayan adventure for 8-31 days; Great Overland Encounter, a 20,000 journey across Asia & Africa, traveling through 20 countries, 29 weeks camp-

ing; Amazon jungle, 19 days, see wildlife plus the Inca sites at Cuzco; the Great Wildlife Safari, camping 7 weeks; Galapagos & Amazon, 18 days; many other options and tours available.

Alaska Discovery, 369 S Franklin St, Juneau AK 99801. (907) 586-1911. FAX # (907) 586-2332. This company believes that we need not live at odds with our environment and that our use of the wilderness should not conflict with the needs of its present inhabitants. Their tours give instructions on low impact camping so that each area remains, as much as possible, in the same virgin state in which it was found.

Numerous wilderness trips are available, some of which are: sea kayaking in Glacier Bay National Park; sea kayaking in the Russell Fiord Wilderness Area; Ice Bay kayak and hiking expedition; Tatshenshini/Alsek River; Kongakut River-Artic National Wildlife Refuge; heart of the Tongass canoe trek; Alaska photo expedition; Baranof Wilderness Lodge kayak base camp; many many more.

American Hiking Society, 1015 31st St NW, Washington DC 20007. (703) 385-3252. This organization encourages volunteerism in trail building and maintenance. They also educate the public in the appreciation of walking and protect the interests of hikers. Hiking has always been ecologically sound touring.

American River Touring Association, Inc. (ARTA), Star Route 73, Groveland CA 95321. 1-800-323-2782. Wilderness whitewater vacations throughout the West: Utah, California, Oregon, Idaho. One to sixteen day trips. Educational and environmentally-sensitive style. Free information.

Basic Foundation, Inc./Basic Publishing & Promotions, PO Box 47012, St. Petersburg FL 33743. (813) 526-9562. Their immediate focus is on saving tropical rainforests. They offer tours to Belize (11 days), Costa Rica (12 days), & Ecuador (9 days). These tours focus on visiting tropical rainforests and observing the natural resources within them, including the wildlife.

More in "Organizations" chapter.

Bikecentennial, PO Box 8308, Missoula MT 59807. (406) 721-1776. Bike touring is an ecologically feasible alternative to regular recreation. This is a membership organization that promotes and supports bicycle touring, bicycle education, safety, and advocacy.

Membership benefits include: participation in the development of a national network of bicycle touring routes; the *Bike Report,* a magazine available to members only that covers topics about upkeep of equipment, tour routes, and networking information; *The Cyclists' Yellow Pages,* a 95-page resource guide to tours state by state, country by country, including hostels information, cycling organizations, cycling periodicals, national network, cycling books, and other resources; *Cyclosource,* a 4-page catalog for cyclists who are touring; and the Bicycle Forum, a periodical 16-page newsletter for cycling professionals and local advocates. Individual membership is $22; various kinds of memberships available including seniors/ students/ family.

They also have a catalog of planned Bikecentennial Tours, such as: Trans-America from Williamsburg, Virginia to Portland, Oregon; TransAm Trainer (West Coast) from Portland, Oregon to Missoula, Montana; TransAm Trainer (East Coast) from Williamsburg, Virginia to Carbondale, Illinois. How about the North Star Expedition, from Missoula, Montana to Anchorage, Alaska? There are trips just on the West Coast, or just on the East Coast, or the Teton-Yellowstone Loop. You can't beat the variety offered here if you are a bicycle enthusiast.

Biological Journeys, 1696 Ocean Drive, McKinleyville CA 95521. Toll-free reservation number 1-800-548-7555. Or make arrangements with Eureka Travel Agency at (707) 445-0861, FAX #(707) 445-5957, 1-800-228-1973, TELEX 4952863. This company offers marine natural history tours featuring close encounters with wildlife, solid education, and fun. Naturalist guides share their knowledge and enthusiasm of the places they love. Tours include: 8-day or 9-day whale-watching in Baja California or out of San Diego (various tours available); the Great Barrier Reef of Australia, 22 days; wildlife of the Galapagos, various tours available, 14 to 22 days; Ecuadorian Amazon tour available; Alaska and the Inside Passage tours, 8-11 days, to see grizzlies, glaciers, whales, old-growth forests.

Cheesemans' Ecology Safaris, 20800 Kittredge Rd, Saratoga CA 95070. (408) 741-5330. Their philosophy is that people in power in governments in the third world should realize what natural biological resources they have and that by taking interested citizens to these marvelous places that they will become involved with conservation organizations and help to try to save the planet. Economics seem to be the bottom line and eco-tourism is one way to make governments and people aware of what marvelous ecological diversity they have before they destroy it.

Tours are arranged and led by Doug Cheeseman, Professor of Zoology, Ecology and Gail Cheeseman, naturalist and birder. Doug is the Director of the DeAnza College Environmental Study Area, a native plant garden or arboretum. Doug and Gail have been program chairpersons for the Santa Clara Valley Audubon Society for the past 8 years. Gail is also the co-chairperson of the Environmental Action

Committee for that Audubon chapter.

Trips are non-smoking safaris and include areas such as: The Naturalist's Costa Rica, 16 days; Kenya Wildlife Safari , 22 days; Alaska, 14 days; The Natural History of Northern India, 29 days; Amazon Basin and Galapagos, 29 days; Australia's Incredible Wildlife, 23 days; day trip for blue whales and migrating seabirds; day trips for whale watching in Monterey Bay; Red Sea for diving and snorkeling, 7 days.

More information in "Seminars, Workshops and Speakers" chapter.

Explorers at Sea, Inc., PO Box 51, Main St, Stonington ME 04681. (207) 367-2356. This is an experienced sea kayaking services that gives hourly lessons, half day trips, day trips, 3 day trips, and up to 9 day trips. Sea kayaking is a great way to explore Maine's coast and to observe wildlife in a natural setting. Their programs include instruction on low-impact camping and wildlife identification for an all-around skills package.

Forum International (Worldwide) Inc., 91 Gregory Lane, Suite 21, Pleasant Hill CA 94523. (415) 671-2900. FAX # (415) 946-1500. (More information in "Organizations" chapter.) Forum Travel International and Eco-Tourism International have become this organization's professional travel branch for many programs, conferences, field studies, and other travel-related activities which have been developed. Since 1965, they have created over 1200 different top-quality nature, wildlife, adventure & cultural tours, expeditions, hiking, biking and other programs in which environmental and social responsibility are paramount. In one of their documents, they have stated, "We must rethink culture. We must rethink education." Their 4 main requirements for responsible tourism are: minimum environmental impact; minimum impact on—and maximum respect for—host cultures; maximum economic benefits to host country; and maximum "re-creational" satisfaction to participating tourists.

Off the Deep End Travels, PO Box 7511, Jackson WY 83001. (307) 733-8707. Toll-free 1-800-223-6833 outside Wyoming. This company's tours are generally self-propelled by bike, raft, kayak, hiking. This minimizes pollution from touring. Camping is low-impact. Examples of tours: Tahiti Bicycling Adventure; Papua New Guinea, hiking and cycling; Polynesian tour starting with square rig sailing, continuing with biking on enchanted isles (now that's ecologically sensitive!); Cycling Alpine Wonderlands; Bighorn Mountain Range (Wyoming) hiking with llamas carrying gear; Lapland Whitewater; Cycling Thailand; and many more.

Sanctuary Travel Services, Inc., 3701 E Tudor Rd, Anchorage AK 99507. (907) 561-1212. FAX # (907) 563-6747. Toll-free 1-800-247-3149. A full-service travel agency located in Anchorage. They share 20% of their commissions with local environmental organizations. The first three years of operation enabled them to raise over $100,000 for these organizations. Their advertising budget has been replaced by their fundraising program, so they rely heavily on word of mouth.

Voyagers International, PO Box 915, Ithaca NY 14851. (607) 257-3091. Telex 887181. FAX # (607) 257-3699. An environmentally-sensitive tour operator, this company organizes travel programs for leading non-profit organizations in the United States and Canada to international destinations. The tours emphasize in-depth experiences that are environmentally sound and culturally sensitive. An examples of the organizations with whom they have worked includes Cornell and Harvard Universities, Toronto Zoo, Academy of Natural Sciences, Massachusetts Audubon Society, American Birding Association, National Association of Biology Teachers, and more.

Tours are kept small, often no more than 12 people, for low impact travel. The focus of the trips is natural history, including visits to nature preserves, sanctuaries, and national parks. Local guides are used to support local economies. Their newsletter includes information on environmental news and conservation projects. Also assists in fundraising for the East African Wild Life Society and the Darwin Research Station.

Some example of recent tours: Detroit Audubon Society's trip to Belize (March 1991); A photographic safari to India with Leonard Lee Rue III

Chapter Four: Eco-tourism

"How can you have a headache? We're an endangered species!"

(March 1991); Massachusetts Audubon Society's trip to the Galapagos (March 1991).

Wilderness: Alaska/ Mexico, 1231 Sundance Loop, Fairbanks AK 99709, (907) 452-1821. Ron Yarnell is your guide for environmentally-sensitive wilderness trips to Alaska's Brooks Range and Mexico and Belize. Tours such as: Hulahula backpack (8 days); Artic refuge backpack (11 days); Kongakut backpack (8 days); Killik River backpack and kayak (8 days); Noatak backpack & kayak (8 days); Kobuk River (8 days). Long list of references of people who have taken the trips.

Chapter Five:
Educational Materials

There are some great environmental educational materials available, including curriculum materials and teaching aids for classrooms—posters, visual aids, videos, slides, audio cassettes, and more. There are educational materials and courses for adults as well as children.

The Acid Rain Foundation, Inc., 1410 Varsity Drive, Raleigh NC 27606. (919) 828-9443. Founded to foster a greater understanding of the acid rain problem and to help bring about its resolution. They have developed curriculum for kids: Quiz for Kids, grade 4-8, $5.95; Word Find, grades 4-8, $7.95; Science Projects, grades 5-12, $9.95; The Air Around Us, grades 5-12, $9.95; Curriculum, acid rain, grades 4-8, $19.95; and more, including puzzles and posters.

They have a list of audio-visual materials (slides, audio cassettes, video cassettes, films, filmstrips, transparencies) available on the acid rain problem.

More in "Organizations" chapter.

Baubiologie Hardware, 207 16th St, Unit B, Pacific Grove CA 93950. (408) 372-8626. They call themselves the "healthful" hardware store. Their

catalog is an education in itself! For instance, on page 3, they say, "Followers of Baubiologie principles avoid electromagnetic radiations whenever possible." They explain how to reduce of eliminate much of the electromagnetic radiation commonly found in homes. Products are found in the catalog to do this.

They offer a "Bau-biologie Correspondence Course" that's a translation of the popular teachings of Professor Anton Schneider, founder of the German Institute for Baubiologie und Okologie in Neubeurn, West Germany. It has been translated into English by German Architect Helmut Ziehe, Managing Director of the International Institute for Bau-biologie™ and Ecology. Thousands of Europeans have already taken this course. The course consists of 22 course packs totaling approximately 800 pages and requires about 1 year to complete. Students receive a regular newsletter and offered a yearly compendium. Course: $750.

More information found in "Books," "Energy Conservation," "Clean Air, Clean Water," and "Household & Personal Use Products" chapters.

Caribbean Conservation Corp., PO Box 2866, Gainesville FL 32602. (904) 373-6441. Dedicated to the protection and preservation of the marine sea turtle and its habitat, specifically in Costa Rica and the Caribbean. Projects: Educational video *National Audubon Society Special: Sea Turtle,* 58 minutes, $35.95 plus $3.50 for shipping. More information in "Organizations" chapter.

Center for Science in the Public Interest, 1875 Connecticut Ave NW #300, Washington DC 20009. (202) 332-9110. FAX # (202) 265-4954. The issues they are presently working on are organic and sustainable agriculture, food additives, nutrition and ingredient labeling, deceptive food and beverage advertising, fast food, and they serve as a watchdog of government and industry.

Educational books available are: *Eat, Think & Be Healthy* ($8.95) for kids with 56 activities; *Creative Food Experience for Children* ($7.95) has practical games, recipes and activities for children, 256 pages.

Slide guides are handy little charts small enough to take along shopping.

These slide guides are very popular because of the huge amount of information they provide in a very handy format. Titles: *Eating Smart Fat Guide* lists the fat and saturated fat of over 200 foods; *Eating Smart Additive Guide* tells you which additives are safe, which to avoid and which are poorly tested; *Eating Smart Fast Food Guide* lists calories, fat, sodium, sugar and a GLOOM rating for over 250 fast foods. Each slide guide is $3.95. Quantity discounts available.

Their line of "Life Saving Guides to Eating Right" posters are each 18" x 24". There are available in standard paper ($4.95) or laminated plastic ($9.95). Titles: *LifeSaver Fat & Calorie Guide Poster; New American Eating Guide; Anti-Cancer Eating Guide; Chemical Cuisine Poster; Nutrition Scoreboard Poster, Fast Food Eating Guide;* and more.

Nutrition Wizard by Michael Jacobson is software that analyzes the nutrients in your meals. Using data on more than 1,800 foods, the program tells you how much of what is in your diet. It also calculates optimum weight and nutritional requirements, and gives menus a "GLOOM" rating. IBM compatible, $99.95; Apple IIc/e $189.95; Apple IIgs $207.95.

More information in "Organizations" and "Books" chapters.

Co-op America, 2100 "M" St NW, Suite 403, Washington DC 20063. (202) 872-5307. Toll-free 1-800-424-2667. This is a non-profit, member-controlled, worker-managed association linking socially responsible businesses and consumers in a national network, a new alternative marketplace. Co-op America allows consumers to align buying habits with values. Basic information found in "Organizations" chapter.

Educational materials from their catalog: *365 Ways to Save Our Planet in 1991* page-a-day calendar with a little reminder each day how we can make a difference, $9.95; Hugg-a-Planet toy made of 100% cotton, $18.95; *A Kid's Point of View of the Environment* is songs from Michael Mish based on what kids told him about the environment, audio cassette, $9.95; Arcobaleno (rainbow) is a puzzle and a construction toy in one, ages 3-8, from Learning Materials Workshop, $39.50; "Endangered Species" ($29.50) or "Ocean" ($27.50) are very unique puzzles in layers, ages 3 to adult, by Coyote Collections of Oregon.

Products from the catalog are found in "Recycling," "Energy Conservation," "Books," " Organically Grown," "Household & Personal Care Products," "Paper Products, " and "Baby & Children's Products" chapters.

Creative Printing & Publishing, 712 N. Hwy 17-92, Longwood FL 32750. (407) 830-4747. Toll-free outside Florida 1-800-780-4447. Educational materials: RecycleSaurous™ coloring and activity booklet. Call or write for free catalog on RecycleSaurous™ products.

Eco Source™, 9051 Mill Station Road Bldg #E, Sebastopol CA 95472. (717) 829-7957 or (707) 829-8345. Catalog of products for a cleaner, safer world. Includes educational materials such as: "Save the World" cooperative environmental board game that educates players about ecological problems and gives them hope that they can be solved, $21.40; "Man of the Trees" video of Richard Baker's vision of how to heal the earth, $19.95; Hugg-A-Planet, a stuffed soft earth that shows physical features or political boundaries, 6 inch for $9.95, 12 inch (physical or political features) $19.95; "AC-DC," the game of electricity, $7.95; The Earth Puzzle from a NASA photo, $4.95.

Other products in their catalog found in "Household and Personal Use," "Recycling," "Books," "Energy Conservation," and "Clean Air, Clean Water" chapters.

Energy Store, PO Box 3507, Santa Cruz CA 95063-3507. (408) 464-1938. Toll-free 1-800-288-1938. This is a mail order business specializing in energy conserving products. Free catalog available by calling toll-free number. Educational product: *Weatherstripping and Insulation Video* that explains in detail the easiest and more effective ways to make your home more energy efficient through insulation and weatherstripping, $14.

More products listed in "Books," "Baby & Children's Products" and "Energy Conservation" chapters.

Environmental Action Coalition, 625 Broadway, New York NY 10012. (212) 677-1601. Publishers of Eco-News, an informative, cartoon-illustrated newsletter about the environment for children grades 4-6. Each 8-page issue explores a different environmental them that youngsters can relate to, and is packed with learning activities for young people to do either on their own or together with classmates and teachers. Issues cost 50¢ each; quantity price is 40¢ per copy for 20 or more copies. Add 25% of the amount of the order for postage. There are 65 issues available. Examples of themes: "Making & doing with garbage," "City trees need your help," "Summer fun and the environment," "Ecological apple activities," "Environmental bingo," "Math & solid waste problems," "How should we use energy?"

More information in "Organiza-

tions" chapter.

Environmental Hazards Management Institute, 10 Newmarket Rd, PO Box 932, Durham NH 03824. (603) 868-1496. FAX # (603) 868-1547. This organization provides environmental information to private citizens, industry, non-profit agencies, government, and schools. Their most widely-known educational tool has been the "Environmental Educational Wheels." These educational wheels are eye-catching, informative and easy-to-use. There are three kinds: "Recycling Wheel™" "Household Hazardous Waste Wheel™" and "Water Sense Wheel™".

The Recycling Wheel has on one side the categories of items that can be recycled (plastic, glass, paper, etc) and as you turn the wheel to that category, it will tell you about options for recycling that product, how it's collected for recycling, what recycled products can be made from it, the percentage that product occurs in the waste stream, and more. On the backside, there's another group of categories with additional information. These wheels are $2.75 each, quantity discounts available. Each of the wheels contain similar information about their respective titles.

Another educational product available from this organization is the "Enviro-Bookcovers" for elementary and secondary school books. These are bookcovers with colorful artwork combines with the environmental message: "Rethink The Way We Live," plus a list of "Ways You Can Change the World Today!" Price of the bookcovers: 35¢ each in quantities of 1000-1499; larger quantities have discounts on the price.

More information in "Organizations" chapter.

Freshwater Foundation, PO Box 90, Navarre MN 55392. (612) 471-8407. Videos available include: *When the River Runs Dry* (grades 5-9), comes in a packet with teaching guide & 4-color poster, $50; *How to Protect Your Private Water Well,* $37; *Water Pollution ... Where Does It Come From?* $37.

More in "Organizations" chapter.

Household Hazardous Waste Project, 901 South National Ave, Box 108, Springfield MO 65804. (417) 836-5777. Their booklet *Guide to Hazardous Products Around the Home* has been recognized and used throughout the United States and by the United Nations Environment Programme. It has also been endorsed by Greenpeace, The Cousteau Society, Seventh Generation and *McCall's* Magazine. This manual helps you understand product labels, helps you select safer products before bringing toxic chemicals into your home, helps minimize waste leaving your home, and helps you located recycling options in your community for some types of hazardous waste. $9.95, 178 pages.

Brochures available to the public: *Consumer Tips,* 50¢; *Pesticides,* 50¢; *Safety Equipment,* 75¢. Bulk discounts available.

A short educational video program is available, outlining the problems and solutions for household hazardous waste, VHS, $28 ppd.

More information in "Organizations" chapter.

Illinois Environmental Protection Agency, 2200 Churchill Rd, PO Box 19276, Springfield IL 62794-9276. (217) 782-2829. Educational and children's materials available: "The Land We Depend On" education packet; *Earth Trek ... Explore Your Environment; Let's Recycle,* lesson plans for Grades K-6 or 7-12; *Teaching Soil & Water Conservation: A Classroom & Field Guide;* "Water: The Liquid of Life" education packet; "The Air We Breathe" education packet. More materials listed in "Magazines, Newsletters & Brochures" chapter.

The Institute for Earth Education, PO

Box 288, Warrenville IL 60555. (708) 393-3096 or (509) 395-2299. Since 1974, Earth Education has been in the process of helping people live more harmoniously and joyously with the natural world. This organization is composed of people who work at trying to live more lightly on the earth. They emphasize environmental learning programs: Sunship Earth™; Earthkeepers™; Earth Caretakers™; and SUNSHIP II™. These programs have information packets ($1 each) to explain how the programs work. The organization sponsors International Earth Education Conferences in which children and adults can experience the various programs and catch up on latest developments in newer programs. Membership starts at $20 and includes the quarterly publication *Talking Leaves*.

Write for free catalog "The Earth Education Sourcebook," which tells about their organization, their programs, and has various interesting products for sale, such as: books, activities, supplemental educational materials, props, posters, seals, cassette tapes, and T-shirts. Many of the materials are designed for children as well as adults. One interesting book title is *The Earth Speaks* ($10.95) by Steve Van Matre and Bill Weiler. This is a collection of images and impressions by those "who have listened to the earth with their hearts," including Rachel Carson (author of *Silent Spring*), poet Walt Whitman, essayist Henry David Thoreau, naturalist John Muir, and more.

An interesting product offered is "Earthwalks" ($10.95) which is a packet of nature activities, applicable for children as well as adults. There's also an "Earth Education Slide Show" ($100) that contains 120 slides and lasts 20 minutes, designed for 10-12 year olds. T-shirts ($11.50) include such mottos as "Your Mother [earth] is in Trouble," and "This Body is Made out of 100% Recycled Materials." Many more services available, including workshops and speakers.

Also listed under "Organizations" chapter and "Seminars, Workshops, and Speakers" chapter.

Institute for Local Self-Reliance, 2425 18th St NW, Washington DC 20009. (202) 232-4108. FAX # (202) 332-0463. *Worms Eat My Garbage,* 100 pages, descriptions for setting up and maintaining small scale vermicomposting operations, ideal for school project, $6.95. More information in "Organizations" chapter.

Institute of Scrap Recycling Industries, Inc., 1627 "K" St NW, 7th floor, Washington DC 20006-1704. (202) 466-4050. FAX # (202) 775-9109. TWX 710 822 9782. EasyLink 620 23427. The group provides public education about the benefits of recycling. Publications available to the public: *The Scrap Map: An Environmental Publication for Grades K-6,* a colorful 6 x 9 brochure that explains the concept of recycling and illustrates recycling of automobiles, aluminum cans and newspapers, $15 for package of 30; *The Scrap Map Teachers' Kit,* includes one copy of *The Scrap Map* and also an environmental poster with bulletin board suggestions, Teachers' Guide, information brochures, a list of ISRI chapters, and the booklet *Scrap: America's Ready Resource,* $5 per kit to teachers, schools, libraries and non-profit organizations. Write order on organizational letterhead and enclose payment.

Phoenix: Voice of the Scrap Recycling Industries is a magazine covering recycling processing activities and issues. Published 2-3 times a year; free to government officials, educators, libraries and environmentalists. Write subscription request on organizational letterhead.

"Who is Making a World of Difference for Our World?" brochure available to the public; single copies free.

More information in "Organizations" chapter.

Jade Mountain, PO Box 4616, Boulder CO 80306. (303) 449-6601. FAX # (303) 449-8266. Toll-free 1-800-442-1972. Large selection of energy saving and appropriate technology products. Educational product: 4 in 1 Solar Construction Kit for children at least 4 years old. The child can build solar-powered windmills, airplanes, watermills and helicopter with the bright plastic pieces in this kit. $15 postpaid.

Newsletter/catalog (80-page) subscription, $3 for one year. Also listed in "Paper Products," "Household & Personal Care Products," "Clean Air, Clean Water" and "Energy Conservation" chapters.

The Land Institute, 2440 East Water Well Rd, Salina KS 67401. (913) 823-5376. A private, non-profit organization devoted to sustainable agriculture and good stewardship of the earth. Educational videocassettes may be checked out from the organization for $5 to cover postage and handling. Titles: *The Earth is the Lord's: Ecology as a Religious Concern,* a one-hour NBC-TV documentary produced for the Jewish Theological Seminary that discusses man's responsibilities for his environment; *Market to Market* produced by Iowa Public TV, 1988; *The Promise of the Land,* produced by Smithsonian World, 1987; *Uncertain Harvest* by PBS, 1985.

The heart of the Land Institute community is the internship program. For 43 weeks, a group of 8 to 10 post graduates from a variety of background and academic traditions carry out experiments in agroecology and investigated the potential of living in a sustainable society. Students work closely with the staff on experiments, and research is reported annually in *The Land Institute Research Report.*

More information in "Organizations" chapter.

Land Stewardship Project, 14758 Ostlund Trail North, Marine on St. Croix MN 55047. (612) 433-2770. FAX # (612) 433-2704. Offers educational videos, cultural programs, and music about sustainable agricultural practices and land stewardship ethics. Videos are: *Excellence in Agriculture* ($40, also in book format) contains interviews with 10 Minnesota farm families who are stewards of the land; *Planting in the Dust* ($90) a popular one-woman drama about a farm woman's love and concern for the land. *Iowa Natural Heritage Magazine* said that this play "expresses the need for a new attitude toward both the land and farming on the part of all who eat." Live performances are available of this drama as well.

A Song for the Earth is an environmental puppet show for both children and adults. It shows that Mother Earth is sick; yet there is hope for the future. A representative from St. Therese School said that the show was "Extremely enlightening. Good program for all ages. It has made an impact on the students—they remembered a lot."

Music of the Land is a live musical tribute to the earth in song and slides, performed by Bret Hesla of Minneapolis. He uses a variety of instruments (some made out of recycled materials) to serenade the earth with love songs, old favorites and his own original tunes. Earth Ethics said "Bret's songs spoke to my heart and mind—and my sense of whimsey. His water cycle song tells us unforgettably why we must work for clean water."

More information in "Organizations" chapter.

Malachite School & Small Farm, ASR Box 21, Pass Creek Rd, Gardner CO 81040. (719) 746-2412. They teach about leading a sustainable lifestyle and becoming a more responsible citizen of the world. Their programs teach about conservation, waste reduction, recycling practices, self-reliant food sources, and energy efficient homes. Programs available are: field trips, Malachite Elderhostel, Malachite farmstays, Malachite retreats, Malachite weeks, Malachite hostel program; and Malachite internships.

Malachite recently sponsored an educational presentation for Gardner School. Students learned about global warming, acid rain, endangered animals, and rain forest destruction.

Malachite is an educational organization and welcomes donations. Newsletters sent to all donors.

National Arbor Day Foundation, 211 North 12th St, Lincoln NE 68508. (402) 474-5655. Dedicated to tree planting and conservation. Educational programs include "Grow Your Own Tree" and "Trees are Terrific" designed for grades K-6. More information in "Organizations" chapter.

National Audubon Society, 950 Third Ave., New York NY 10022. (212) 832-3200. *Audubon Society's Video-Guide™ to the Birds of North America* is a 5-part videocassette series on over 500 North American birds. This project has taken 5 years in the making, and is an incredible guide. The videos can give you the experience of being there. There are computer graphics such as maps showing bird migration patterns, colored-coded references and indexes, making the videos easy to use for bird identification. The set is $144.75 plus $5 for shipping and handling, or 5 monthly installments (on credit card) of $29.95. Available VHS or Beta. Ordering address for this set is: The Easton Press, 47 Richards Avenue, Norwalk CT 06857.

More information about the Audubon Society in the "Organizations" chapter.

The Nature Company, PO Box 2310, Berkeley CA 94702. 1-800-227-1114. FAX (415) 849-0465. Beautiful full-color catalog full of interesting items for people who love nature. The educational materials in this catalog explain and explore nature, and are wonderful for showing the beauty we are trying to save. Examples: *Water, Gift of Life* a video journey filmed by world-renowned marine cinematographer Al Giddings that traces this magical substance through all its realms, approx 50 minutes, $39.95; original music from this video available on CD ($19.95) or cassette ($14.95); "The Daily Planet 1991" is the new version of the hit that was acclaimed Most Educational Calendar of the Year, includes beautiful illustrations with 365 fascinating daily facts about animals and plants, printed on recycled paper, $18.95; "Leaf Discovery Kit" turns outdoor walks into great adventures, $9.95; *World Alive* video with dolphins, gazelles, tortoises, includes 16-page booklet, $34.95; paint-it-yourself rainforest poster that's educational and fun, includes 12 large and 12 narrow tips, plus separate chart that identifies the animals $16.95.

Other items in the catalog described in "Books," "Household & Personal Care Products," and "Recycling" chapters.

New Alchemy Institute, 237 Hatchville Rd, East Falmouth MA 02536. (508) 564-6301. Dedicated to an ecological future. Located on a 12-acre farm on Cape Cod, Massachusetts, New Alchemy serves students, teachers, gardeners, small-scale farmers and communities with research and education projects on food, energy, water and waste treatment systems. Educational programs include on-site tours, courses, school and community programs and publications. Internships are available, as well are volunteer opportunities. Their Green Classroom is a garden-based science program in the Falmouth, Massachusetts, schools. This program can be used throughout New England. A teachers' manual is available. More information in "Organizations" chapter.

Old Mill Farm School of Country Living, PO Box 463, Mendocino CA 95460. (707) 937-0244. Offers an apprenticeship in an alternative organic farm homestead of 40 acres with an emphasis on the following: alternative energy; solar heat; solar electric biodynamic intensive raised vegetables, grains, fruit trees and herbs; organic goat's cheese; non-chemical treated wool products. Free brochure.

Pennsylvania Resources Council, PO Box 88, Media PA 19063. (215) 565-9131. Specializes in recycling information. Classroom materials available: *Spike & His Friends Recycle,* preschool to third grade, story coloring book, $1.50 each or $80 for 100 copies; Teachers Guide to Spike & His Friends Recycle, $1; Spike Poster shows benefits of recycling, 11" x 17", $1 or $37.50 for 100 copies; Spike skit ($1); Spike slides ($50 deposit, $5 rental); Spike video ($50 deposit, $5 per week rental); Spike kit has storybook, teacher's guide, poster and skit, $3.75.

More classroom aides on recycling: *Recycling's No Puzzle* with Teachers' Guide for grades 5-12 has 10 original puzzles from crosswords to cryptograms to challenge language skills as they teach recycling, $3.50 ea or $100 for 50 copies; *Recycling Makes Sense for Your School* outlines the steps to starts a recycling program at your school, 25¢; *Reusable Math* with Teachers' Guide for grades 1-8 has math problems relating to recycling, $3.50 ea or $100 for 50 copies; *Teacher's Guide to Recycling Curricula* is an annotated bibliography of curricula resources and activities on recycling, 8 pages, $2.50; Recycling Lesson Plans for grades K-12 is seven lesson plans on waste reduction and recycling, free with postage; Recycle Your Board Game for ages 10-adult has players form recycling companies, purchase property and market recyclables, $15.

Litter control classroom materials: *Take Me to Your Litter* (in English and Spanish) is a story coloring book about fighting litter, for grades K-4, $2.50 ea or $70 for 100 copies; Teacher's Guide for *Take Me to Your Litter* has suggestions for study units in social studies, math, English, science and health based on the coloring book, $1.50.

More information in "Organizations" and "Magazines, Newsletters & Brochures" chapters.

Planet Drum Foundation, Box 31251, San Francisco CA 94131. (415) 285-6556. Planet Drum is planning to open a Green City Center (projected date fall 1991), which will be a place to demonstrate techniques and activities of urban sustainability and which will educate the public about them and influence municipal policies.

For more information, see the "Organizations" chapter.

Public Broadcasting Service, 1320 Braddock Place, Alexandria VA 22314-1698. (703) 739-5380. 1-800-424-7943. Amway sponsored ICE-WALK, a 1989 International North Pole Expedition. Icewalk's mission was to focus the world's attention on pollution and global warming and to emphasize the need for international cooperation and individual initiative for protecting the environment. A four-part PBS educational video series was produced about Icewalk. The series shows how the 8-member team each hauled 250 pounds of food and equipment for 10-12 hours a day across more than 2000 jagged ice ridges. The team fought 70-mile an hour winds and temperatures as low as 70 degrees below zero.

The video series shows how fragile the frozen seas are; how deadly is a storm of acid snow; and shows about the vanishing ozone and its effects. The school kit ($150) includes: a teachers guide; reproducible student handouts; discussion questions; before-and-after viewing activities; and supplemental readings. Single programs are $39.95.

PBS also has a service called PBS VideoFinders. If you are looking for a hard-to-find video, or if you need to know the availability of public television titles for your school or library, there's now a 900 number to answer your questions. Call 1-900-860-9301 within the continental U.S. Callers are charged $3 for the first minute and $1 for each additional minute.

Rainforest Action Network, 301 Broadway, Suite A, San Francisco CA 94133. (415) 398-4404. FAX # (415) 398-2732. Educational materials: Slide show with 78 slides and a script showing rainforest ecology and destruction, $85; *Tropical Rainforest Press Brief,* a press kit with quotable quotes, maps, news clipping, bibliography, contacts, questions and answers, $14.95. More information is in "Organizations" chapter.

Refuse Industry Productions, Inc., PO Box 1011, Grass Valley CA 95945. (916) 272-7289. Outside California call toll-free 1-800-535-9547. Offers a complete solid waste education & public awareness program emphasizing the three R's: Reduce, Reuse, Recycle! They have K-12 curriculum, videos, educational aids, colorbooks, wallcharts, stickers, and supplementary materials.

Save the Planet Shareware, PO Box 45, Pitkin CO 81241. (303) 641-5035. Producers of "Save the Planet" computer software for PC compatibles (512 K RAM, 5.25 or 3.5 inch formats) and Macintosh computer (using Hypercard). This program provides up-to-date information on global warming and ozone depletion as well as a wealth of environmental action resources. Topics covered: recycling and energy saving ideas, shopping suggestions to reduce pollution and waste, fossil fuel combustion, population explosion, forest destruction, climate modeling showing greenhouse warming estimated by scientists, and more. Program contains lists of conservation organizations. There's also a database of all 535 members of Congress so users can use it to write letters to Congress. A summary of environmental voting records is included. This software package is only $15.

Save the World, PO Box 84366, Los Angeles CA 90073. (213) 450-3134. Save The World game is a board game which takes the position that the planet's other inhabitants are just as important as people and have equal survival rights, and is a game that attempts to show solutions to the serious ecological problems facing us. Players learn about problems such as: the threat of nuclear war, overpopulation, the greenhouse effect, pollution, rainforest destruction, ozone depletion, as well as solutions such as: catalytic converters, recycling resources, co-generation, permaculture, reverse vending machines, and even some that are as yet visionary. This game is designed for older kids and adults. Game was designed by Don Strachan, who writes a regular ecology column in the *LA Whole Life Monthly*. Game is $16, make checks payable to Bongers.

This company also has a comic book called "How You Can Save the Planet," featuring nine great stories featuring eco-hero Mr. Green and his hydrogen-powered jet pack. This is 60-pages full of good ideas for concerned global citizens. $4.75 postpaid, make checks payable to Bongers at the above address.

Seventh Generation, Colchester VT 05446-1672. (802) 655-3116. FAX toll-free # 1-800-456-1139. Order toll-free 1-800-456-1177. Customer service toll-free 1-800-456-1197.

Seventh Generation is one of the most well-known companies for environmentally safe consumer products. Their 48-page catalog "Products for a Healthy Planet" ($2) contains an extraordinary variety of products. They also practice what they preach. For instance, they recycle their office paper, and reuse cardboard boxes for shipping. They have a 1% fund that goes to environmental organizations.

Educational materials include: a child's paper recycling kit and book ($24.95); Hugg-a-Planet, their bestselling toy ($19.95, baby $11.95);

solar educational kit ($14.95); bird feeder and book ($19.95); The Green Game, a board game with questions on the environment ($29.95).

Environmental books for children listed under "Baby & Children's Products" chapter.

There are so many products in this catalog that additional information can be found in these chapters: "Baby and Children's Products," "Books," "Household & Personal Care Products," "Paper Products," "Recycling," "Energy Conservation," and "Organically Grown."

Sisters' Choice, 1450 6th St, Berkeley CA 94710. (415) 524-5804. Cassette tape called *All In This Together* (Candy Forest, Nancy Schimmel and the Singing Rainbows Youth Ensemble, ages 9-15, with special guests Laurie Lewis & Rosie Radiator) is 15 ecology songs for the whole family. The songs are folk, jazz & rock numbers about the disappearing rain forest, pet overpopulation, endangered species, the urban forests and other songs about the environment. Some of the song titles are: "My Sister's a Whale in the Sea," "Must Be Johnny Appleseed," "Eating Up the Forest." This tape was a 1990 Parents' Choice Gold Award Winner. Cassette is $10. The company is in the process of developing and testing a study guide to go along with this tape, so inquire about these if you're interested.

The company also has a book called *Frogs That Sing: An Ecology Songbook* which has the song from *All*

In This Together plus other songs on the environment by Malvina Reynolds. Melody lines with guitar chords or piano arrangements. Available 1991, $10.

See also "Seminars, Speakers & Workshops" chapter.

Sprout House, 40 Railroad St, Great Barrington MA 01230 (413) 528-5200. Kits and courses for growing organic foods at home. Introductory course ($79) gives you an indoor vegetable kit; 2 flaxseed sprout bags; a book *Recipes from the Sproutman*; the beginners dozen seeds (in half pound bags); and the book *Growing Vegetables Indoors*. A complete course ($139) adds 7 guidebooks and 8 classes on audio cassette. Individual audio cassettes are available for $9 each and includes titles such as "Juice Fasting I"; "Vegetarianism"; "Indoor Gardening." Individual kits are available, such as Flaxseed Sprout Bag ($12.95) which is a bag made from the natural, raw linen fibers of the flaxseed plant and perfect for growing sprouts; or the Indoor Vegetable Kits ($29.95) that contains seeds and custom-designed bamboo sprouters. *The Sprout House Newsletter* is published 5 times a year ($10). Contains information about new seeds, how to maintain the best sprouts, clean water information; workshop schedules; more.

More information in the "Organically Grown" chapter.

Trees for Life, 1103 Jefferson, Wichita KS 67203. (316) 263-7294. A non-profit organization that helps people worldwide plant and maintain trees. Food-producing trees not only protect the environment but also feed the hungry. "Project Trees for Life" creates and awareness and provides trees for the world. This project is for grade school children and includes a planting carton for each child, non-toxic seeds, and a teacher's workbook about hunger facts and planting instructions plus other activities. The cost is $10 postpaid for 15 students, $15 postpaid for 30 students. Sample kit is $2 ppd.

More information available in "Organizations" chapter.

Union of Concerned Scientists, 26 Church St, Cambridge MA 02238. (617) 547-5552. *Greenhouse Crisis: The American Response* is a award-winning video (Bronze Medal at the International Film & TV Festival in New York) that explains how the use of energy in the United States may be contributing to global warming and provides positive steps individuals can take to help fight this environmental threat. Designed for a general audience and accompanied by a discussion guide. VHS, 11 minutes, $14.95. More information in "Organizations," "Books," and "Magazines, Newsletters & Brochures" chapter.

University Research Expeditions Program (UREP), University of California, Berkeley CA 94720. (415) 642-6586. This program provides hands-on field research experiences to students, teachers and the general public by supporting important University of California research at sites around the world. There are worldwide field research projects in the natural and social sciences, including environmental studies, animal behavior, archaeology, arts, anthropology and marine studies. Scholarships for teachers and students are available. Free catalog of expeditions and seasonal updates.

Wildlife Games Inc., PO Box 247, Ivy VA 22945. (804) 972-7016. Producers of The Whale Game™ survival at sea, a board game with an objective of building a whale family and guiding it home. Carefully researched "Whale Facts" on game cards make this educational as well as fun. $19 postpaid.

Wildlife Information Center, Inc., 629 Green St., Allentown PA 18102. (215) 434-1637. The Center is actively involved in public lectures and wildlife walks. There are courses for public school teachers dealing with hawk migrations, urban wildlife, world wildlife conservation and other topics. Hundreds of teachers have completed one or more of these courses. In 1987 the Center hosted a national conference with the theme of raptors and public education.

Wildlife Protector is a computer software prepared as a HyperCard stack for Macintosh users. Seven basic sections are: about the Wildlife Information Center; CITES; endangered species; hunting; laws & enforcement; reading list; and wildlife. Member's price, $15; non-member, $25; corporation price, $35.

More information in "Organizations" chapter.

Xerces Society, 10 SW Ash St, Portland OR 97204. (503) 222-2788. Dedicated to the preservation of invertebrate protection, especially butterflies. Educational materials: *Butterflies of the American West: A Coloring Album,* $5.45 ppd; *Butterflies of Eastern North America: A Coloring & Activity Book,* $6.45 ppd. Also self-help sheets: *Railways & Butterflies,* 75¢; *Create a Community Butterfly Reserve,* 75¢; *Butterfly Gardening,* $2.50; *Endangered Mission Blue Butterfly of California,* 75¢; *Butterfly Gardening—One Way to Increase Urban Wildlife,* 75¢; *Endangered and Extinct Butterflies—Why?,* $1; *Why Save An Insect?* $1; more on endangered species. More information in "Books" and "Organizations" chapters.

Chapter Six:
Energy Conservation

Energy conservation products are numerous. Water conservation includes products such as low flow showerheads, faucets, and toilet dams. Solar electricity products are easily obtainable no matter how remote you are. Most of these companies provide education and information as well as products; some even offer system design and planning.

Aatec Publications, PO Box 7119, Ann Arbor MI 48107. (313) 995-1470. Specializes in books on photovoltaics (solar electricity) and other energy conservation books. See listings in "Books" chapter.

All South Energy Control, 29 Barnes St, Marietta GA 30060. (404) 426-9652. This company specializes in developing and installing products to reduce energy costs and make the living and working environment more pleasant. In addition to consultation and energy analysis, these are services and products they can provide: solar control film; sun screen and shade screen; insulation, electrical energy conservation systems, more.

Baubiologie Hardware, 207 16th St, Unit B, Pacific Grove CA 93950. (408) 372-8626. Energy-saving compact fluorescent bulbs offered in their catalog. These bulbs are manufactured using no radioactive materials, so they cost more, but are more user-friendly than most.

Other energy conservation products in their catalog include: IFO cascade that saves toilet water, $265; shower water saver, $16.95; kitchen water saver, $5.75; bath sink water saver, $2.75; point-of-use water heater, 2.5 gallons, $189.

Their catalog is extensive, so be sure to see all listings for this company. More information found in "Books," "Household & Personal Care Products," "Clean Air, Clean Water," and "Educational Materials" chapters.

Biomass Publications of America, Box 69333, Portland OR 97201. (503) 246-4436. FAX # (503) 452-0595. Supplies a range of information about the pellet and solid fuel (wood stove) industry. Their 14-page brochure, *Pellet Primer,* is an introduction to heating with wood pellets, $2. Quantity discounts available. Other information: *Buying Guide to Pellet Stoves,* $5.95; *Energy Evaluator* fuel calculator, $4.95; dealer *Check List for Pellet Stoves,* $2.95; *Appliance Manufacturers* (who sells the stoves), $1.95; *Pellet Mills* (for finding the fuel), $1.95.

Conservation & Renewable Energy Inquiry & Referral Service (CAREFIRS), PO Box 8900, Silver Spring MD 20907. 1-800-523-2929. CAREFIRS is operated by Advances Sciences Inc, under contract by the US Department of Energy to aid technology transfer by responding to public inquiries on the use of renewable energy technologies and conservation techniques for residential and commercial needs.

The goal of this organization is to assist the general public in determining the feasibility of using these technologies by providing basic and special information. For more technical information, CAREFIRS maintains and refers people to an extensive network of government agencies and organizations whose areas of expertise cover the entire range of energy technologies.

The group operates a nationwide toll-free telephone services and a post office box to receive public inquiries.

Topics covered by CAREFIRS include: active and passive solar heating; photovoltaics; wind energy; biomass conversion; solar thermal electric; geothermal energy; small-scale hydroelectric; alcohol fuels; wood heating; ocean energy; and all energy conservation technologies. CAREFIRS provides more than 150 publications, fact sheets, and bibliographies; many are furnished and approved by government organizations.

Co-op America, 2100 "M" St NW, Suite 403, Washington DC 20063. (202) 872-5307. Toll-free 1-800-424-2667. This is a non-profit, member-controlled, worker-managed association linking socially responsible businesses and consumers in a national network, a new alternative marketplace. Co-op America allows consumers to align buying habits with values. Basic information found in "Organizations" chapter.

Energy conservation products from their catalog: water saving showerheads; The Incredible® line of Tapsavers; non-electric carpet sweeper from Real Goods Alternative Energy Company, $35; solar battery charger, $26.95; compact fluorescent light bulbs.

Products from the catalog are found in "Recycling," "Energy Conservation," "Educational Materials," "Books," " Organically Grown," "Household & Personal Care Prod-

Dahon folding bike—take it anywhere!

ucts," "Paper Products," and "Baby & Children's Products" chapters.

Dahon, The Folding Bicycle People, 901 Corporate Center Dr, Suite 508, Monterey Park CA 91754. (213) 264-7969. FAX # (213) 264-8042. The Dahon folding bicycle is a truly unique way to save energy and keep the air clean. You can take this bike with you nearly everywhere because of its technology that allows it to be folded up. It can even be transported in its own carrying case!

Devices & Services Company, 10024 Monroe Dr, Dallas TX 75229. (214) 902-8337. Has instruments for solar energy users that measure reflectance, absorbance, transmittance and emittance. Write for their catalog.

Ecco Bella, 6 Provost Square, Suite 602, Caldwell NJ 07006. (201) 226-5799. FAX # (201) 226-0991. Toll-free 1-800-888-5320. This company manufactures and sells products that are cruelty-free and environmentally sound. The Ecco Bella line of products is extensive and featured in their own catalog, but there are other products featured as well. Energy conservation products: compact fluorescent lightbulbs; earthbulb; Spa 2000 low-flow showerhead; kitchen faucet aerator; water conservation kit that has 4 conservation products.

More items listed in "Paper Products," "Recycling," "Organically Grown" and "Household & Personal Care Products" chapters.

Echo Energy Products, 219 Van Ness Ave, Santa Cruz CA 95060. (408) 423-2429. Manufacturers of Echolite™ modular photovoltaic mount. This mount is detachable and portable so you can use it where you need it. It is easily expandable and has padlock security. This strong mount can withstand winds up to 125 miles per hour.

Eco Source™, 9051 Mill Station Road Bldg #E, Sebastopol CA 95472. (717) 829-7957 or (707) 829-8345. Catalog of products for a cleaner, safer world. Includes energy conservation products such as: Ecoworks energy-efficient

Chapter Six: Energy Conservation

Photo: Ed Carlin/THE PICTURE CUBE

Energy conservation saves more than money.
The very air we breathe depends on it!

 Chapter Six: Energy Conservation

lightbulbs, 4 bulbs for $5.98; Dulux "EL" compact light bulbs that are 75% more efficient than incandescents; compact fluorescent lightbulbs and floodlights; faucet aerators from $5.95; Rainshower filter removes chlorine and conserves water, $68.95; toilet dams to conserve water, 2 for $11.50; low-flow showerheads from $9.95.

Other products found in "Books," "Household & Personal Care," "Clean Air, Clean Water," "Educational Materials," and "Recycling" chapters.

Elemental Enterprises, PO Box 928, Monterey CA 93942. (408) 394-7077. They supply water heater maintenance and repair. Their main thrust is to teach people that they can make their water heaters last instead of having them develop leaks and then needing to replace them. Longer-lived water heaters mean fewer new ones need to be made—so less raw materials are needed, less pollution occurs from the manufacturing process, and less waste at the landfills. Also, additional energy savings occur from having a more efficient water heater. They will send free information for a business-size SASE.

Energy Federation, Inc., 354 Waverly St., Framingham MA 01701. (508) 875-4921. FAX # (617) 451-1534. Toll-free 1-800-876-0660 outside Massachusetts. Toll free eastern Massachusetts 1-800-752-7372. The organization was formed in 1982 by 6 non-profit community energy organizations to coordinate bulk purchases of quality energy conservation materials. Since then, the group has focused on providing superior service and skilled technical assistance to its customers.

The objectives of EFI are: to provide significant savings on the cost of energy conservation materials; to provide access to quality products; to provide reliable, quick service; and to provide technical expertise and information.

EFI serves a variety of customers: non-profit conservation groups; low-income weatherization program; contractors performing public or utility financed conservation works; utility companies requesting energy conservation products; public housing authorities; buying co-op members; municipalities; and retail/ mail order customers.

EFI inventories more than 200 reliable conservation products, such as: caulking and glazing materials; energy efficient lighting products; pipe insulation; radon test kids; setback thermostats; water and hot water saving products; weatherstripping for doors and windows; and more. Catalog available.

Energy Keeper Kap Company, PO Box 2202, Farmington Hills MI 48333. (313) 553-3173. Manufactures the "Keeper Kap," a top-sealing chimney cover/damper. This cover will save money because it keeps out freezing, windy cold at the chimney top where it originates and the air in the chimney stays warm. This cover overlaps the flue liner, protecting the mechanism from freezing shut and lays flat so that

Chapter Six: Energy Conservation ★

A large variety of energy conservation products are available from The Energy Store.

debris, snow, and water can't fall in the chimney when the cover is opened. The cover is spring loaded and opens automatically. There's a remote control chain for closing the cover from inside. Installation is quick and easy. This Keeper Kap can be ordered direct from the company. Prices start at $65.95, depending on the size of your chimney.

Energy Store, PO Box 3507, Santa Cruz CA 95063-3507. (408) 464-1938. Toll-free 1-800-288-1938. This is a mail order business specializing in energy conserving products that enable homeowners and small businesses to reduce utility bills. Free catalog available by calling toll-free number. Wholesale pricing available for dealers.

Their 16-page catalog contains: The BatteryMate, a solar battery charger, $48; Slim Charger, a pocket battery charger, $28.45; Energy Monitor II Plus, a programmable thermostat, $66; set-back thermostat, $48; water heater time, $34; air conditioning timer/controller, $45; compact fluorescent bulbs; low flow showerheads; faucet aerators; toilet dams; Sunfrost energy efficient refrigerator; composter, composting tool; solar emergency light, $32.

One very interesting product is the TourLite cargo cart to pull behind your bike. What a great way to shop without polluting the air! The basic TourLite is $285.

More products listed in "Books," "Educational Materials" and "Baby & Children's Products."

F-Chart Software, 4406 Fox Bluff Rd,

Middleton WI 53562. (608) 836-8536. Energy analysis software for active/passive solar system analysis and for photovoltaic systems analysis.

Fowler Solar Electric Inc, PO Box 435, 13 Bashan Hill Road, Worthington MA 01098. (413) 238-5974. Catalog of solar electric items (including many kits), inverters, batteries, charge controllers, DC pumps, generators, lighting, and more. Front of the catalog says that "We will match or beat any sale price on any Arco or Solarex module, Trace inverter, Trojan battery, Sibir refrigerator, or any other item we sell." Catalog $2.

Energy efficient lighting available: Osram light bulbs, Thinlite fluorescent fixtures; DC incandescent light bulbs; and reflector fixtures.

See also "Books" and "Seminars, Speakers & Workshops" chapters.

Jade Mountain, PO Box 4616, Boulder CO 80306. (303) 449-6601. FAX # (303) 449-8266. Toll-free 1-800-442-1972. Large selection of energy saving and appropriate technology products: solar electric systems; super energy efficient lighting; water saving fixtures; water purification; recycled paper products; solar water pumping; drip irrigation; demand water heaters; more.

Examples of products available: 110 watt power modules, $489; Hoxan 48-watt solar electric panel, $288; Osram Dulux El light bulbs; Toto low flush toilet, $165; Quantum pressurized low flush system, $250; Incredible Head low-flow showerheads, $17;

solar powered toys and gifts (such as solar cool cap, solar tea jar, solar clock); tankless water heaters; solar water package systems; space heaters; woodstove accessories; pole mounts and adjustable solar mounts; wind generators; inverters; batteries; DC fluorescents; the James hand washing machine with wringer; much more.

Newsletter/catalog (80-page) subscription, $3 for one year. Also listed in "Paper Products," "Household & Personal Care Products," "Clean Air, Clean Water" chapters.

Los Alamos Sales Company, PO Box 795, Los Alamos NM 87544. (505) 662-5053. Suppliers of solar products and hardware.

Microphor®, Inc., 452 East Hill Road, PO Box 1460, Willits CA 95490. (707) 459-5563. FAX # (707) 459-6617. Microphor manufactures plumbing products and is the importer for TOTO plumbing products for the U.S. Microphor products: Microflush® 2-quart low-flow toilet, saves up to 90% of normal water requirements for the toilet; model LF-220 ultra low-flow toilet operated on 12-volt DC and is ideal for RVs, boats; low flow showerhead made of solid brass with triple chrome/nickel plating.

TOTO energy conservation product: TOTO model LF-16 low-flow gravity flush toilet uses only 1.6 gallons per flush and is approved by the City of Los Angeles and the State of Massachusetts.

Photocomm Inc., Consumer Division, 930 Idaho-Maryland Rd, Grass Valley CA 95945. Toll-free 1-800-544-6466. ARCO Solar® electric systems—full line of solar electric power modules.

Plenum Publishing Corp, 233 Spring St, New York NY 10013-1578. Publishers of *Advances in Solar Energy: An Annual Review of Research and Development,* Volume 5, 1989, $125.

Real Goods Trading Company, 966 Mazzoni St, Ukiah CA 95482. (707) 468-9214. FAX # (707) 468-0301. Order toll-free 1-800-762-7325. This company has an extensive 106-page catalog full of energy-saving equipment and supplies. Examples of items offered: high efficiency lighting; low-flush toilets; solar battery chargers and rechargeable batteries; solar air conditioning; Sunfrost energy efficient refrigerator; solar panels; photovoltaics power system kits; wind generators; hydro-electric systems; inverters; 12-volt Christmas tree lights; water and pool heaters; waterless composting toilets; 12-volt appliances—including a 12-volt mini washing machine. There's more listed in "Books," "Household & Personal Care Products," "Clean Air, Clean Water," "Baby & Children's Products," "Paper Products" and "Recycling" chapters.

Resources Conservation Inc., PO Box 71, Greenwich CT 06836. (203) 964-0600. FAX # (203) 324-9352. Toll-free 1-800-243-2862. Manufacturers of several energy & water savers. Their

Incredible Head™ low flow shower rated excellently in a *Consumer Reports* ratings on low-flow shower heads. Other products are: The Incredible Tap Saver Deluxe™ faucet aerator; The Incredible SuperBowl™ toilet tank water saver; and the Incredible Soap-up Saver™ that fits all showers.

Robbins Engineering, Inc., 1641-25 McCulloch Blvd, #294, Lake Havasu City AZ 86403. (602) 855-3670. Series 1100 PV (photovoltaics) support structures carries 4 to 12 modules; all steel construction; easily assembled; can handle wind up to 100 miles per hour. Available via UPS shipment.

RPL Energy Enterprises Inc., 96 Elgin Ave., Manchester NH 03104. (603) 669-0836. Authorized dealer/ applicator of energy control products such as: "Switch-o-Matic®," a switch that turns the lights on automatically when you enter the room, and off after you leave; Scotchtint® Plus All Season Window Film (a 3-M product) that cuts energy costs year-found by reducing both heat loss and heat gain through windows; and Silverlux® Reflectors (a 3-M product) that let you remove as many as half your fluorescent lamps while maintaining optimum lighting levels.

Sennergetics, 8751 Shirley Ave, Northridge CA 91324. (818) 885-0323. Wholesale solar equipment supplier such as: pre-designed complete solar water heater kits; pool heating kits; photovoltaic components; solar engineering and computer services.

Low-flow showerheads from Resources Conservation (above) and Vanderburgh Enterprises (below).

Seventh Generation, Colchester VT 05446-1672. (802) 655-3116. FAX toll-free # 1-800-456-1139. Order toll-free 1-800-456-1177. Customer service toll-free 1-800-456-1197.

Seventh Generation is one of the most well-known companies for environmentally safe consumer products. Their 48-page catalog "Products for a Healthy Planet" ($2) contains an extraordinary variety of products. They also practice what they preach. For instance, they recycle their office paper, and reuse cardboard boxes for shipping. They have a 1% fund that goes to environmental organizations.

Energy conservation products available include: compact fluorescent light bulbs, several kinds and styles; energy efficient lighting fixtures; alert

Chapter Six: Energy Conservation

sensors to turn your lights off automatically; outlet covers to make your outlets not only energy efficient by child proof as well; set-back thermostat; water-saving aerators for kitchen, bath; toilet dams; low flush toilet; and low flow showers.

There are so many products in this catalog that additional information can be found in these chapters: "Baby and Children's Products," "Books," "Educational Materials," "Paper Products," "Recycling," "Household & Personal Care Products," and "Organically Grown."

Solar Components Corporation, 121 Valley St, Manchester NH 03103. (603) 668-8186. FAX # (603) 627-3110. Their 60-page catalog ($2)called "The Energy Saver's Catalog," contains strictly solar energy products, and a wide variety of them. There are solariums; greenhouses & accessories; Sun-Lite® solar glazing; Sun-Lite® accessories; Sun-Lite passive solar water heater; solar storage tubes; energy efficient skylights; Suneye™ natural energy control system; solar water heater systems & accessories; pool heating systems; window insulation; photovoltaic supplies.

Solar Development Inc., 3630 Reese Ave, Riviera Beach FL 33404. (407) 842-8935. FAX # (407) 842-8967. Solar collectors, solar water heaters, design services, solar pool heaters, tanks, pumps, controllers, PV panels.

Solar Electric Engineering, Inc., 116 4th St, Santa Rosa CA 95401. (707) 542-1990. FAX # (707) 542-4358. This is a publicly owned corporation that has been committed to bringing to the marketplace environmentally sound products at affordable prices to the consumer. Solar Electric has ongoing research into solar powered and electric cars. They sell practical electric vehicles. They also design and build homes that are powered partially or entirely by solar power.

They have a 40-page "Environmental Catalog," with many energy conservation products, including: compact fluorescent lamps and bulbs; Tapsaver water flow reducer for faucets; Superbowl™ Toilet Tank water saver; Aqualine toilets; clothes lines; 12-volt bet warmer; solar panels; solar chargers for RV and homes; solar kits for home and RV systems; inverters; batteries; solar cooker; solar shower; hydroelectric power systems; wind machine; Vitalizer fuel saver; electric water heater timer; passive solar water heating systems; Sunfrost refrigerator (can be used in solar-powered home); solar safari hat or baseball cap, more.

Two particularly interesting solar products are: the Naturelite Solar Powered Address Number that runs all night on just one hour of sunshine and will run even after rainy and cloudy

Suneye™ natural energy control system can function as a passive solar heating system or a natural lighting system.. Available from Solar Survival.

days, shows up to five digits of your address, $89; and the Solar Light Guard is a solar powered motion sensitive light, the solar panel is detachable, $59.95.

More items listed in "Books," "Recycling," "Paper Products," "Clean Air, Clean Water," "Baby & Children's Products," and "Magazines, Newsletters & Brochures."

Solar Electric Specialties Company, PO Box 537, 101 North Main St, Willits CA 95490. (707) 459-9496. Toll-free 1-800-344-2003. Solar/ Cell Photovoltaic Batteries series of sealed, maintenance-free, deep cycle lead-acid batteries designed for long life in stand-alone power systems.

Solarex, (An Amoco Company), PO Box 548, Santa Cruz NM 87567. (505) 753-9699. FAX # (505) 753-8474. Manufacturers of solar water pumping systems: Flowlight® Booster Pump; Solar Slowpump™; Flowlight® Micro-submersible; and Solaram™ Surface Pump.

Solar Industries, 1985 Rutgers University Blvd, Lakewood NJ 08701. (201) 905-0440. Toll-free outside New Jersey 1-800-227-7657. Solar Industries Pool Heating Systems has a solar pool collector for residential, commercial, or public pools and spas. Distributorships available.

Solar Research, PO Box 869, Brighton MI 48116. (313) 227-1151. Refrigerant charged solar systems.

Solar Survival, PO Box 250, Cherry Hill Rd, Harrisville NH 03450. (603) 827-3811. The work of this company involves many areas of simple passive solar design involving: house plans; intensive gardening; solar food hydration; domestic water systems; window/ shutter systems; and masonry stove systems. Designer Lea Poisson, an incredible child prodigy-turned-solar designer, has patented several products for energy efficiency. One of the most popular of his designs has been the Solar Survival™ dehydrator. This product dries and preserves food using the simplest and most natural method—solar energy. No added energy needed. *Mother Earth News* said, "After researching several solar dehydrators, Mother's shop crew settled on a tried and true design." Also reviews in *Organic Gardening Magazine* and *Yankee Magazine.* The do-it-yourself plans are $15.

Poisson's Solar Cone™ has also been very popular. This cone is the 20th century improvement of the original "cloche," a French intensive gardening device. The solar cone stretches the gardening season by 4-6 weeks on either end, and can also be used to accelerate the germination process of heat-loving plants. Can also be used to protect vulnerable plants from frost, insects, hail, predators, and wind. Stacks neatly when not in use. Other designs for solar greenhousing are: the Solar Frame™, the Solar Pod™ (plans $11) and the Trisol ™ Greenhouse.

The Trisol greenhouse method can be learned one of several ways: through his book *The Solar Greenhouse Book* (Rodale, $10.95); through purchase of a kit ($3500); through a Trisol brochure with floorplans, photographs and descriptive material ($10); through a license and blueprint specifications ($300 for 1200 sq ft model or $350 for 1500 sq ft model); or through a seminar and gardening workshop at the research center in Harrisville, New Hampshire (tuition $30 per person, $50 per couple).

Poisson has designed the Suneye™ natural energy control system which can function as a passive solar heating system, a natural lighting system, and includes a fully adjustable R-20 insulating shutter window to fine tine solar heat gain and prevent heat loss.

They also have a Solartank™ for passive solar domestic water heating ($380-$480) or plans for $7. Dealer inquiries welcome. Their Siberian Stove™ is a stove design that optimizes the use of heat from burning wood. Plans are $27. Hardware kit is $350.

Other books available are: *Home Food Hydration*, $3.50; *How to Dry Food*, $10.50.

Specialty Concepts Inc., 9025 Eton Ave, Canoga Park CA 91304. (818) 998-5238. FAX # (818) 998-5253. Telex 662914 SCI CNPK. Photovoltaic controls, such as the SCI Monitor Mark III (DM3), a flush mounted digital monitoring system for alternative energy systems.

Sunelco®, the Sun Electric Company, PO Box 1499, 100 Skeels St, Hamilton MT 59840. (406) 363-6924. FAX # (406) 363-6046. 1-800-338-6844. This company has a 76-page catalog devoted to sun energy products, so you can imagine how extensive their product line is. The catalog also has numerous helpful hints about sun energy. Their design people are also available for consultations by phone.

An interesting feature of their catalog is that entire systems (RV, vacation home, cabin, etc) are graphically presented so that you can easily determine what you need.

The product available are: batteries, battery chargers, controllers, generator hybrid systems, hydro electric generators, inverters, lighting systems, meters, mounts & trackers, photovoltaic modules, RV systems packages, refrigerators, twelve volt appliances, water pumps, water heating, wind generators, and more.

Sunnyside Solar, RD 4 Box 808, Green River Road, Brattleboro CT 05301. (802) 257-1482 (in Vermont). 1-800-346-3230. Catalog of photovoltaic equipment including components, batteries, and end use equipment. Includes: photovoltaic modules from Solarex that are multicrystal, glass-covered anodized aluminum frame, various sizes; Arco Solar panels that are single crystal glass cover, aluminum frame, various sizes; Sovonics™ panels; Zomeworks mounting systems for various sizes; controllers; switches; inverters from Trace, Heart, Heliotrope and PowerStar™; pumps; fans.

Chapter Six: Energy Conservation ★

More information in "Books" and "Seminars" chapters.

Sun Selector, PO Box 1545, Parkersburg WV 26101. (304) 485-7150. FAX # (304) 422-3931. Sun Selector® Linear Current Booster™ will enhance the performance of any small DC water pumping system which requires up to 10 amps. Simple to install.

SunTrak™, 2350 E 91st St, Indianapolis IN 46240. (317) 846-2150. SunTrak™ is a portable sun locator that shows the sun's path above the horizon for any day and any place in the world; the time and direction of the sun at sunrise and sunset; solar and clock time. Instruction book accompanies instrument. SunTrak and book, $79 plus $6 shipping.

SunWatt®, RFD Box 751, Addison ME 04606. (207) 497-2204. Solar energy products offered: photovoltaic modules; rechargeable batteries; solar battery chargers. Also listed in "Books" chapter.

Synerjy, PO Box 1854/ Cathedral Station, New York NY 10025. This is a directory of renewable energy published every six months. This publication lists thousands of articles, books, plans, patents and government reports published, as well as research groups, facilities, manufacturers and conferences. One year subscription is $45; back issues available.

Separate lists may be purchased of renewable energy manufacturers and distributors, organized by geographic area. There are four separate lists included: solar (collectors, greenhouses and sunspaces, heating and cooling, photovoltaics) $6; biomass (wood stoves, alcohol and methane production, refuse-derived fuels) $5; small scale electric (wind, hydroelectric, advances batteries, fuel cells, electric vehicles, inverters and controls) $5; and heat conservation (recovery and transfer, temperature controls, insulation) $5. All four lists can be purchased for a total of $18.

Satisfaction guaranteed.

TESS (Thermal Energy Storage Systems Inc), RR 1 Box 3, Beanville Road, Randolph VT 05060. (802) 728-4485. FAX # (802) 728-9582. 1-800-323-TESS. TESS offers brochures featuring its line of modular, efficient, heat-storing fireplaces; glass doors and fireplace accessories. TESS fireplaces incorporate multiple flues and a masonry heat-exchange area above the fire chamber. These fireplaces have been tested for efficiency and emissions. The results showed that TESS fireplaces were about 4 times more efficient than the best masonry fireplace available. The emissions testing showed the TESS to be an extremely clean-burning device, emitting a very low amount of particulates into the air.

Thermo Dynamics Ltd, 81 Thornhill Dr, Dartmouth, Nova Scotia, Canada B3B 1R9. Call Collect (902) 468-1001. Solar Boiler™ domestic water

TESS fireplace doors are available in antique brass, polished brass and black finishes. Fireplace doors save energy.

heating appliance will deliver 65% of the requirements for a family of four. G-Series collectors (4 x 10) are rated for 65,000 BTUs for a clear day.

3-Day Solar Store, (Monday-Wednesday), Box 23, Capella CA 95418. (707) 485-0588. FAX # (707) 485-0831. Offers information packages and completely designed systems on solar electrics, standby electric systems, RV & boat electric systems, water pumping systems, wind electric systems, hydro electric systems, and solar hot water and space saving systems. The information packages are $7.50 each, refundable upon system purchase.

3-M Energy Control Products, Bldg 225-4S-08 3M Center, St. Paul MN 55144-1000. (612) 736-2388. Scotchtint® Plus All Season Window

Film that cuts energy costs year-found by reducing both heat loss and heat gain through windows; and Silverlux® Reflectors that let you remove as many as half your fluorescent lamps while maintaining optimum lighting levels.

US Sky, 2907 Agua Fria, Santa Fe NM 87501. FAX # (505) 471-5437. Toll-free 1-800-323-5017. Producers of SureSeal™ glazing system, perfect for skylights, sunspaces, view glass. Send $7.95 for kit with 7 extrusions, 24 pg. application manual, prices and order forms.

Vanderburgh Enterprises, Inc., PO Box 138, Southport CT 06490. (203) 227-4813. Manufacturers of LoVo MaxiMizer™ ME4000 low flow shower head that has a unique "accelerating" feature that gives a remarkable massage-like sensation and controls water flow to a mere 2 gallons per minute. The result is water and energy savings up to 75%. This non-aerating shower differs from other low flow showers in that it does not introduce or force air to mix with the water to create an illusion of extra volume. According to this company, aerating cools the water so that the bather turns up the hot water, decreasing energy savings. Money back guarantee. The standard MaxiMizer is $14.95; several style available. Other models and styles of low flow showers available.

Other energy conservation products include faucet aerators and toilet dams.

Vermont Castings, Prince St, Randolph VT 05060. (802) 728-3181. Manufacturer of clean-air certified wood stoves. These hearth products represent the state-of-the-art in heating efficiency and clean-burning technology. There are many styles of these stoves. For a full-color magazine-style catalog, send $4 and request *The Fireside Advisor,* Volume III. This catalog shows products by Vermont Castings and by Consolidated Dutchwest. It also gives decorating ideas for how to incorporate these stoves into your home, as well as an installation planner. A list of local dealers is included.

WaterFurnace International Inc., 4307 Arden Drive, Fort Wayne IN 46804. (219) 432-LOOP (5667). FAX # (219) 432-1489. Manufacturers of energy-efficient, environmentally safe geo-thermal heating and cooling systems. Geothermal technology harnesses the energy available from the underground temperature that stays relatively constant all year. It is a renewable, natural supply of energy that can be used for heating, air conditioning and hot water. In winter, water circulating through a loop of underground pipe absorbs heat from the earth and carries it to the geo-thermal unit which extracts the heat, compresses it to a higher temperature, and distributes it throughout your home. In summer, the unit extracts heat from your home and transfers it back to the circulating water in the underground loop system, where it is dissipated into the cooler earth. Geothermal systems are extremely energy efficient because they use electricity only to power the pump, compressor and fan.

This company has several models of WaterFurnace. One is the Premiere AT Series™ WaterFurnace that is as technologically advanced as any geo-thermal furnace. Several sizes to choose from; strong warranties from the company. They offer a computer energy analysis before you buy to let you see the actual performance of a WaterFurnace unit compared with other types of systems. It even estimates annual utility savings. Water heaters can be incorporated into your geothermal system.

The Watt Stopper, 296 Brokaw Rd, Santa Clara CA 95050. (408) 988-5331. FAX # (408) 988-5373. Toll-free 1-800-879-8585. Manufactures a line of "occupancy sensors" for energy management. Their Passive Infrared Wall Switch detects whether or not a room is occupied and automatically turn the lights of when the area is left unoccupied for a specified length of time. The LightSaver Controller turns lighting systems on and off according to natural light levels. Other products in the line are the Passive Infrared Sensor, Ultrasonic Sensors, Power and Slave Packs, and the Illuminometer.

Zomeworks Corp, PO Box 25805, Albuquerque NM 87125. (505) 242-5354. FAX # (505) 243-5187. Track Rack™ Company products: pole mounted fixed racks for 1 to 12 modules; ground and roof racks, 1 to 12 modules; side-of-pole racks for 1 to 4 modules. Cool Cell™ Battery Boxes.

EARTH: OUR GREATEST TREASURE

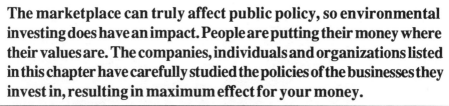

Chapter Seven: Environmental Investing

The marketplace can truly affect public policy, so environmental investing does have an impact. People are putting their money where their values are. The companies, individuals and organizations listed in this chapter have carefully studied the policies of the businesses they invest in, resulting in maximum effect for your money.

Affirmative Investments, Inc., 129 South St, 6th floor, Boston MA 02111. (617) 350-0250. FAX # (617) 350-6629. Investment advisor providing professional advice on privately-placed, socially positive investments. This company recommends projects such as low-income housing, economic democracy and alternative energy.

Calvert Group, 4550 Montgomery Avenue, 10th floor North, Bethesda MD 20814. (301) 951-4820. 1-800-368-2748. Offers socially and environmentally responsible funds, including Calvert-Ariel Appreciation Fund, Calvert Ariel-Growth Fund as well as Calvert Social Investment Fund, made up of money market, bond, equity and balanced portfolios. The Calvert Social Investment Fund seeks to invest in companies which deliver safe products and services that sustain our natural environment; is managed with participation throughout the organization; negotiates fairly with its employees; and fosters a commitment to human goals. The fund will not invest in any company that is involved in business activities with South Africa, is involved in the manufacture of nuclear energy, or is a manufacturer of weapons. Call or write for prospectus.

Catalyst, 64 Main St, 3rd Floor, (05602) PO Box 1308, (05601) Montpelier VT . (802) 223-7943. An organization connecting economics, ecology and human rights. They offer the book *Economics as if the Earth Really Mattered: A Catalyst Guide to*

Socially Conscious Investing (New Society Publishers, 260 pgs, $10.95) that shows ways in which people are using their consumer power as a vehicle for their values, such as ecology and fighting hunger or injustice.

More information in "Organizations" chapter.

Clean Yield Group, PO Box 1880, Greensboro Bend VT 05842. (802) 533-7178. This company manages money for environmentally sensitive clients. They produce *The Clean Yield,* an environmentally sensitive stock market newsletter. Companies are screened for involvement in South Africa, weapons production, environmental practices, labor and community relations, affirmative action, tobacco production and gambling, nuclear power generation and corporate frankness. Those companies that are able to successfully mix financial prosperity with social responsibility and whose stocks show above average promise are profiles and actively followed. The newsletter provides advice and recommendations on when and at what price to buy and sell these stocks. According to the *Hulbert Financial Digest,* an independent monitoring service, The Clean Yield's Model Portfolio was one of the top ten performing newsletter portfolios of 1988. Subscription, $85 1 year, 12 issues.

Environmental Economics, 1026 Irving Street, Philadelphia PA 19107. (215) 925-7168. Publishers of the third annual *Directory of Environmental Investing,* 1990. This directory helps investors know about the health of environmental services industry—an area in which the profit picture improved in 1989 and early 1990. This industry is showing remarkable strength in an otherwise sluggish economic. Along with material about the environmental industry, the directory looks at how the environmental restructuring of the economy is affecting operations in key industries such as petro-chemicals, banking, real estate, health care, agriculture, and utilities. Michael Silverstein, the author of the book, is also the author of *The Environmental Factor.* He writes a daily Environmental Report the the UPI and does regular "Green Economics" columns for several business publications. The book is 150 pages, $60.

Financial Network Investment Corporation, 605 1st Ave, Ste 505, Seattle WA 98104. (206) 292-8483. They offer socially and environmentally responsible investing in the form of stocks, bonds, mutual funds and annuities.

First Affirmative Financial Network, 1040 S. 8th St, Suite 200, Colorado Springs CO 80906. (719) 636-1045. FAX # (719) 636-1943. Toll-free 1-800-422-7284. Broker dealing in stocks, bonds and mutual funds involving investments that include recycling, alternative energy and pollution control. Free financial planning review offered. Write or call for more information.

New Alternative Fund, 295 Northern Blvd, Great Neck NY 11021. (516) 466-0808. This is a mutual fund concentrating in alternative energy, solar energy, conservation, cogeneration, non-nuclear utilities, geothermal, recycling and resource recovery investments. Minimum investment $2650. Write or call for more information.

PAX World Fund, 224 State Street, Portsmouth NJ 03801. (603) 431-8022. Toll-free 1-800-767-1729. PAX World Fund is a mutual fund that invests in companies that: exercise pollution control; produce life supporting goods and services; are not involved in weapon production; have fair employment practices; promote some international development. IRA and Keogh plans are available. Minimum investment $250. This company is affiliated with a foundation that supports tree planting in areas of the deforested Third World. A prospectus will be sent to you upon request.

Robert Berend, Attorney at Law, Registered Investment Advisor, Stockbroker, 6611 W. 5th St, Los Angeles CA 90048-4601. (213) 651-2375. Specializing in socially and environmentally responsible investments since 1983. Long-range comprehensive estate planning, retirement planning, tax considerations, and financial planning. He helped found the Southern California Socially Responsible Investment Professionals, is an attorney, a registered investment adviser, stockbroker and member of the Social Investment

Valdez Principles

In 1989 the group CERES (Coalition for Environmentally Responsible Economies) published the Valdez principles, a set of standards for evaluating the actions of corporations that affect the earth. The principles call for:

✓ Protection of the air, water or earth.

✓ Sustainable use of natural resources.

✓ Minimizing waste.

✓ Energy conservation practices.

✓ Use of technologies and manufacturing of products that are safe for employees and the communities.

✓ Compensation for damage done to the environment.

✓ Disclosure of incidents that cause environmental harm.

✓ Including one member on the board of directors who represents environmental interests.

✓ An annual assessment of the company's progress implementing these principles.

For more information, contact the Social Investment Forum.

Forum. His book, called *New Investor's Compass* ($20, 135 pgs) is available directly from him.

Social Investment Forum, 430 1st Ave N, Suite 290, Minneapolis MN 55401. (612) 333-8338. This is a national nonprofit trade association of financial professionals and individuals that spe-

cialize in socially responsible investing. Basic membership is $35 and
benefits includes a quarterly newsletter, a listing guide of members, performance updates on social & environmental investments, and quarterly
meetings.

**Social Responsibility Investment
Group, Inc.,** 127 Peachtree St NE,
Atlanta GA 30303. (404) 577-3635.
FAX# (404) 577-4496. This group
invests in socially responsible companies. Their criteria for investments includes looking at a company's employee relations, energy & environmental policies, weapons policies, and
involvement in South Africa. Minimum
investment $200,000. One of the part-
ners of this company, Hugh Kelley,
was one of the founders of the Valdez
principles.

Working Assets Money Fund, 230
California St, San Francisco CA
94111. (415) 989-3200 (call collect for
information). FAX # (415) 989-5920.
Toll-free 1-800-533-3863 for Prospectus. This company offers a money-
market fund that invests in short-term
commercial paper of companies with
good environmental and labor records.
They refrain from investing in companies that have involvement in South
Africa, defense, or nuclear power.
They also select government agencies
that finance student housing, small
businesses and farm loans. They select
banks that finance community housing
or investment programs. Minimum
investment $1000. Call collect or write
for more information, or call their toll-
free number for a prospectus.

They also offer a socially responsible VISA credit card, travel services,
and Sprint long-distance service. Each
time the card is used, 5¢ is donated to
nonprofit groups working for peace,
human rights, for the hungry, or for the
environment. For more information on
the credit card, travel and Sprint services, call toll-free 1-800-522-7759.

Chapter Eight:
Household & Personal Care Products

This extensive chapter covers many companies that carry nontoxic and cruelty-free products. Most of the products are available through mail order, although more and more of them are becoming available through natural food stores or health products stores. Kinds of products found in this chapter are: household and laundry cleaners, body and bath care products, cosmetics, pet care, paint and stains, clothing and bedding from 100% cotton grown with no pesticides, and gift items such as T-shirts, stickers, posters. Reusable shopping bags can be found here and in the "Recycling" chapter.

***This chapter has an additional feature that companies who make an extra effort to define their environmental concerns are highlighted.

A Clear Alternative, 8707 West Lane, Magnolia TX 77355. (713) 356-7031. Offers detergents, cleaners and sprays containing no chlorine, CFCs, phosphates or other ingredients harmful to the environment. All are 100% biodegradable.

Amberwood, Rt 1, Box 206, Milner GA 30257. (404) 358-2991. Cruelty-free products for home and personal use. Their policy is that any item offered by them will be animal-free, and

that a statement will be obtained from the manufacturer affirming this. Periodic checks are made on labels for verification.

Products include skin care, hair care, toothpaste, deodorant, cosmetics, perfumes, wallets, belts, vitamins, cleaners, books and specialty items.

Examples: Sirena Fresh Coconut Soap, 4 oz, 85¢; Aubrey Organics jojoba meal and oatmeal facial scrub and mask, 4 oz, $5.50; Beauty Without Cruelty after-sun moisturizer, 3+ oz,

✳Environmental Excellence✳

Acorn Designs

This company has a clearly defined environmental policy. They strive to do business in a manner that does as little harm as possible to the environment while informing people about the ecology of various species and natural systems. They research the materials they use and choose those which are the least toxic and resource intensive, passing this information along to customers. They recycle all paper materials and use recycled paper exclusively in all of their products. They encourage the recognition of indirect environment costs (such as transportation pollution) with a voluntary "green tax" which is donated to environmental organizations. **Listed in "Paper" chapter.**

$8; Rainbow natural henna haircoloring, 4 oz, $5.25; Golden Lotus shampoo, 18 oz $5; Home Health Products sole relief medicated foot lotion, 2 oz, $4.45; Viva Vera aloe oil free foundation, 1 oz, $6.95; Paul Penders cream blush, $5.95; canvas belts, $3; Golden Lotus all purpose cleaner, 32 oz, $5.50; Nature's Gate herbal pet shampoo, 12 oz, $3.

Specialty items include rubber stamps that say "Be Kind to Animals, Don't Eat Them," $5.50; wildlife notecards, pack of 4, $2; postcards from PETA (People for the Ethical Treatment of Animals), 4 postcards for $1; animal liberation labels, 100 for $2; Christmas cards that say "Peace on Earth ...

Goodwill to all that dwell therein." 20 cards for $7.50.

More in "Books" chapter.

American Merfluan, Inc., 3479 Edison Way, Menlo Park CA 94025. (415) 364-6343. FAX # (415) 365-8772. Merfluan European toothpowder is fully biodegradable except for the natural inorganic minerals used; it is cruelty-free; formulated from traditional, time-proven ingredients such as baking soda, seasalt, myrrh, and peppermint. Available at natural foods stores.

Amway Corporation, 7575 Fulton Street East, Ada MI 49355-0001. (616) 676-6000. FAX #(616) 676-8140. 1-800-544-7167. Products from Amway have always reflected a concern for the environment. From the very beginning, their first product L.O.C. (Liquid Organic Cleaner) contained only biodegradable surfactants

✳Environmental Excellence✳

American Merfluan

This company has developed a well-founded environmental policy, which is probably the most important reason to use their products. Their environmental policy states that they as a company will use recycled shippers; they recycle all materials they cannot reuse; they create no by-products and their manufacturing processes have an extremely low impact on the environment.

✶Environmental Excellence✶

Amway Corporation

Amway Corporation has a strong commitment to the environment. They have an official "environmental mission statement" in which they announced that "Amway recognizes its responsibility and role in both fostering and promoting sound environmental stewardship." The company has an internal Environmental Task Force composed of executives from manufacturing, research & development, marketing and other areas. Company environmental sponsorships have included ICEWALK, a 1989 International North Pole Expedition. Icewalk's mission was to focus the world's attention on pollution and global warming and to emphasize the need for international cooperation and individual initiative for protecting the environment. A four-part PBS educational video series was produced about Icewalk. (For information on how to obtain the PBS videos, see listing for "Public Broadcasting Service" under "Educational Materials" chapter.)

Amway is one of only two corporations to receive the United National Environment Programme Award for Achievement. They received this award for their sponsorship of ICEWALK.

Amway was one of the first sponsors and participants in the American Forestry Association's Global Releaf project. The company is also the founding corporate sponsor of the Aspen Global Change Institute, which was formed in 1990 to study global change and develop educational materials and outreach programs to inform the public about environmental issues.

and no phosphates, solvents, or caustic material. Today, surfactants used in all of Amway's cleaning products are biodegradable. Amway's SA8 Liquid Laundry Concentrates are free of phosphates, and the powder is available in a phosphate-free version as well. Most Amway products are concentrated, meaning they last longer and need less packaging materials. The net benefit is 50-75% less packaging for disposal.

Amway eliminated all animal testing as of June 1989.

More information in "Clean Air, Clean Water" chapter.

Aura Cacia, Inc., 1401 Main St, PO Box 399, Weaverville CA 96093. (916) 623-3301. FAX # (916) 623-2626. Producer of body care products that are cruelty-free with an emphasis on true botanical, non-synthetic fragrance. Product line: natural body powders (from flowers and herbs in a corn starch base); botanical perfume oils; mineral baths; bath soap; sun care; and essential oils. Many fragrances to choose from.

Baubiologie Hardware, 207 16th St, Unit B, Pacific Grove CA 93950. (408) 372-8626. They call themselves

Chapter Eight: Household & Personal Care Products

the "healthful" hardware store. Their catalog is an education in itself! For instance, on page 3, they say, "Followers of Baubiologie principles avoid electromagnetic radiations whenever possible." They explain how to reduce of eliminate much of the electromagnetic radiation commonly found in homes. Products found in the catalog to do this are: computer shield protection (model NoRad DB60) that comes flat or curved or even custom made, starts at $129; an electromagnetically balanced waterbed heater, $65; apron for protection against electrical fields (developed by an inventor to protect his pregnant wife and unborn child while she worked on her computer and other tasks that would expose them to the effects of electromagnetic pollution), $29.95; electromagnetic radiation meter, $99.

The catalog includes environmental test kits, such as the Comprehensive Environmental Test Kit, $159.95; Electromagnetic Radiation Test Kit, $149.95; Water Analysis Kit, $150 basic kit; Watercheck water test, $150; LeadCheck Swabs for checking lead in your plumbing, house paint, ceramic dishes, toys, furniture, 12 for $24.95; Verify Water Test, $9.95; Carbon Monoxide Tester, $19.95; Mold Testing Kit, $25; Formaldehyde Tester, $56; Radon Gas Detector, $25.

Natural linoleum is available (one of their most popular products). You can order a kits of 24 sample color chips of their linoleum for $5. They also have a safe adhesive for laying their safe linoleum! Other safe household products include their line of AFM paints, primers, sealants, solvents, caulking, spackling, wood stain, floor wax, floor polish, and carpet cleaner.

Cleansers in the catalog include: AFM Super Clean, $6.95 qt; Allens All Purpose Cleaner, $5.95 qt; AFM Safety Clean for anti-bacterial and anti-fungal cleaning, $8.50 qt; Golden Lotus Winter White Liquid Laundry Detergent, $7.95 qt; Golden Lotus Soft 'n Fresh Fabric Softener, $5.95 qt; Golden Lotus Glass Mate Glass Cleaner, 20 oz, $4.85; Allens Cruelty-Free Automatic Dishwasher Detergent, 64 oz, $14.95; Allens Fabric Softener, $5.95 qt; Granny's Power Plus laundry concentrate, $5.25 qt; Granny's Soil Away stain and soil remover, $5.75 qt; more.

Natural animal care products include: POW flea powder, $3.95; herbal pet shampoo, $3.95; flea collar, $5.95. Natural insect control products offered.

More information found in "Books," "Energy Conservation," "Clean Air, Clean Water," and "Educational Materials" chapters.

Beehive Botanicals, Rt 8, Box 8258, Hayward WI 54843. (715) 634-4274. Products for body care, supplements and specialties using pure and natural ingredients, and are cruelty-free. All ingredients are listed right in the brochure. Products: Propolis Derma Cream; Conditioning Shampoo & Moisturizing Conditioner; Propolis Lip Balm; Propolis Granules; Propolis Capsules; Propolis Chewing Gum; Propolis Tincture; Pollen Plus; Royal

Cedar-Al Pet Shampoo is gentle castile soap scented with Western Red Cedar oil to keep pets flea-free.

Jelly; Royal Jelly Facial Cream; and Propolis Toothpaste.

Member of the International Bee Research Association.

Ben & Jerry's, Route 100, PO Box 240, Waterbury VT 05676. (802) 244-5641. Manufacturers of Rainforest Crunch Ice Cream. **Profiled in Part I of this book.**

Body Love Natural Cosmetics, PO Box 7542, 303 Potrero St #4, Santa Cruz CA 95061. (408) 425-8218. 1-800-873-3076. Pure, natural, cruelty-free skin care products: Amazing Grains skin cleanser, 8 oz, $8.50;

Aromatherapy Bath Beads, $6.50; Aroma Lotion, 2 fl oz, $2.95; Love Mitts, $3.75.

Botanicus, Inc., 7920 Queenair Drive, Gaithersburg MD 20879. (301) 977-8887. Toll-free 1-800-282-8887. They manufacture natural, non-toxic, and cruelty-free products. This company doesn't just say that their products are "natural;" they also explain exactly what the word "natural" means to them. Product lines: skin care; hair care; fragrance; bath & shower; and gifts.

Carole's Cosmetics—The Caring Catalog, 2973 Harbor Blvd, Suite 174, Costa Mesa CA 92626. (714) 842-0454. Catalog of cruelty-free natural cosmetics and household products, which are phosphate-free and environmentally safe. Catalog is $1, refundable on first order.

Cedar-al Products Inc., HCR 63 Box 6, Clallam Bay WA 98326. (206) 963-2601. Toll-free order line 1-800-431-3444 from 8-4 pm Pacific time, Mon-Fri. They manufacture a line of pet beds filled with Western Red Cedar shavings, which help control fleas, ticks and odors. (Fleas don't like the smell of this cedar.) The regular pet pillows are covered with burlap (medium) is 25" x 33" and $20.95; (large) is 30" x 40" and $25.95. Deluxe pet pillows are covered with all-cotton chamois cloth, medium is $32; large is $39. They also make Cedar-al Pet Shampoo that is gentle Castile soap scented with Western Red Cedar oil to help keep pets flea-free, 12 oz, $8.95. Also available is Cedar Oil spray, 16 oz for $12.95; Cedar-al Freshener for carpets, 16 oz for $10.95. Fresh cedar shavings can be purchased separately to freshen the pet pillows for use in pet cages; 5 lbs, $8.

For those concerned about the great Northwest old-growth forests, we'd like to add that these products are produced from mill wastes, which previously were burned or buried in landfills. No trees were cut to make these products.

Also listing in "Recycling" chapter.

Chempoint Products Company, 543 Tarrytown Rd, White Plains Ny 10607. 1-800-343-6588. Manufacturers of Citra-Solv, the natural citrus solvent. Natural citrus extracts are the main ingredients of this non-toxic, biodegradable solvent that dissolves grease, gum, tar, oil and ink and eliminates pet odors and stains. It is non-caustic and contains no chlorinated solvents or alkalines.

C.H.I.P. Distribution Company, 1139 Dominquez St., Unit E, Carson CA 90746. (213) 603-1114. A distributorship created to promote environmentally safe cleaning products. They went into business specifically to offer products that will do the job without posing a threat to people or to the environment. Their principle product, CON-LEI is a biodegradable non-caustic cleaner created in 1982. This concentrated cleaner can provide heavy degreasing of floors, walls, upholstery, glass, plastics, and heavy equipment. This pro-

duce has been used by custodial services, schools, universities, hotels, hospitals, restaurants, and manufacturing facilities. Testimonials from these customers are available. Available to the consumer through mail order: 8 oz, $7; 16 oz, $8.50; 32 oz, $12; or 1 gal, $22. Other cleaning products available, such as brushes and scrubbing utensils.

Clothcrafters, Inc., PO Box 176, Elkhart Lake WI 53020. (414) 876-2112. A catalog of products for "conservation living"—using materials that can be washed and reused, rather than throwing things away, doing some things the old-fashioned way that some people never gave up, but is now fashionable again now that we realize the impact to the environment.

Examples of the types of things they sell: bags made from cheesecloth to use instead of plastic, keeps lettuce longer, 14 x 16, six bags for $4.50; 100% cotton coffee filters, reusable, washable, 12 for $4.25; pure Castile soap from Bocabelli; natural fiber bedding and baby bedding; cloth diapers; market tote made of denim so it's tough and lays flat, long handles, has outside pocket for keys, grocery list, 18 x 16, $10; also a child's tote ($8) and city tote ($8).

Cloverdale, Inc., PO Box 268, West Cornwall CT 06796. Cloverdale is a concentrated all-purpose cleaner and degreaser that is biodegradable, non-toxic, non-phosphate, & environmentally safe. It works on counters, floors, linoleum, plastic, stone, steel, appliances, machinery, toilets, sinks, vinyl upholstery, cars & trucks, and more. This cleaner is a concentrate, which also is more environmentally-sound since it uses less packaging materials per amount of cleaning product provided. Sold in quarts, gallons, and 5 gallon pails. Safety sealed; child-proof caps. Has been reviewed in *Home* magazine in their green products review (twice!) and in *Buzzworm: The Environmental Journal*. Available for distributorships. Individual orders can be placed through The Sprout House, listed in this chapter.

Community Products Inc., RD #2, Box 1950, Montpelier VT 05602. (802) 229-1840. Their premier product is Rainforest Crunch, a very popular snack made of cashew and Brazil nuts harvested in the Amazon rainforest and combined with an all-natural buttercrunch recipe. This company is the creation of Ben Cohen of Ben & Jerry's Ice Cream of Vermont. The product aids the rainforest in many ways. First, the nuts are purchased directly from forest peoples, providing them with three to ten times the normal income from their labor. Second, the profits of Rainforest Crunch are distributed to rainforest preservation organizations (40%) and for peace (20%). More explained in "Ben & Jerry's" profile, part I of this book.

The Compassionate Consumer, PO Box 27, Jericho NY 11753. (718) 445-4134. Cruelty-free products for the home. All products in their catalog are guaranteed free of any animal derived ingredient or by-product. No product has been tested on animals. Popular brand names include Paul Penders, Aubrey Organics, Kiss My Face, Body Love, Orjene Natural Cosmetics, Weleda, Vita Wave, Tom's of Maine, Autumn Harp, Green Ban, Mountain Fresh, Ecover, and Warm Earth. Examples: After Shave Lotion, 6 oz, $7.95; Seaware Facial Cleanser, 4 oz, $5.25; Orange Blossom Freshener, 6 oz, $6.50; Aloe Moisturizer, 16 oz, $6.50; Oil-Free Shampoo, 16 oz, $4.89; Anti-Perspirant Deodorant, 2 oz, $4.75; Water Base Make-up, 2 oz, $8.50; Sparkle Glass Cleaner, 25 oz, $3.65; Green Ban for People, 2.5 oz, $5.75; and Herbal Flea Collar, $1.50.

Durable nylon shopping bag, $3.50; toilet dam to save water, $7.95; The Compassionate Consumer tote bag, made of canvas, $8.97; The Compassionate Consumer T-shirt, $7.95; "Vegetarian" button, $1; Anti-fur button proclaims "To Wear Fur is a Shame," $1. Catalogs are $1.

See also "Books" chapter.

Co-op America, 2100 "M" St NW, Suite 403, Washington DC 20063. (202) 872-5307. Toll-free 1-800-424-2667. This is a non-profit, member-controlled, worker-managed association linking socially responsible businesses and consumers in a national network, a new alternative marketplace. Co-op America allows consumers to align buying habits with values. Basic information found in "Organizations" chapter.

Household products from the catalog: eco-filter is a reusable cotton filter for coffee; T-shirts that say "We Don't Inherit the Earth," "A Breath of Fresh Air," $22 each; T-shirt "If You're Not Recycling, You're Throwing It All Away," from Environmental Defense Fund, $14; T-shirt "In Wildness is the Preservation of the World," $14; T-shirt "Save the Rainforest,: $12.50; T-shirts "Think Globally, Act Locally" or "Recycle or Die" or "Good Planets are Hard to Find" $9.95 each.

Household cleaners in the catalog: Clean and Safe products such as Con-Lei general purpose cleaner, window cleaners, etc; Ecco Bella cleaners for laundry, non-chlorine bleach, dishwashing liquid; all-purpose cleaner; Ecover® toilet cleaner and cream cleaner.

Tote bags come with slogans "Make a World of Difference" or "Co-op America," 1 large and 1 small for $12.

Keep your closet moth-free with cedar moth balls, $12.50 from Hummers of Texas. Other natural cedar products available.

Products from the catalog are found in "Recycling," "Energy Conservation," "Books," " Organically Grown," "Paper Products, " and "Baby & Children's Products" chapters.

The Cotton Place, PO Box 59721, Dallas TX 75229. (214) 243-4149. Naturalguard™ barrier cloth, bedding, clothing, fabrics, yarn & more. Free catalog.

Country Comfort, PO Box 3, 28537 Nuevo Valley Dr, Nuevo CA 92367. (714) 657-3438. This company makes pure and natural lip cremes and herbal salves. No preservatives are used in their formulas.

Desert Essence Cosmetics, PO Box 588, Topanga CA 90290. (213) 455-1046. FAX # (213) 455-2245. Committed to enhancing the beauty of the individual without harming the beauty of the planet. They use pure, natural ingredients that are cruelty-free. Products: 100% pure jojoba oil; jojoba-aloe vera hand and body lotion; lip balm; skin care products (facial scrub, mask, moisture cream); jojoba shampoo & conditioners; jojoba massage oil; tea tree oil.

Deva Lifewear, Box GEF1, Burkittsville MD 21718-0438. (301) 663-4900. FAX # (301) 663-3560. Toll free order line 1-800-222-8024. A cottage industry with a network of friends and neighbors that manufacture pure cotton apparel for men and women. Examples: popular buccaneer shirt, various colors, $31; cozy waffle sweater, various colors, $45; hooded sweater, cream or purple heather, $76; denim jumper, $36; padre shirt, $29; kimono, $5, "Share the Earth" T-shirt, $13; "Save the Rain Forest" T-shirt, $14; many more interesting designs. Cotton lingerie also available. Catalog free; send $1 for fabric samples.

Dona Designs, 825 Northlake Drive, Richardson TX 75080. (214) 235-0485. Cotton pillows and bedding made with no pesticides, herbicides or defoliants.

Dry Creek Herb Farm, 13935 Dry Creek Road, Auburn CA 95603. (916) 878-2441. Shatoiya's handmade all natural skin care products made with organically grown herbs. Includes cleansing grains, herbal splash, dry skin cream, herbal balm, eye care, trauma-aid, and massage oil. Free catalog. See also "Seminars, Speakers & Workshops."

Earth Science, PO Box 1925, Corona CA 91718. (714) 524-9277. FAX # (714) 524-5705. Manufacturer of skin care, hair care, vitamins and nutrients that are biodegradable, do not contain aerosols, and do not use animal ingredients or do animal testing.

Their product line is extensive. Some examples: Mild Apricot Scrub Creme; Almond Aloe Light & Silky Moisturizer; Clarifying Facial Wash; Mint Tingle Masque; Lip Protector; Moisture Plus Shower & Bath Gel; Aloe 'n E Tanning Lotion; Herbal Astringent Shampoo & Conditioner; Sculpting Gel Glaze; Mousse (non-aerosol); and much more.

They have a line of skin care and body care products for men. Some of these products are: Almond Treatment Scrub (pre-shave); Aloe/ Herbal After Shave; Azulene Moisturizing Shave Cream; Follicare Hair and Scalp Treatment; more.

An interesting item in their product line is their Liken™ deodorant. This deodorant is made from the natural odor-preventing extract from the tiny lichen plant. It's safe and environmentally sound. There are no irritants, no alcohol, no aerosol, no aluminum or zirconium sales, no artificial colors, and no excessive paperboard box packaging.

Ecco Bella, 6 Provost Square, Suite 602, Caldwell NJ 07006. (201) 226-5799. FAX # (201) 226-0991. Toll-free 1-800-888-5320. This company manufactures and sells products that are cruelty-free and environmentally sound. The Ecco Bella line of products is extensive and featured in their own catalog. Ecco Bella products include the following: cosmetics, fragrances; body care; bath care; skin care; men's skin care; aromatherapy & massage oils; hair care; herbal carpet freshener; laundry powder; laundry liquid; non-chlorine bleach; citrus solvent; dishwashing liquid; pet shampoo; and more.

The Ecco Bella catalog contains items from other manufacturers as well: Ecover cream cleaner; Ecover floor soap; Ecover toilet soap; Nature's Miracle stain and odor remover; and more. There's biodegradable cellulose food storage bags.

Gift items in catalog: "Respect Your Mother" T-shirt, $14; "Save the Rainforest," "Save Our Planet," "Save Our Wildlife" T-shirts, $21 each. Or give them an Ecco Bella gift certificate so that they can choose their own environmentally safe products.

More items listed in "Paper Products," "Recycling," "Organically Grown" and "Energy Conservation" chapters.

Eco Design Company, 1365 Rufina Circle #1, Santa Fe NM 87501. Telephone orders 1-800-621-2591. Free 32-page catalog on environmentally sound products. Includes such products as Livos shoe polish (no animal ingredients), 3.4 oz, various colors, $5.95; Healthy Cleaner biodegradable all natural skin cleanser, 4 oz, $2.95; Ecologne Unisex cologne and aftershave, non-toxic, all natural, low allergy, recycled, no animal testing, 1 oz, $12.50; book *Saving the Tropical Forests* $24.95; Gellos-Wax Crayons, set of 7 colors, $4.85; Alis furniture polish, 8.50 oz, $5.95, and more.

The Ecology Box, 425 East Washington, Ann Arbor MI 48104. (313) 662-9131. Free catalog of safe, non-toxic

Environmental Excellence

Ecco Bella
They believe in recyclable and biodegradable packaging. They donate 10% of their profits from their catalog to animal and environmental protection organizations.

products including cleaners, shampoos, deodorants, paints, foods and cotton pillows. Books also available on allergy prevention, and making your home allergy-free.

EcoSafe Products Inc., PO Box 1177, St. Augustine FL 32085. 1-800-274-7387. Manufacturers of a line of natural flea control products: rechargeable flea collar; insect shoo recharging for the collar; yeast & garlic bits; herbal shampoo and dip; coat enhancer, a spritz with aloe, walnut leaves, orange oil, sesame oil, and citronella oil; herbal flea powder containing only dried pyrethrum flowers; herbal formula for pet diet; Gentle Dragon for deworming the natural way; environmental cedar spray that repells insects; pyrethrum insect powder to fight ants, ticks, silverfish, fleas, flies, moths, spiders, lice without the use of chemicals; diatum dust for sprinkling on pets, furniture to discourage fleas; personal insect repellant containing citronella, cedarwood, lavendar and geranium.

EcoSource™, 9051 Mill Station Road Bldg #E, Sebastopol CA 95472. (717) 829-7957 or (707) 829-8345. Catalog of products for a cleaner, safer world. Includes energy efficient lighting, non-toxic paints, biodegradable household cleaners, recycled paper and products, water purifiers, solar products, clean air products, pet and garden products, more.

Examples from catalog: Recycle tote bag, 16", that says "If You're Not Recycling You're Throwing It All Away," $19.95; EcoSource™ all-purpose cleaner, 32 fl oz, $5.95; EcoSource™ laundry detergent, 1 gal, $17.95; solar nicad battery charger, $25.95; super solar shower for camping, $11.95; EcoWorks light bulbs, 4 bulbs for $5.98; "Save the Rainforests" T-shirts for $14.95; *Earth Book for Kids* from The Learning Works, $9.95; "Save the World" cooperative game, $21.50; Earth Puzzle, $4.95; Snado shoe polish, various colors, 3.4 oz, $5.95.

Non-toxic building supplies include AFM Safecoat paint, 1 gal, $26.95; AFM Safecoat water-based wood stain, 1 gal, $30.95; AFM 3-in-1 adhesive, 1 qt, $11.95; water seal, 1 qt, $7.95; Leinos citrus thinner, 33.8 fl oz, $7.95; handi-gloves mate from pure Malaysian latex, 20 per pkg, $2.00; natural linoleum from $2.60 per square foot.

Includes a very interesting "RCI Environmental Test Kit" that contains everything you need to collect samples to find out if you have pollutants in and around your home. After collecting the samples, you mail them to the lab in the containers provided. Kit $49.95.

More products listed under "Books," "Recycling," "Energy Conservation," "Clean Air, Clean Water," "Paper Products" and "Educational Materials" chapters.

Genesee Natural Foods, Inc., RD 2 Box 105, Genesee PA 16923. (814) 228-3200. FAX # (814) 228-3638. Mostly organic foods (see "Organically Grown" chapter) but also carries Ecover soaps and cleaning products.

Gentle Strength Co-op, 234 West University Drive, Tempe AZ 85281. (602) 968-4831. This store handles many environmentally sensitive lines of products. Household products: non-toxic, biodegradable cleaners for bathroom, rugs, glass, dishwashing such as Ecover, Brownies, Allens Naturally, LifeTree and Country Safe; cruelty-free and non-toxic body care and bath care products, such as Sun Feather Herbal Soap Company's bar shampoo; Paul Penders cosmetics and facial care; Pet Organics nontoxic flea control; New Moon vitamins in glass bottles with no preservatives; Air Therapy room fresheners; and Today's Choice women's hygiene products that are made with unbleached, recycled material.

More products found in "Baby & Children's Products," "Organically Grown," "Paper Products," "Books," and "Magazines, Newsletters & Brochures" chapters.

Gold Mine Natural Food Company, 1947 30th St, San Diego CA 92102. (619) 234-9711. 1-800-475-FOOD (3663). Free 40-page organic foods mail order catalog. and teas. Nontoxic cookware is available in the catalog includes: ceramic cooking pot with pressure cooker insert; Genmai Donabe cooking pot; & natural stone pot. Natural body care from catalog: Dentie toothpowder made from powdered eggplant and sea salt.

Organic products listed in "Organically Grown" chapter.

See ad page 161.

Green Fields Inc., 30770 Buck Heaven Rd, Hillsboro OR 97213. (503) 538-8738. Fire to Go™ firelogs, 100% recycled content, certified by Green Cross certification. These logs can be burned in place of wood for heating, camping, cooking, and BBQ. The whole manufacturing process adds no pollutants to the air or water, and saves hardwood scrap from being sent to landfills. You can have a cheery fire, yet never cut down a tree. Mail order kit (12 logs, 2" x 9", with kindling and paper, burns about 4 hours) is $2.99 plus shipping for 15 pounds from Oregon.

Growing Naturally, PO Box 54, 149 Pine Lane, Pineville PA 18946. (215) 598-7025. FAX # (215) 598-7025. Catalog of products for organic gardening. This catalog also contains nontoxic pet care products: Safer® Flea & Tick Spray, 24 oz, $5.90; Safer® Pet Odor Eliminator, $5.50; Natural Con-

ditioning Pet Shampoo, 8 oz, $4.25; and pyrethrum powder for flea and tick control, 7 oz, $8.50.

Healthy Kleaner, PO Box 4656, Boulder CO 80306. (303) 444-3440. Sales 1-800-EARTH29 (3278429). Healthy Kleaner is a non-toxic, non-abrasive, biodegradable, healthy alternative to petroleum and chemical based cleaners. This product uses only natural products—oranges, glycerine, jojoba oil, grains, and other food grade ingredients. There are no animal by-products and it has not been tested on animals. This cleaner can be used to remove permanent ink, oil, grease, adhesive, glue, crayons, shoe polish, odors, makeup, gum. Reviewed in *Buzzworm, the Environmental Journal,* May/ June, 1990. An 8-oz bottle costs $4.49 plus shipping.

Heart's Desire, 1307 Dwight Way, Berkeley CA 94702. Catalog $1. Cruelty-free products: makeup; personal care; household cleaners, gifts.

Heavenly Soap, 5948 E 30th St, Tucson AZ 85711. (602) 790-9938. Heavenly Soap is a gentle, non-drying, totally cruelty-free product. It also contains no chemicals or harmful substances and is completely biodegradable. The bars of soap come in a variety of scents: apricot, coconut milk and honey, oatmeal unscented, oatmeal sandalwood, oatmeal vanilla, rose glycerine, and unscented. Unwrapped soaps are $1 each; wrapped soap $1.25; bath/ body oil $3; and herbal salve $3.

Environmental Excellence

The Hummer Nature Works

This company has produced over 45,000 items from wood yet they have never cut down a live tree nor used boards gained from the harvesting of live timber. All of the products, which include boxes, chests, turnings, desk & kitchen accessories, are fashioned only from the dead wood that they gather from the Texas hill country. They also fashion a line of cedar products (moth balls, closet fresheners, oil, incense) without using any live cedar trees—again, harvesting only the dead trees. And they utilize a full 95% or more of each piece of deadwood they gather!

Available by mail order only. Distributorships available.

Home Service Products Company, PO Box 269, Bound Brook NJ 08805. (201) 356-8175. Manufacturers of Professional® household cleaning products that are cruelty-free, contain no animal ingredients, and are safe for the environment. Professional Brands have been awarded the Beauty Without Cruelty, PETA (People for the Ethical Treatment of Animals) and NAVS (National Anti-Vivisection Society) seals. The product line is: laundry powder, laundry liquid, all fabric non chlorine bleach, fabric softener, automatic dishwashing powder, liquid dishwashing detergent, and all purpose spray cleaner. All product sold in case lots. Satisfaction guaranteed.

Humane Alternative Products, 8 Hutchins St, Concord NH 03301. (603) 224-1361. Fully guaranteed products with no animal testing and containing no animal ingredients. Line of products includes home care, hair care, skin care; cosmetics; perfumes; bath care; mouth care; deodorants; pet products; sun care products; and more.

Examples: Allen's Naturally dishwasher compound, concentrated, 4 lbs, $10; Golden Lotus Winter White Liquid Laundry Soap, 32 oz, $6; Tom's of Maine Aloe & Almond Hair Conditioner, 12 oz, $4.75; Aubrey Organics Jojoba & Aloe Hair conditioner, 8 oz, $5.50; Vita Wave creme hair colors; Paul Penders Peppermint Hops Shampoo, 8 oz, $5.50; Weleda baby oil, 2 oz, $5.50; Beauty Without Cruelty Rose Petal Skin Freshener, 120 ml, $9; Aura Cacia body powders; Beauty Without Cruelty cosmetics; Lightning dog spray with a blend of citrus oils, 16 oz, $6.49; much more.

Humane Street USA, Offices & Store: 985 Terra Bella Ave, Mountain View CA 94043. Orders & Mail: PO Box 807, Mountain View CA 94042. (415) 965-8441. Cruelty-free products for household & personal use. These products have not been tested on animals nor do they have animal-derived ingredients (with the occasion exception of some beeswax or lanolin). Most of the products have no added fragrances and are free of harmful chemicals. Product lines in the catalog are skin care, cosmetics, cosmetic accessories, hair care, fragrance, body care, sun care, health care, baby care and household. Some companies represented are Natural Bodycare; Beauty Without Cruelty, Ltd; Paul Penders, Delore Nails; Giovanni; Eastern Star Cremes; Sirena; Allens Naturally; SolarCare; Autumn Harp; Liberty Products; and Ecover.

The Hummer Nature Works, Reagan Wells Canyon Box 122, Uvalde TX 78801. (512) 232-6167. Examples of their products: the Forest Box, fashioned to appear as natural as possible yet be smooth to the touch, from $7 to $34; Forest Canticle, a natural container from the forest, $6 to $36; Forest Chest, from $16 to $44; Forest "Love" Chest, each drawer cut in the shape of a heart, $19 to $47.50; Forest "Dove" Chest with two draws in the shape of a dove, $46.50 to $76; Hummer Original Chest with secret compartment, $22 to $56.50. Aromatic products include Texas Moth Balls, 14 to a bag; Hanger Hangers fresheners, 4 to a bag; Closet Fresheners, 2 per bag, more.

They also distribute other products, such as: Green Ban Herbal Insect Repellants, EcoSafe Natural Flea Control, Natrapel Natural Insect Repellant, Citra-Solv Natural Citrus Solvent.

Ida Grae Natures Colors Cosmetics, 424 LaVerne Ave, Mill Valley CA 94941. (415) 388-6101. Cosmetics that use all naturally derived ingredients: no synthetic preservatives, dyes, detergents, emulsifiers; no petro chemicals; no irradiation; and totally cruelty-free products. Products: Earth Rouge; Creme Rouge; Eye Shade Powders; Translucent Powder; Creme Foundation; Venus Moisturizer; and Lip Creme. Cosmetic accessories also available: brush sets, maple boxes, and tester displays. These products have medical recommendations, such as: Dr. Alan Levin, an allergist; Debra Dadd, author of ecology books and publisher of *The Earthwise Consumer;* and Dr. Sherry Rogers, lecturer and physician.

IFM, 333 Ohme Gardens Rd, Wenatchee WA 98801. (509) 662-3179. 1-800-332-3179. Free catalog called "Products and Services for Natural Agriculture." Organic flea and tick controls available, such as Safer® Insecticidal Pet Soap or Indoor Flea Guard. More much listed in "Organically Grown" chapter.

Jade Mountain, PO Box 4616, Boulder CO 80306. (303) 449-6601. FAX # (303) 449-8266. Toll-free 1-800-442-1972. Large selection of energy saving and appropriate technology products. Household products include: Ecover dishwashing liquid (32 oz, $4.50); Ecover laundry powder (6 lbs, 9 oz, $16); Life Tree laundry liquid (32 oz, $7); EcoSafe pyrethrum insect powder (7 oz, $12); and shopping bag, $9.

Newsletter/catalog (80-page) subscription, $3 for one year. Also listed in "Paper Products," "Energy Conservation," "Clean Air, Clean Water" chapters.

Environmental Excellence

J. R. Carlson Laboratories

What is particularly interesting about this company is that is has taken the effort to publish the company's environmental policy, which states: the company's facilities were designed to conserve energy (time controlled thermostats, passive solar energy used to help reduce heating requirements, extra insulation); the company has intensive recycling efforts (employees bring aluminum for recycling, computer paper recycled, scratch pads made from discontinued literature, packaging reused and recycled); their product plastic bottles are recyclable; and they are a member of the "Green Committee" which actively promotes legislation to protect the environment.

Jantz Design & Manufacturing, PO Box 3071, Santa Rosa CA 95402. (707) 823-8834. Organically grown cotton available from this company to other businesses and individuals.

This company sells 100% certified organic cotton futons and pillows. Mattress pads and comforters made with pure, untreated lambswool batting and prewashed muslin. Free catalog.

Jason Natural Products, 8468 Warner Drive, Culver City CA 90232-2484. (213) 838-7543. FAX # (213) 838-9274. Manufacturer of cruelty-free, environmentally-safe products for hair, skin, nails, body and bath. Includes: Duck Oil™ waterproof sun block; Sunbrellas of Jason™ line of sun protection and sun tanning products; A Fresh Step™ natural foot care system; Envirobiometics™ anti-stress skin care products; plus shampoos, conditioners, henna hi-lights; hairspray, hair gel, and more.

J. R. Carlson Laboratories, Inc., 15 College Drive, Arlington Heights IL 60004. (708) 255-1600. This company manufactures a full line of Vitamin E products.

Karen's Nontoxic Products, 1839 Dr. Jack Road, Conowingo MD 21918. (301) 378-4621. 1-800-KARENS-4. Write or call toll-free number for catalog of truly natural, environmentally-safe, cruelty-free and energy building items for family, home and health. These products must meet strict guidelines before they are included in Karen's catalog: no synthetic colors; no synthetic fragrances; all products must be natural, pure, and if possible, organic; whenever possible paper, cellophane or glass have been substituted for plastic. Items included are: natural makeup & natural fragrances, holistic health care, personal care, cleansers, herbs, plant & pet care, wooden toys and crafts, books, nontoxic construction materials and much more.

Cellophane bags are a good substitute for plastic bags. These come in various sizes, including an extra large size.

Try using unbleached cotton muslin coffee filters instead of the paper

Chapter Eight: Household & Personal Care Products

**LaCrista Face & Body
natural oil moisturizer**

Kiss My Face Corporation, PO Box 224, Gardiner NY 12525. (914) 255-0884. FAX # (914) 255-4312. Manufacturers of products that are 100% biodegradable and cruelty-free. Products lines are: pure soaps; moisturizers; aftershave; shampoo; conditioner; facial cleanser; facial masque; astringent; toner. Available by mail order directly from the company, through health food stores, and through other catalog companies.

Examples: pure olive soap (fragrance free) 8 oz packet of 3, $6.75; olive & aloe shampoo, 16 oz, $4.95; cool mint moist shave, 16 oz, $5.95; olive & aloe moisturizer, 16 oz, $6.95; olive & aloe cleanser, 4 oz, $5.95; citrus essence astringent, 8 oz, $4.95. Many of the products are available in 16 ounce family size, 1 ounce travel tubes, 4 ounce personal size, or 64 ounce refill size.

KSA Jojoba, 19025 Parthenia #200, Northridge CA 91324. (818) 701-1534. FAX # (818) 993-0194. Cruelty-free, animal-free products that use jojoba oil in place of sperm whale oil. Products in the catalog include: jojoba oil for pets; bulk jojoba oil; jojoba glycerin soap; jojoba lip balm; lotions & creams; shampoos & creme rinse; perfumes; and more. Also sells a rubber stamp with a mother and baby whale that says "Save Our Whales" $5.50.

LaCrista, Inc., PO Box 240, Davidsonville MO 21035. (301) 956-4447. Cruelty-free Face & Body natural oil moisturizer ($5 ppd) and Face &

kind. This catalog offers two brands, and the filters fun from $2.30 to $4.25 each, and will last for months.

Cotton shopping bags are offered. These are made from 100% pure American cotton, machine washable, and will last for years. The Garden Sacs are good for produce, 2 for $4.95; the Eurosac expands to the size of a grocery bag, $4.95.

Livos brand of nontoxic putty, adhesives, spackles, shellac, varnish, oil primers, finishes and sealers are available.

See also "Books" & "Paper Products" chapter.

Lillian Vernon's classic French style string shopping bag.

Body cleanser/ masque ($6 ppd). Available at Giant Food, Drug Emporium, Safeway Pharmacy stores, Peoples Drug, and health food stores, or order by mail.

Lakon Herbals, 4710 Templeton Rd, Montpelier VT 05602.(802) 223-5563. Personal care products that are created from ingredients that are completely cruelty-free. The ingredients they use are all botanical derivatives, and are tested so that they do not use anything potentially toxic or allergenic. Product line: body, bath and massage oils; salves, ointments & liniments.

Lillian Vernon Corporation, 510 S. Fulton Avenue, Mount Vernon NY 10555. (914) 699-4131. The catalog offers a "classic French-style string shopping bag" that eliminates the need for plastic shopping bags. Woven to hold up to 10 pounds; has two reinforced handles; folds to fit into pocket or purse. 100% cotton; washable. Still at the same price as in 1986: 2 bags for $7.98. Order #398748. See also "Recycling" chapter.

Livos Plant Chemistry, 1365 Rufina Circle, Santa Fe NM 87501. (505) 438-3448. **See Eco Design Company.**

Mercantile Food Company, 4 Old Mill Road, PO Box 1140, Georgetown CT

06829. Ecover® brand bio-degradable household cleaning products are manufactured in Belgium and imported into the United States by Mercantile Food Company. Ecover makes dishwashing liquid, automatic dishwasher powder, laundry powder, liquid launder wash, wool wash liquid, fabric conditioner, cream cleaner, floor soap, and toilet cleaner. Ecover does not use animals in any kind of testing and requires that its suppliers confirm that they also do not test on animals. Ecover uses recycled cardboard for its outer cases of packaging of the powders.

See also "Organically Grown" chapter.

Mia Rose Products, Inc., 1374 Logan Unit #C, Costa Mesa CA 92626. (714) 662-5465. Toll-free 1-800-292-6339. Non-toxic, chemical-free, cruelty-free, 100% natural products for air freshening, pet odors, and cleaning. Air Therapy® all natural air purification products are made from "Real Citrus," eliminate odors, smoke, airborne bacteria, allergy-causing pollen, and insects, yet they are safe to use around food, children and pets. Pet Air® freshens pet bedding, carpets, kennels and cages. Citri-Shine® Total Home Cleaner is made from pure organic plant-derived soap and citrus, is an all-purpose cleaner for dishes, laundry, floors, walls, cars, and more.

Mountain Fresh Products, (formerly Golden Lotus), PO Box 40516, Grand Junction CO 81504. (303) 434-8434. FAX # (303) 434-8395. This company

✷Environmental Excellence✷

Mountain Fresh Products (formerly Golden Lotus)
Winter White™ packaging won a design award from Packaging Association of America and is made from recycled material, biodegradable ink, and includes a codegradable plastic inner liner. Mountain Fresh company is one of the largest employers of the handicapped in western Colorado.

has been making environmentally friendly and cruelty-free products for more than 17 years. The products are distributed in over 14,000 health food stores, super markets and discount stores across the United States, Canada and Mexico.

Their product lines are Winter White™ (Pre-wash for laundry, Soft N Fresh™, Powdered Bleach, Cool Wash™, Non-chlorine Liquid Bleach, Liquid Laundry Detergent, Powdered Detergent, Kleer™ dishwashing detergents, Glass Mate™, Kleen™ All-

Purpose Cleaner); Golden Lotus™ (hair and skin care); baby massage™ (shampoo & conditioner, lotion, creme & oil); Aloe Gold™ and Vegelatum™. All Winter White™ products are phosphate-free, petroleum-free, perfume-free, dye-free and super concentrated. One 48-oz box equals the cleaning power of a normal detergent's 147 oz.

The Nature Company, PO Box 2310, Berkeley CA 94702. 1-800-227-1114. FAX (415) 849-0465. Beautiful full-color catalog full of interesting items for people who love nature. Household items offered are the re-usable lunch bags, made of washable waterproof fabric with Velcro closure, $6.95; and mesh reusable shopping bag that folds to fit into pocket or purse, $4.95. Also offered is a pin that says "Treat the earth well," enamel on brass, $5.95.

Other items in the catalog described in "Books," "Recycling," and "Educational Materials" chapters.

Nature's Colors, 424 LaVerne Ave, Mill Valley CA 94941. Sell's Ida Grae's all natural unscented cosmetics: moisturizer, foundation, translucent face powder, eyeshadows, creme rouge, lip gloss, blusher. No animal testing. Natural colorings used. For brochures, send business size envelope plus 4 first class stamps.

North Country Soap, 7888 Hennepin County Rd #6, Maple Plain MN 55359. (612) 479-3381. FAX # (612) 476-8527. Orders toll-free 1-800-328-4827 ext 2153. Their products are non-

toxic, non-allergenic, cruelty-free. Ingredients: vegetable shortening, coconut oil, caustic soda, various herbs and oils. They have many kinds, sizes, and specialties in their soaps, so send for the brochure.

The Peaceable Kingdom, 1902 W 6th St, Wilmington DE 19805. (302) 429-8687. (302) 652-7840. A store in Wilmington, Delaware, that offers cruelty-free cleaners, beauty & health aids, and cosmetics. Hours: Tuesday through Saturday, 11 to 4.

Pets 'N People, Inc., 5312 Ironwood Street, Rancho Palos Verdes CA 90274. (213) 373-1559. Manufacturers of environmentally sensitive cleaning products for the pet industry, janitorial services, veterinarians, groomers, and professional rug cleaners. They are on the approved list by PETA (People for Ethical Treatment of Animals).

Nature's Miracle™ gets rid of stains and odors, and is safe for children and pets. This product was tested by Monsanto on their Wear Dated® Carpet with Locked-in Stainblocker and found compatible as a cleaning formula for that carpet.

Nature's Miracle™ Dog Body Deodorizer Cleaner & Dander Remover works by neutralizing odors, no temporary perfume odor cover-up. Nature's Miracle™ Litter Deodorant is guaranteed to prevent litter odors, even with small animals such as rabbits, weasels and hamsters. And of course, there's Nature's Miracle® Skunk Odor

Remover for those special problems!

Nature's Miracle® Glass Cleaner, Polisher and Protector is another environmental improvement product. For air freshening, try Nature's Miracle® Air Freshener/ Deodorant Gel Cup.

Mother's Little Miracle is a formula for quickly and safely cleaning up baby's messiest messes. Deodorizes and removes stains.

Plasco Press Company, Inc., 16037 Foothill Blvd, Azusa CA 91702. (818) 969-1545. Bottlesack™ plastic shopping bag, 30% recycled content, certified by Green Cross Certification.

Rainbow Concepts, Rt 5, Box 569-H, Pheasant Mountain Rd, Toccoa GA 30577. (404) 886-6320. They strive to find products that are: environmentally safe; cruelty-free; safe and healthful; the best quality and value. Their 16-page catalog contains a wide variety of cosmetics, facial care, body care, sun care, hair care, products for men, personal care, essential oils; and household products.

Examples from their catalog: Sombras China Clay Foundation; Paul Penders lip color; Earth Science apricot mild facial scrub; Earth Science Azulene desensitizing eye creme; KSA jojoba oil; Earth Science hair treatment shampoo; Rainbow Research Corporation henna hair colors; Earth Science problem after shave formula; Tom's of Maine natural toothpaste; Merfluan Natural European Toothpowder; Earth Science Liken Deodorant; Autumn Harp fresh comfrey salve; Aura Cacia

essential oils; and more.

They carry Allens Naturally fabric softener; Professional automatic dishwashing compound; and more Allens Naturally cleaners.

There's a string shopping bag that folds to fit into pocket or purse, $4.98.

Real Goods Trading Company, 966 Mazzoni St, Ukiah CA 95482. (707) 468-9214. FAX # (707) 468-0301. Order toll-free 1-800-762-7325. This company has an extensive 106-page catalog full of energy-saving equipment and supplies. Products for the home include household non-toxic cleaners: liquid wax, 8.5 oz, $7; shoe & leather polish, clear, brown or black, $7; Ossengal stick spot remover, $4; Oasis Laundry detergent, $12 qt.

For fun, there's: T-shirts, "Harvest the Sun," "peace in the World," "Give Peas a Chance," "Recycle or Die," "Think Globally, Act Locally," $12.50 each; solar clock, $49; gift certificates; bumper stickers "Stop Solar Energy, Mutants for Nuclear Power, Village Idiots for a Toxic Environment," $2; bumper sticker "I Get My Electricity From the Sun," $1; solar radios; night sky star stencil to look at the stars from inside the home even when there's clouds—just turn out the lights and voila!; solar safari hat, $42; solar cool cap, $21; "All One People" button, $2; "Good Planets are Hard to Find," post card, 25¢.

More items listed in "Books," "Energy Conservation," "Baby & Children's Products," "Paper Products," "Clean Air, Clean Water" and

Chapter Eight: Household & Personal Care Products

Safer® has the pest control products that are safe to use around children and pets.

"Recycling" chapters.

Ringer Corporation, 9959 Valley River Road, Eden Prairie MN 55344. (612) 941-4180. FAX # (612) 941-5036. 1-800-654-1047 for ordering. Manufacturers of products for the organic gardeners. People-safe, pet-safe, natural products for a healthier lawn and garden.

Flea and Tick Attack® effectively kills fleas and ticks in the pet areas frequented by your dog or cat. The active ingredient is pyrethrum from the Chrysanthemum plant. It can be sprayed directly on pets. 1/2 gallon ready-to-use, $11.98.

Write for their 32-page color catalog of gardener's supplies. Much more information in "Organically Grown" chapter.

Safer, Inc., 189 Wells Ave, Newton MA 02159. (617) 964-2990. Safer® has the kind of pesticides that Americans want—the kind that are safe to use

around children and pets. The active ingredient in every Safer pesticide product is derives from sources found in nature. Many of the products contain fatty acids, which disrupt the cell membranes of some pests, causing them to die on contact. Other products contain pyrethrins, extracted from the flowers of a species of chrysanthemum, which kill a wide range of pests. Others contain biological strains which come from the soil and stop the feeding of harmful pests.

Product lines include: BioSafe™ Lawn & Garden Insect Control, Safer® Natural Pesticide Applicator; Safer® Household Pest Killer; Safer® B.t. Leaf Beetle Killer; Safer® Insecticidal Soap; Safer® Rose & Flower Insect Killer; ForEverGreen® Plant Protectant; Sharpshooter® Weed Killer; Safer® Housefly Trap; Safer® Indoor Flea Guard™; and more.

Schaefer Applied Technology, 200 Milton St, Unit 8-R, Dedham MA 02026-2917. (617) 320-9900. Order toll-free 1-800-366-5500. Manufactures the Model EM1 Electromagnetic Field Detector, a low-cost, accurate, easy-to-use meter for measuring environmentally-hazardous ELF magnetic fields in and around homes, schools and businesses. Recommended by *Family Circle*. Price: $89.95 plus $5 for shipping. Educational booklet included with product.

Seventh Generation, Colchester VT 05446-1672. (802) 655-3116. FAX toll-free # 1-800-456-1139. Order toll-free 1-800-456-1177. Customer service toll-free 1-800-456-1197.

Seventh Generation is one of the most well-known companies for environmentally safe consumer products. Their 48-page catalog "Products for a Healthy Planet" ($2) contains an extraordinary variety of products. General categories of products found in the catalog are: baby, bags, books/calendars, cleaners, clothing, coffee filters, energy savers, hardware, organic food, personal care products, recycled paper, recycling equipment, sheets and towels, toys, and water savers.

They have several alternatives to plastic grocery bags: 100% unbleached cotton string bags like the ones used in Europe, 4 for $16.95; canvas grocery bag that says "Seventh Generation: Products for a Healthy Planet" that's washable, $7.95; trash bags made from recycled plastic; and trash bags made from recycled paper.

For food storage use cellulose bags. They come in various sizes or you can buy a combo back.

Seventh Generation has their own lines of non-toxic cleaners that contain no phosphates, no petroleum-based detergents and no chlorine bleach. They come in containers made of recycled plastic. There is laundry powder, laundry liquid, non-chlorine bleach, wool wash, fabric softener, toilet cleaner, nonabrasive cream cleanser, and glass cleaner. They also carry Citra-Solv super cleaner.

Other types of cleaners include petroleum-free furniture polish,

EnvironmentalExcellence

Seventh Generation

Seventh Generation is one of the most well-known companies for environmentally safe consumer products. They also practice what they preach. For instance, they recycle their office paper, and reuse cardboard boxes for shipping. They have a 1% fund that goes to environmental organizations.

An interesting note is how the company was named. In Iroquois Indian lore, one of the factors that tribal elders would use in decision-making is how that decision would affect the next generation, the generation after that, the generation after that, and so forth—up to the seventh generation. Thus Seventh Generation continues the policy of providing products that are safe for the planet and that we can be sure will not harm the seventh generation to follow.

Ecover floor soap, and Seventh Generation dishwashing liquid.

For cars, there's non-toxic windshield cleaner, non-toxic hand cleaner, and environmentally-safer motor oil (oil that is made using less re-refined oil and thus less polluting to manufacture).

Speaking of less polluting, there's a portable grill, and a unique device called the "charcoal starter" to start your charcoals without using lighter fluid—a necessity if you live in the Los Angeles area, where they are considering banning lighter fluid.

Rechargeable batteries, battery chargers using solar energy, and even a solar radio are available.

Personal care products include toothpaste, shampoo, conditioner, shave cream, soap, moisturizing cream, and more. One unique item is the cotton balls, swabs and pads made from 100% cotton that is bleached without chlorine. In addition, panty liners and maxi pads are available that are bleached without chlorine. Unbleached coffee filters also available.

Just for fun, or for gifts, there's: "Save the Rainforest" T-shirt; Women's Environmental Network T-shirt; global warming poster; World Wildlife Fund rainforest calendar; Peter Max 1990 Earth Day poster; New York City Earth Day poster; green datebook; "Seventh Generation" T-shirt; Greenpeace calendar.

There are so many products in this catalog that additional information can be found in these chapters: "Baby and Children's Product," "Books," "Educational Materials," "Paper Products," "Recycling," "Energy Conservation," and "Organically Grown."

Shahin Soap, PO Box 8117, 427 Van Dyke Ave, Haledon NJ 07538. (201) 790-4296. They make 100% pure olive oil soap without animal ingredients or animal testing. They use only paper for wrapping—no plastic.

Shaker Shops West, 5 Inverness Way, PO Box 487, Inverness CA 94937. (415) 669-7256. FAX # (415) 669-7327. Their catalog contains items of

✷Environmental Excellence✷

Signature Art

They produce the award-winning For-The-Earth Bags™ that eliminate the need for plastic shopping bags. For-The-Earth Bags™ were recently selected by *Ecologue: The Consumer's Guide to Environmentally Safe Products* as one of the top ten products. Signature Art received an *Ecologue* Award for being an "Earth Conscious Company" and for "products and practices for a safe planet." The company's goal is to offer environmentally sound alternatives to ecologically damaging behavior patterns, with a focus on shopping habits. Signature Art contributes 10% of its profits to environmental organizations. Environmental groups receive a 5% discount on their wholesale purchases.

interest to the environmentally-concerned: goat's milk soap, set of 2, $5.75; Shaker natural potpourri, 1.7 oz in tin cannister or glass spice jar, $6.95; milk paint in various early-American colors, qt, $13.50; Shaker fabric chair tape made of 100% cotton in various colors (tape samples sent free of charge), comes in 1" (70¢ per yard) or 5/8" width (55¢ per yard); herbs and herbal teas.

Shikai Products, PO Box 2866, Santa Rosa CA 95405. (707) 584-0298. Outside California 1-800-448-0298.

Manufacturers of hair and body care products—all of which are biodegradable, packaged in recyclable plastic bottles, and cruelty-free. These products are sold in health food stores.

Signature Art, PO Box 801, Wilder VT 05088. (802) 295-3291. They produce the award-winning For-The-Earth Bags™ that eliminate the need for plastic shopping bags. These bags are made in the USA of sturdy cotton canvas in natural and bright colors. They feature a large interior pocket for carrying extra bags. The straps are the perfect length for both shoulder and hand carrying. Beautiful nature scenes are silk screened on the side. Businesses may custom order their own logo. These bags are ideal for the beach, gym, school, work, toddler, overnighter, and carry-on, as well as grocery and clothes shopping.

Styles available in these bags are: Lily, Palm Lagoon, Earth, Turtle, Fluorescent Palm Lagoon, Sunburst, Penguins, Rainforest and Savanna.

Another product from the company is a Russian string shopping bag, called "Avoska." These bags are traditionally made by the blind. They have a wide neck opening and are available in cotton and rayon in variety of colors. They fold conveniently to fit into pocket or purse.

When calling or writing for information, please specify wholesale or retail catalog (minimum wholesale quantity is 24). Also listed in "Recycling" chapter.

See ad page 132.

Simmons Handcrafts, 42295 Hwy 36, Bridgeville CA 95526. (707) 777-3280, ext 6074 (radio phone). Free catalog of pure castile and vegetarian soaps, scented and unscented. Examples: castile in various scents and vegetarian in various scents, $1.50 each; aloe vera shaving soap, 2 oz $1; citronella camping soap with scent to repel mosquitos, 2 oz $3. Bath and bodycare products: bath oils, various scents, 8 oz $6; Garden Empress lotions, 4 oz $5; Rosemary's Garden lip balm, various flavors, $2; natural boar bristle bath brush, $7.20; ayate natural washcloth, $4.95. See also "Clean Air, Clean Water" chapter.

Simply Delicious, 243-A North Hook Rd, PO Box 124, Pennsville NJ 08070. (609) 678-4488. This is a retail natural food store that offers organic cereals, grains, beans and more from Health Valley, Arrowhead Mills and other major product lines. Also carries household cleaning products from Golden Lotus, Ecover and Mountain Fresh. Also listed in "Organically Grown" and "Paper Products" chapters.

Sinan Company, PO Box 857, Davis CA 95617-0857. (916) 753-3104. They offer natural building materials. All of their products contain no petroleum based, cruel oil or plastic ingredients. Their extensive line of Auro® products include: varnishes, waxes, laquers, paints, glues, cleansers, polishes, and more. Their catalog contains a "User's Guide for the Most Important

Ranges of Application for Paints, Wood Finishes, etc."

Solar Electric Engineering, Inc., 116 4th St, Santa Rosa CA 95401. (707) 542-1990. FAX # (707) 542-4358. This is a publicly owned corporation that has been committed to bringing to the marketplace environmentally sound products at affordable prices to the consumer. They have a 40-page "Environmental Catalog," with household products, including: Earth Rite® all-natural non-toxic All Purpose cleaner, $3.95; and the Rainforest Crunch T-shirt, $14.

More items listed in "Energy Conservation," "Recycling," "Paper Products," "Clean Air, Clean Water," "Baby & Children's Products," and "Magazines, Newsletters & Brochures."

Spare the Animals, Inc., PO Box 233, Tiverton RI 02878. (401) 625-5963. A mail-order source for cruelty-free, animal-free environmentally-sound personal care and household products, including cosmetics, oral care products, shampoos, soaps, dishwashing liquid, laundry detergent and all-purpose cleaners. Free brochure. Mastercard/Visa accepted.

Product examples: Tom's of Maine Anti-Perspirant Roll-On, 2 oz, $4.75; Beauty Without Cruelty cosmetics; Weleda products; Golden Lotus products; Sirena Fresh Coconut Soap, three 4 oz bars, $2.39; Life Tree Home-Soap All-Purpose Cleaner, 16 oz, $4.59.

Sunrise Lane, 780 Greenwich St., New York NY 10014. (212) 242-7014. Catalog of cruelty-free and biodegradable products for personal use and for the home. Examples: Dr. Bronner's Plain Castile Soap, 16 oz, $4.25; Autumn Harp Talc-free Baby Powder, 4 oz, $4.45; LifeTree Dishwashing Liquid, 16 oz, $3.50; Winter White's Kleen full strength liquid cleaner, 32 oz, $6.25; Ecover cream cleaner, 33.8 oz, $4.85; Weleda Natural Salt Toothpaste, 2 oz, $3.75.

Products offered are soaps, hair care, hair styling, facial cleansers and masques, body care (lotions & treatments), deodorants, suntan lotions, makeup, laundry and dish detergents, air fresheners, glass cleaners, all-purpose household cleaners, perfumes, mouth care, and salves. The popular lines carried are made by Autumn Harp, LifeTree, Paul Penders, Sleepy Hollow Botanicals, Earth Science, Golden Lotus, Vita Wave, Nutri-metrics, Winter White, Ecover, and Weleda.

This company also publishes a bimonthly newsletter called *Sunrise Gazette* which carries current news on the animal rights and ecology movements; offers special discounts on their merchandise; and offers new merchandise not yet in their catalog. Subscription $8 for 6 issues.

Tender Corporation, PO Box 290, Littleton Industrial Park, Littleton NH 03561. (603) 444-5464. FAX # (603) 444-6735. Toll-free 1-800-258-4696. Manufacturers of Natrapel® Insect Repellant with Natural Ingredients.

✳Environmental Excellence✳

Tender Corporation

Natrapel® Insect Repellant has earned the EPA and Good Housekeeping approval. Independent tests by Shuster, Inc. prove Natrapel a safe and non-toxic repellant. This company donates to environmental causes based on the sales of this product.

This natural repellent contains citronella, aloe, and water with a preservative to keep the aloe fresh.

Treekeepers, 249 South Hwy 101, Ste 518, Solana Beach CA 92075. (619) 481-6403. FAX # (619) 481-2305. They offer shopping bags that are an alternative to paper and plastic. Styles: the Canvas Lunch Sack with "I'm a Treekeeper" logo, flat strap for carrying, 7" x 11" x 3", $6 each; the old fashioned flour sack, cotton drawstring, 12" x 16", $2.50; the mesh produce bag, 12" x 16", $4; European style string bag, $5. Also T-shirts that say "I'm a Treekeeper!" in blue, white, black or green, $9.

The Vermont Country Store, Inc., PO Box 3000, Manchester Center VT 05255. (802) 362-2400. Their 1990 catalog is called "Voice of the Mountains: The Strength of the Hills is in the People." Founded in 1946 by Vrest Orton, this company carries an interesting array of products. It's kind of a nostalgic trip to the past to browse

Treekeeper's European style string bag.

through the catalog. There's plenty of 100% cotton and natural fiber clothing, bedding, & pillows.

This catalog offers a natural herb moth repellent that has no chemicals and makes clothes smell good. Package of 8 sachets: $9.95. They have a re-cycled tire tread doormat. This type of doormat has been around since after WW II when "worn-out car tires began growing into mountains." This woven mat is very good for scraping shoes clean and letting the mud and snow fall through. Size 29" x 20" is $19.95 and 36" x 24" is $25.95.

Their grocery tote is made of 100% cotton canvas. It has strong web handles and double-stitched seams for long life. Tote is 18" x 12" x 8", $9.95. They also offer an oval willow shop-ping basket. This basket is reinforced with wire and has reinforced handles. Measures 13" x 10' at top and is 10" tall, $19.95.

They have 100% cotton floursack towels, which was an old-fashioned necessity. Use these instead of paper towels. Many other uses. Set of 6, $9.90. Natural citrus cleaning solvent has no chemicals but lots of cleaning

 Chapter Eight: Household & Personal Care Products

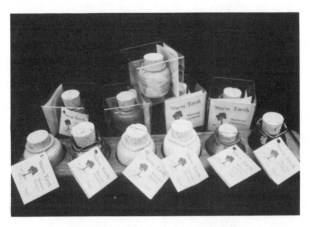

∗Environmental Excellence∗

Warm Earth Cosmetics

Their products are packaged exclusively in their own pottery vessels, which are useful after the cosmetics are gone, thus there's no empty packaging to throw away. As a company, they are also environmentally responsible. They use recycled boxes that they acquire from local business friends and reuse existing packaging material instead of creating more waste.

power, 32 oz bottle, $10.95.

See also "Recycling" chapter.

Warm Earth Cosmetics, 2230 Normal Ave, Chico CA 95928. (916) 895-0455. FAX # (916) 342-8223. This small company manufactures blush and eye shadow cosmetics that are not tested on animals nor use any animal products. These products are also fragrance free. Their products are packaged exclusively in their own pottery vessels, which are useful after the cosmetics are gone, thus there's no empty

packaging to throw away.

Weleda Inc., 841 S. Main St, PO Box 769, Spring Valley NY 10977. Pharmacy (914) 352-6145. Bookkeeping, Wholesale, & Inquiries. (914) 356-4134. FAX # (914) 356-5270. Manufacturers of a line of natural body care products that are very popular. This 70-year old company has also never participated in animal testing, making their products cruelty-free all of these years. Many of the plants used in the products are grown in Weleda's own gardens,

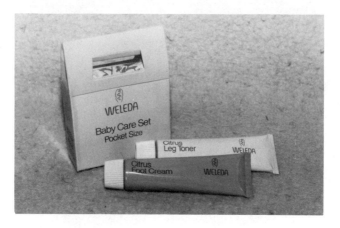

Many of the plants used in Weleda's natural body care products are grown in Weleda's own gardens.

using the biodynamic method. They never use chemical fertilizers, pesticides or herbicides. Proper packaging insures that the products stay fresh without additives. They do not add artificial coloring agents or synthetic preservatives.

Product lines include: mouth care; hair care; skin care; soaps & baths; body care; baby care; natural colognes; candies; fruit syrups; herbs; herbal tea blends; and anthroposophical/homeopathic medicine.

Products can be ordered directly from them or from other catalog companies. Send for their catalog.

Chapter Nine:
Magazines, Newsletters & Brochures

There are excellent environmental magazines available on newsstands and by subscription. There are also numerous newsletters and brochures available to those who are interested.

Alcoa Recycling Company, 1150 Riverview Tower, 900 S. Gay St, Knoxville TN 37902. (615) 971-1907. Free information about aluminum recycling.

The Alliance to Save Energy, 1725 "K" St NW, Suite 914, Washington DC 20006-1401. (202) 857-0666. FAX # (202) 331-9588. Publications available to the public: *Good for You, Good for the Planet* brochure on energy-efficient compact fluorescent light bulbs, $1; fact sheet on energy-efficient products for the home, $1; fact sheet on "flame retention" burners for oil-heated homes, $1; *Helping Communities Thrive: A Resource Guide for Economic Development Through Energy Efficiency,* $10; and more. Additional information in the "Organizations" chapter.

American Solar Energy Society, 2400 Central Ave, B-1, Boulder CO 80301. (303) 443-3130. A national society for professionals and others involved in the fields of solar energy. Their newsletter is *Solar Today,* published bimonthly. Each issue has articles on various issues of solar technology, as well as giving updates on organizational news. Back issues available. Nonmembership subscription is $25 per year.

Biomass Publications of America, Box 69333, Portland OR 97201. (503) 246-4436. FAX # (503) 452-0595. Supplies a range of information about the pellet and solid fuel (wood stove) industry. Their 14-page brochure, *Pellet Primer,* is an introduction to heating with wood pellets, $2. Quantity discounts available. Other information: *Buying Guide to Pellet Stoves,* $5.95; *Energy Evaluator* fuel calculator, $4.95; dealer *Check List for Pellet Stoves,* $2.95; *Appliance Manufacturers* (who sells the stoves), $1.95; *Pellet Mills* (for finding the fuel), $1.95.

Buzzworm, Inc., 1818 16th St, Boulder CO 80302. (303) 442-1969. *Buzzworm: The Environmental Journal* is a bimonthly full-color magazine reporting on national and international environmental issues. The word "Buzzworm" is an old term for rattlesnake, a creature that "buzzes" and you reaction. They thought that this was a very appropriate term in view of how they perceive their purpose: to "buzz" about the environment and create a similar reaction toward the preservation of our natural resources. The magazine contains articles on international ecological problems and solutions with special reports. $3.50 per issue or by subscription, $18 per year (6 issues).

COGNITION, c/o Tomas Nimmo, COGnition Director of Advertising, Heidelberg, Ontario, Canada N0B 1Y0. (519) 699-4481. FAX # (519) 747-5660.
COGnition is the quarterly educational magazine of the Canadian Organic Growers organization with an estimated 5500+ readers per issue. The magazine is sold in natural foods stores, book stores and other eco-con-

scious outlets.

Concern, Inc., 1794 Columbia Rd NW, Washington DC 20009. (202) 328-8160. Booklets available: *Household Waste, Waste, Farmland, Drinking Water, Groundwater,* $3 each; bulk rates available. More information in "Organizations" chapter.

Cultural Survival, Inc., 53 Church St, Cambridge MA 02138. (617) 495-2562. *Cultural Survival Quarterly* magazine is the organization's publication and back issues are available, $2 each. Other publications available: *Indigenous Peoples and Tropical Forests: Models of Land Use and Management from Latin America,* 1988, $8.

More information in "Organizations" and "Books" chapters.

Discover, 3 Park Ave, New York NY 10016. (212) 779-6200. *Discover: The World of Science* is a science magazine for the adult layman. It's written in easy-to-understand language, not scientific jargon. Environmental issues are frequently explored. The April, 1990 issue was devoted to "The Environmental Dilemma: The Struggle to Save Our Planet." Often found in newsstands, $2.95 per issue.

Earth Action Network, Inc., 28 Knight St, Norwalk CT 06851. (203) 854-5559. Non-profit organization that publishes *E, The Environmental Magazine.* This bimonthly full-color magazine was formed for the purpose of acting as a clearinghouse of informa-

tion, news, and commentary on environmental issues for the benefit of the general public and in sufficient depth to involve dedicated environmentalists. Available on some newsstands. Magazine address: PO Box 5098, Westport CT 06881.

The Earthwise Consumer, PO Box 279, Forest Knolls, CA 94933. (415) 488-4614. *The Earthwise Consumer* is a 12-page newsletter published 8 times a year that helps consumers decide which products are "green" and which are not. Each issue has a feature article exploring a particular kind of product in depth, answers your questions, and introduces new products, catalogs, and books. $20 for 1 year subscription. The editor/ publisher is Debra Lynn Dadd who is also the author of *Nontoxic, Natural & Earthwise: How to Protect Yourself and Your Family from Harmful Products and Live in Harmony with the Earth* ($12.95) and *The Nontoxic Home* ($9.95). These books are published by Jeremy P. Tarcher, but are also available from the Earthwise Consumer. Other books also available from them. More information in "Books " chapter.

Energy Probe Research Foundation, 225 Brunswick Avenue, Toronto, Ontario, Canada M5S 2M6. (416) 978-7014. Examples from the Environment Probe publications list: *The Price of Preservation: The Value of timber in the Carmanah Valley Watershed* by Adam White provides a social cost-benefit analysis of logging in British Colum-

***Greenpeace* magazine is now available on newsstands.**

bia, $5; *Enlisting Trees in Canada to Fight the Greenhouse Effect* by Wendy Hawthorne, $5; *How You Can Help Fight the Greenhouse Effect* is a free pamphlet that contains ideas for projects that can be carried out around the home and in the community; *How Trees Can Help Fight the Greenhouse Effect* is a free factsheet about the Canadian potential to become a net absorber rather than a net emitter of carbon dioxide.

More information in "Organizations" chapter.

Environmental Action Coalition, 625 Broadway, New York NY 10012. (212) 677-1601. Members receive *Cycle,* an 8-page quarterly newsletter with information about their projects and profiles of what people are doing to

protect the environment. Membership starts at $20 for an individual.

More information in "Organizations" and "Educational Materials" chapters.

Environmental Action Foundation/ Environmental Action, 1525 New Hampshire Ave NW, Washington DC 20036. (202) 745-4870. Publications: bimonthly *Environmental Action Magazine,* $20 to individuals and non-profit groups; bimonthly *Powerline,* from their Energy Project, $20; quarterly *Wastelines* from their Solid Waste Alternatives Project, $10; *Wrapped in Plastics,* a report on the environmental impact of plastics, $10; *Acid Rain and Electricity Conservation,* $20; *Global Warming* fact pack, $4; *Making Your Home Energy Efficient,* fact pack, $4;

Pesticides fact pact, $4; *Global Warming and The Car,* 10 copies for $2. More information in "Organizations" chapter.

Environmental Planning Office, Hawaii State Department of Health, 5 Waterfront Plaza, Suite 250, 500 Ala Moana Blvd, Honolulu HI 96813. (808) 543-8337. This office has brochures available to the public: *Recycling: It's in the Bag; Needed: Clean Water; Needed: Clean Air; America's Clean Water Act; Everybody's Problem: Hazardous Waste; Hazardous Waste: What You Should & Shouldn't Do; Everyone's Problem: Backyard Oil Barrels; Motor Oil Recycling & Hints on Changing Your Oil; Groundwater Why You Should Care; Nature's Way: How Wastewater Treatment Works for You; Clean Water: A Bargain at Any Cost; Our Marine Environment: Guidelines for Using Anti-fouling Paint; Unleaded Gasoline: The Only Way; Lead and Your Drinking Water; Protect Your Family from Lead Poisoning: A Special Publication for Rainwater Catchment Users.*

Freshwater Foundation, PO Box 90, Navarre MN 55392. (612) 471-8407. Publications available to the public include: *Agrichemicals & Groundwater: Perspectives & Solutions,* an overview of concerns and responses related to the potential of agrichemicals for contaminating groundwater, seeks an awareness of possible solutions, $10; *Understanding Your Shoreline: Protecting Rivers, Lakes & Streams,* 30¢;

Waste is a Water Problem: What You Can Do About Solid Waste, 30¢; *Groundwater: Understanding Our Hidden Resource,* 30¢; *Water Filters: Their Effect on Water Quality,* 30¢; *Hazardous Waste in Our Homes—and in Our Water,* 30¢; *Understanding Your Septic Systems,* 30¢; *Nitrates & Groundwater: A Public Health Concern,* a 13-page brochure, 50¢; *A Citizens' Guide to Lake Protection,* $2; more. Quantity prices available.

More information in "Organizations" chapter.

Friends of the Earth, 218 "D" St SE, Washington DC 20003. (202) 544-2600. FAX # (202) 543-4710. EcoNet ID—foedc. Newsletters: *Friends of the Earth* 10 times a year, a 32-page general newsmagazine about the issues affecting the environmental; *Atmosphere,* a quarterly ozone newsletter; *Groundwater News,* a periodic newsletter, and *Community Plume,* a periodic chemical safety newsletter.

Additional publications: *Saving Our Skins—Technical Potential & Policies for the Elimination of Ozone-Depleting Chlorine Compounds,* 167 pgs, 1988, $24 postpaid; *Bottled Water: Sparking Hype at a Premium Price,* 74 pgs, 1989, $23 postpaid; *The Strip Mining Handbook,* 150 pgs, 1990, $11.95 ppd.

Additional information in "Organizations" chapter.

Gentle Strength Co-op, 234 West University Drive, Tempe AZ 85281. (602) 968-4831. This store handles many environmentally sensitive lines of products. Magazines handled: *Greenpeace, Buzzworm, Garbage, Earthwise Consumer,* more.

More products found in "Household & Personal Care Products," "Organically Grown," "Paper Products," "Books," and "Baby & Children's Products" chapters.

Heldref Publications, 4000 Albemarle St NW, Washington DC 20016. Subscription toll-free 1-800-365-9753. Publishers of the magazine *Environment,* a magazine about environmental issues of interest to the public. Available at some newsstands ($3 per issue), or by subscription, $24 per year (10 issues).

Home Energy, 2124 Kittredge St, #95, Berkeley CA 94704. (415) 524-5405. *Home Energy: The Magazine of Residential Energy Conservation,* is a bimonthly publication with a rather technical emphasis. It serves as an excellent resource for the latest energy conservation products. The magazine makes it a priority to provide a balanced picture of the many variables affecting energy consumption and conservation. They focus on conservation products and techniques that maximize efficiency without compromising comfort. Advertisers are screened carefully. Subscription: $45 per year (6 issues).

Household Hazardous Waste Project, 901 South National Ave, Box 108, Springfield MO 65804. (417) 836-5777. Their booklet *Guide to Hazard-*

ous Products Around the Home has been recognized and used throughout the United States and by the United Nations Environment Programme. It has also been endorsed by Greenpeace, The Cousteau Society, Seventh Generation and *McCall's* Magazine. This manual helps you understand product labels, helps you select safer products before bringing toxic chemicals into your home, helps minimize waste leaving your home, and helps you located recycling options in your community for some types of hazardous waste. $9.95, 178 pages.

Brochures available to the public: *Consumer Tips,* 50¢; *Pesticides,* 50¢; *Safety Equipment,* 75¢. Bulk discounts available.

A short educational video program is available, outlining the problems and solutions for household hazardous waste, VHS, $28 ppd.

More information in "Organizations" chapter.

Illinois Environmental Protection Agency, 2200 Churchill Rd, PO Box 19276, Springfield IL 62794-9276. (217) 782-2829. This agency has a long list of publications available, of few of which are listed here: *Books for Young People on Environmental Issues; Farming & Protecting the Environment; Starting an Office Recycling Program; Guide to Household Recycling; Recipes for a Safer Home* (how to dispose of hazardous wastes); *Ozone: the pervasive pollutant; Protecting the Nation's Groundwater From Contamination; Dioxin Facts; Radon in*

Homes; and many many more. Also educational materials available.

INFORM, 381 Park Avenue South, New York NY 10016. (212) 689-4040. Publications available: *Garbage: Practices, Problems & Remedies,* 32 pages, useful facts about garbage we create and how we manage it, $3.50; *Toxics in Our Air,* 8 pgs, $4.50; *Trading Toxics Across State Lines, 32 pgs, $7.50; Promoting Hazardous Waste Reduction:: Six Steps States Can Take,* 24 pgs, $3.50; *Controlling Acid Rain: A New View of Responsibility,* 56 pgs, $9.95 and more. Some publications are regionally oriented. Ask for their publications list. *Inform* is a quarterly newsletter that reports on their latest research projects. More information in "Organizations" chapter.

Institute of Scrap Recycling Industries, Inc., 1627 "K" St NW, 7th floor, Washington DC 20006-1704. (202) 466-4050. FAX # (202) 775-9109. TWX 710 822 9782. EasyLink 620 23427. The group provides public education about the benefits of recycling. Publications available to the public: *The Scrap Map: An Environmental Publication for Grades K-6,* a colorful 6 x 9 brochure that explains the concept of recycling and illustrates recycling of automobiles, aluminum cans and newspapers, $15 for package of 30; *The Scrap Map Teachers' Kit,* includes one copy of *The Scrap Map* and also an environmental poster with bulletin board suggestions, Teachers' Guide, information brochures, a list of

ISRI chapters, and the booklet *Scrap: America's Ready Resource,* $5 per kit to teachers, schools, libraries and non-profit organizations. Write order on organizational letterhead and enclose payment.

Phoenix: Voice of the Scrap Recycling Industries is a magazine covering recycling processing activities and issues. Published 2-3 times a year; free to government officials, educators, libraries and environmentalists. Write subscription request on organizational letterhead.

"Who is Making a World of Difference for Our World?" brochure available to the public; single copies free.

More information in "Organizations" chapter.

National Arbor Day Foundation, 211 North 12th St, Lincoln NE 68508. (402) 474-5655. Dedicated to tree planting and conservation. Introductory membership is $10 and the member receives 10 Colorado blue spruce trees as well as a subscription to the bimonthly *Arbor Day* publication. The magazine is packed with how-to tips such as how to become fuel-wood self-sufficient, how to water a tree to maintain its health and vigor, how to keep a Christmas tree fresh and fragrant, and how proper mulching will improve tree growth. More in "Organizations" chapter.

National Audubon Society, 950 Third Ave., New York NY 10022. (212) 832-3200. Bimonthly magazine *Audubon* just $20 for the first year (introductory rate) includes membership to the society. Other membership benefits include membership in one of the 500 local chapters; free or reduced admission to Audubon nature centers; invitations to their ecology camps, workshops, and tours; and discounts on nature books, collectibles and gifts.

Other publications of the society include *American Birds,* an ornithological journal; *Audubon Activist,* a monthly newsjournal available to all those who wish to join Audubon's Activist Network and make a commitment to take action; *Action Alerts* for the activists to advise them of pending legislation; and the annual *Audubon Wildlife Report* that examines federal and state agencies responsible for the management of natural areas and wildlife.

Free to the public are: the Audubon Fact Sheet which describes the organizations philosophy and activities; and Conservation Notebook sheets, one called "Planet Earth: Coming to the Rescue," and another called "Global Climate Change and What You Can Do About It."

More about the Society in the "Organizations" chapter.

National Coalition Against the Misuse of Pesticides (NCAMP), 701 E Street SE, Washington DC 20003. (202) 543-5450. Information about the organization is provided through their newsletters, *Pesticides and You* (about 5 times a year) and *NCAMP's Technical Report* (monthly). A recent issue of *Pesticides and You* included pesticide statistics update, setback for victim rights, a notice that toxic pest strips have returned to the market, more news clips, "chemicalWATCH", and a list of resources. A compilation of back issues is available. Other publications include a *chemicalWATCH* that tracks chemical effects and alternatives, and *State & Local Pesticide Ordinances: A Compilation of Legislation and Regulation Regarding Pesticide Right-to-Know and Posting and Notification,* which includes laws from 16 states. Brochures include "Least Toxic Control of Lawn Pests" and "Pesticides and Your Fruits and Vegetables."

For more information, see the listing in the "Organizations" chapter.

National Parks & Conservation Association, 1015 31st St NW, Washington DC 20007. (202) 944-8530. Dedicated to the protection and improvement of the National Park System. *National Parks* is a beautiful full color magazine that features specials about parks, events and programs. The March, April 1990 issue was a special for "Earth Day." Single copies, $2.50. Subscription comes with basic membership, $25.

National Wildflower Research Center, 2600 FM 973 North, Austin TX 78725. (512) 929-3600. Publications include the membership newsletter *Wildflower* and the magazine *Wildflower, Journal of the National Wildflower Research Center,* published 6 times annually. These are available only to members. Basic individual membership fee is $25. 17,000 members worldwide. More information in the "Organizations" chapter.

Natural Resource Defense Council, 40 West 20th St, New York NY 10011. (212) 727-2700. Membership department, zip 10114-0466. Their "Mothers and Others for Pesticide Limits" program was instrumental in gaining the ban against the use of the pesticide Alar on apple crops. This project publishes a newsletter called *tlc: truly loving care for our kids and our planet.* The newsletter focuses on ideas for a healthier planet, gives update news on their programs, includes resources, and has activities for kids.

Members receive four issues of *The Amicus Journal,* an award-winning magazine of environmental thought and opinion, and five issues of the *NRDC Newsline,* which keeps you informed of NRDC programs and publications. In addition, members receive timely alerts and updates on NRDC work so that you can help influence important environmental policies.

More in "Organizations" chapter.

New Jersey Department of Environmental Protection, Division of Water Resources, CN 029, Trenton NJ 08625. (609) 932-1637. Source for the free pamphlet "The Clean Water Book" that describes nonpoint source pollution, how it affects water systems, and what homeowners can to to prevent this kind of pollution. Designed especially for New Jersey.

New Jersey Department of Environmental Protection, Office of Communications & Public Education, 401 East State St, Trenton NJ 08625. (609) 292-2885. Source for the free teacher's guide to water pollution control called *My World, My Water and Me,* that has specific lesson plans, objectives, skills and activities.

New Jersey Environmental Federation, 808 Belmar Plaza, Belmar NJ 07719. (201) 280-8988. Publications include their quarterly newsletter *Clean Water Action,* which comes with subscribing membership ($24) and monthly New Jersey updates, which come with sustaining membership ($60). Other membership fees includes $2 for a four-month membership (no newsletter) and $6 for annual dues (no newsletter). Another publication is the *Home SAFE Home Chart of Household Alternatives,* an 11 x 17 chart that lists safe alternatives for 20 categories of household products. $2 each, group discounts available. *Lawn Care Without Toxic Chemicals,* a letter-size flyer gives information on non-toxic lawn care including a supplies source list for central New Jersey. 25¢ each, group discounts available. *Every Citizen's Environmental Handbook,* is a 44-page illustrated handbook expanding the information on the Home SAFE Home chart, listing steps consumers can take to further protect the environment, including environmental shopping. There are charts that show specific brand names that are toxic. (Examples: Easy-Off oven cleaner is listed as toxic;

Arm & Hammer washing soda is non-toxic and environmentally safe.) Price: $5, quantity discounts available. For more information, see "Organizations" chapter.

North American Native Fishes Association, 123 West Mt. Airy Ave., Philadelphia PA 19119. (215) 247-0384. *American Currents* is a quarterly magazine featuring articles on finding, collecting, keeping, observing, conserving, and breeding North American fishes; and news about aquaristics, laws, the environment, scientific literature and developments, and other sources of information. *Darter* is a newsletter published approximately six times a year. Membership to NANFA is $11 year, includes the magazine and newsletter. More in the "Organizations" chapter.

Northeast Regional Agricultural Engineering Service, 152 Riley-Robb Hall, Cooperative Extension, Ithaca NY 14853. (607) 255-7654. Source for the brochure *Bottled Waters* that defines the types of bottled waters, their safety and terms used in the bottling industry, $1.

Pennsylvania Resources Council, PO Box 88, Media PA 19063. (215) 565-9131. Publications: *All About Recycling* newsletter updates recycling activities locally and nationally, complimentary copy with SASE; *Become An Environmental Shopper* is a handbook that explains how to shop to reduce waste and protect the environ-ment, $3.50; *50 Ways to Celebrate Recycling Month* contains suggestions for activities for all segments of the community to promote recycling, 25¢; *10 Steps to Organizing a Community Recycling Program,* $2; *Householders Recycling Guide,* $1.50; *Recycling Works. Here's How,* free by calling recycling hotline 1-800-346-4242; *Recycling: The 12 Ways of Christmas* show how to recycle holiday wrap, ribbon, packaging and trees, 20¢; *Household Hazardous Waste,* free with SASE; *Litter Control: Blueprint for Action,* $1.50. More information in "Organizations" and "Educational Materials" chapters.

Planet Drum Foundation, Box 31251, San Francisco CA 94131. (415) 285-6556. (Organizational information included in "Organizations" chapter.) The organization's newsletter is *Raise the Stakes,* with back issues available.

The group has a *Catalogue of Bioregional Primary Sources,* which contains 22 bioregional reprints, ranging in price from 35¢ to $3.15 each. Includes such titles as *Bioregional Green* by Kirkpatrick Sale, *Living There* by Seth Zuckerman, *Why I am a Bioregionalist* by Gene Marshall.

The San Francisco office contains a fine library of bioregional references and other ecology-related material. The organization provides networking services to start new bioregional groups and to find resources. The group maintains a directory of bioregional groups. Planet Drum is planning to open a Green City Center (projected date fall 1991), which will be a place to demonstrate techniques and activities of urban sustainability and which will educate the public about them and influence municipal policies.

PV Network News, Rt 10 Box 86, Santa Fe NM 87501. Quarterly newsletter about photovoltaics with lots of networking information including an annual resource issue. Paul Wilkens, editor. $15 per year.

PV News, Box 90, Casanova VA 22017. Monthly photovoltaics newsletter. $80 per year. Also available are the "PV Yellow Pages." Paul Maycock, editor.

Rainforest Action Movement, 430 E University, Ann Arbor MI 48109. (313) 662-0232. Publication: *Tropical Echoes* 16-page quarterly newsletter, very informative. One recent issue included such articles as: "Hawaii: Is Geothermal Development Really Needed?"; "Mitsubishi: On the Wrong Road," about the company's use of exotic woods and urging boycott of their products; information on Georgia-Pacific and Weyerhauser companies and their importation of exotic hardwoods; "The Ongoing Struggle of the Yanomami," about this Brazilian tribe's struggle for existence. Brochure: "7 things you can do to help save the rainforests." Membership is $10 for one year and includes newsletter; $20 gives you one year membership plus a T-shirt. (More information in "Organizations" chapter.)

Resource Recycling, Inc., PO Box 10540, Portland OR 97210. (503) 227-1319. FAX # (503) 227-6135. 1-800-227-1424. *Resource Recycling* is North America's Recycling Journal. It is published monthly and printed on recycled paper using soy-based inks. This four-color magazine features articles about recycling programs in various cities and counties, new business approaches to recycling, waste collection and waste management features, resources, legislative news, and more. Monthly departments include: state/ province/ federal watch; programs in action, market update, news & views, information sources, recycling showcase, events, and more. Subscription is $42 per year, 12 issues.

The company also published monthly 6-page newsletters called *Bottle/ Can Recycling Update* ($75 per year, 12 issues) and *Plastics Recycling Update* ($85 per year, 12 issues).These newsletters contain news about markets, legislation, research, data, technology, and economics.

Rutgers Cooperative Extension, Publications Distribution Center, Cook College, PO Box 231, New Brunswick NJ 08903. (201) 932-9762. Source for water quality publications for New Jersey, although many of the publications contain information applicable in other areas. Some titles: *Septic System Care—Essentials of Using and Maintaining Your Septc Tank Sewage Disposal System,* $1; *Water From Home Wells—Problems and Treatments,* $1;

Landscaping for Water Conservation—A Guide for New Jersey, $2; *Watering Guide for Home Gardeners,* $1; *A Guide to Designing a Community Water Conservation Program,* $2; *Care of Water for Home Swimming Pools,* $1; *Hazardous Chemicals in Your Home: Proper Use and Disposal,* free; *Drinking Water Treatment and Conditioning,* free; *Where to Get Your Drinking Water Tested in New Jersey,* free; *Recycling Used Motor Oil in New Jersey,* free. Make payment to: Rutgers, The State University.

Seventh Generation, Colchester VT 05446-1672. (802) 655-3116. FAX toll-free # 1-800-456-1139. Order toll-free 1-800-456-1177. Customer service toll-free 1-800-456-1197.

Seventh Generation is one of the most well-known companies for environmentally safe consumer products. Their 48-page catalog "Products for a Healthy Planet" ($2) contains an extraordinary variety of products. They also practice what they preach. For instance, they recycle their office paper, and reuse cardboard boxes for shipping. They have a 1% fund that goes to environmental organizations.

You can order a subscription of the colorful *Earth-based* magazine for kids, written expressly for children 7 to 12 years old. There's comics, puzzles, stories, and more in each issue. Ten issues, 1 year, $14.

Also available is *The Seventh Generation Green Consumer Letter* from the author of The Green Consumer book. Keeps you up-to-date on product developments. 1 year, 12 issues, 8 pages, $27.

There are so many products in this catalog that additional information can be found in these chapters: "Baby and Children's Products," "Household & Personal Care Products," "Books," "Educational Materials," "Paper Products," "Recycling," "Energy Conservation," and "Organically Grown."

Sierra Club, 730 Polk Street, San Francisco CA 94109. (415) 776-2211. Their publications include the magazine *Sierra,* which has been published since 1893 and is an award-winning, four-color publication filled with environmental articles, commentary and photography. Members receive this magazine 6 times a year. Other publications are the *National News Report,* which is a summary of legislative news concerning the environment; *Source Book,* their catalog of brochures, books, videos, posters and other products; and local chapter newsletters. The brochure *Sierra Club Environmental Resources* is an order form for books and brochures with two prices—one for non-members, and a discounted price for members. Categories of publications that can be orders from this form are *Be an Environmental Activist, Politics and the Environment, Environmental Education, Air Pollution, Protecting America's Public Lands, Global Warming,* and more. One brochure that can be ordered for 50¢ is about environmental educational materials (item #206). You can order a clean air poster for $5 (item #303). For $1 you can order *What You Can Do to Save Tropical Rainforests* (item #530). Many more items.

More information about Sierra Club included in the "Organizations" chapter.

Soil & Water Conservation Society, 7515 Northeast Ankeny Rd, Ankeny IA 50021. Source for the brochure *Treasure of Abundance—or Pandora's Box? A Guide for Safe, Profitable Fertilizer and Pesticide Use;* free. More in "Organizations" chapter.

Solar Electric Engineering, Inc., 116 4th St, Santa Rosa CA 95401. (707) 542-1990. FAX # (707) 542-4358. This is a publicly owned corporation that has been committed to bringing to the marketplace environmentally sound products at affordable prices to the consumer. They have a 40-page "Environmental Catalog," with pamphlets about solar electricity, including: *How to Install Solar Electric Panels; All About Inverters; Install a Two-Battery System in Your Vehicle; Getting the Most From Your Batteries; Build Your Own Solar Electric Panel; Convert Your Washing Machine to 12 Volts; Convert Your Dryer to 12 Volts; Build a 12 Volt Nicad Battery Charger; Build Your Own Small Power Plant.* These pamphlets are $4 each or 6 for $22.50.

More items listed in "Energy Conservation," "Recycling," "Household & Personal Care Products," "Paper Products," "Clean Air, Clean Water," "Baby & Children's Products," and "Energy Conservation."

Sprout House, 40 Railroad St, Great Barrington MA 01230 (413) 528-5200. *The Sprout House Newsletter* is published 5 times a year ($10). Contains information about new seeds, how to maintain the best sprouts, clean water information; workshop schedules; more. More information in the "Organically Grown" chapter.

Sunrise Lane, 780 Greenwich St., New York NY 10014. (212) 242-7014. Catalog of cruelty-free and biodegradable products for personal use and for the home. This company also publishes a bimonthly newsletter called *Sunrise Gazette* which carries current news on the animal rights and ecology movements; offers special discounts on their merchandise; and offers new merchandise not yet in their catalog. Subscription $8 for 6 issues. More information about their products in the "Household and Personal Care Products" chapter.

U.S. PIRG (The United States Public Interest Research Group, 215 Pennsylvania Ave SE, Washington DC 20003. (202) 546-9707. Publications of this organizations include the quarterly report, *Citizen Agenda,* which is an 8-page newsletter that provides updates on recent legislation, news briefs, state updates, and profiles of individuals who are making a difference. Newsletter comes with membership.

Numerous publications and reports are available to the public, such as:

DuPont fiddles while the world burns, ($5) about how the CFC industry have fought against regulation of CFCs for the past 15 years; *As the World Burns: Documenting America's Failure to Address the Ozone Crisis* ($5); *Exhausting Our Future: An 82 City Study of Smog in the 80's,* ($10); *Pesticides in Groundwater: EPA Files Reveal Tip of a Deadly Iceberg,* ($10); *Big Green vs. Big Green: Why $16 Million is a Small Price to Pay to Defeat the Environmental Protection Act of 1990,* ($5); *Clean Air PAC Study 1990,* ($1); and more. Send for US PIRG Publications/ Reports list.

Membership starts at $15 for an individual 6-month membership; $25 for an individual 1-year membership.

More information in "Organizations" chapter.

Union of Concerned Scientists, 26 Church St, Cambridge MA 02238. (617) 547-5552. Publications available: *Cool Energy: The Renewable Solution to Global Warming; The Global Warming Debate: Answers to Controversial Questions; The Heat is On: Global Warming, the Greenhouse Effect, and Energy Solutions; How You Can Fight Global Warming: An Action Guide;* and more. Single copies of these brochures are free; additional copies are $3 for 50 copies. More information in "Organizations," "Books," and "Educational Materials" chapters.

U.S. Fish and Wildlife Service, US Department of the Interior, National Fisheries Contaminant Research Cen-

ter, Route 2, 4200 New Haven School Road, Columbia MO 65021. (314) 857-5399. As the nation's principal conservation agency, the Department of the Interior has responsibility for most of our nationally owned public lands and natural resources. This includes preserving the environmental and cultural values of our national parks and historical places. This particular branch has a list of publications in scientific journals concerning fish contamination research.

West Virginia Division of Natural Resources, 1900 Kanawha Blvd, E., Capitol Complex, Building 3, Charleston WV 25305. (304) 348-2754. FAX # (304) 348-2768. Recycling Section: (304) 348-3370. Pamphlets available: *Recycling at Home; Recycling Bookmark; Adopt-A-Highway; Litter Control.* More information in "Organizations" chapter.

Whole Earth Review, PO Box 38 Sausalito CA 94966. (415) 332-1716. *The Whole Earth Review* is a quarterly magazine that is dedicated to a special theme each issue (usually) concerning alternative living. There are articles plus numerous product reviews. Some of the categories reviewed are energy conservation and solar energy.

Wildlife Information Center, Inc., 629 Green St., Allentown PA 18102. (215) 434-1637. Reports available from the organization include: *Pole Traps & Raptors: A Protection Crisis,* 10 pgs, $5; *Tundra Swan Hunting: A Biologi-*

cal, *Ecological and Wildlife Crisis,* 9 pgs, $6; *Wildlife in Traveling Animal Shows: An Examination and Critique,*

12 pgs, $7.

More information in "Organizations" chapter.

If we don't act now to protect our environment, we may find ourselves out on a limb!

GREEN EARTH RESOURCE GUIDE

152

Chapter Ten:
Organically Grown

Organically grown means that the food has been grown, processed, packaged, stored and transported without the use of synthetic fertilizers, insecticides, herbicides, fungicides, fumigants, preservatives, hormones, coloring or wax. Today's organic growers combine state-of-the-art techniques with tried and true methods. There's an amazing array of organic foods available by mail: fresh produce, grains, honey, snacks, wines, cheese, sea vegetables, breads, kosher foods and more. This chapter also contains supplies for organic gardening (such as composting items and biological insect controls), magazines for organic gardening, and consultants.

Arrowhead Mills, Inc., PO Box 2059, 110 S. Lawton St., Hereford TX 79045. (806) 364-0730. They offer a line of organically grown foods. They also promote organic agriculture, use recycled/recyclable packaging materials and office stationary as much as possible, and discharge no pollutants into the air or water. Organic foods available: grains (barley, rice, buckwheat, corn, oats, popcorn, wheat, rye, more); beans (kidney, garbanzos, lentils, pinto, soybeans, more); seeds (alfalfa, flax, sesame, sunflower,

more); cold cereal (apple corns, bran flakes, corn flakes, maple corns, maple nut granola, puffed corn, puffed wheat, wheat bran, more); hot cereals (corn grits, cracked wheat, instant oatmeal, more); flakes (barley, oats, potato, rye, wheat, more); flours (barley, buckwheat, cornmeal, oat, rice, unbleached white, more); mixes (biscuit, muffin, pancake, more); snacks, quick brown rice, oils & condiments, nut and seed butters.

Baldwin Hill Bakery, Baldwin Hill Rd,

 Chapter Ten: Organically Grown

Phillipston MA 01331. (508) 249-4691. They specialize in certified organic sourdough bread hearth-baked on wood-fired brick oven using deep pure well-water, lima seasalt, no sugar, no yeast, and no cholesterol.

Beneficial Insectary, 14751 Oak Run Road, Oak Run CA 96069. (916) 472-3715. Experts in biological control as an alternative to chemical pesticides. They have 20-years experience in combining field releases of beneficial organisms, field monitoring and consulting on many phases of agricultural pest control. Examples of biological pest control: ladybugs are the best known beneficial insect around—they feed on insects that are not too hard shelled, not too fast, or not too large; fly parasites are by nature programmed to attack and kill flies; predatory mites seek and eat spider mites; the praying mantis will attack just about any insect. Detailed information is available about any of their products. They are happy to have you consult them about any particular pest problem you have.

BioIntegral Resource Center, PO Box 7414, Berkeley CA 94707. (415) 524-2567. Dedicated to least-toxic pest management. Projects: BIRC field station; international information gathering program; data bases; integrated pest management design. Members can receive free advice as well as periodicals, booklets and directories. Also listed in the "Organizations" chapter.

BioLogic, Springtown Rd, PO Box

Baldwin Hill Bakery **They are the winners of the Bread & Circus Natural Food Supermarket's "1988 Safe Food Award."**

177, Willow Hill PA 17271. (717) 349-2789. Offers Scanmask™, a natural biological insecticide that is safe for people, pets and plants. The active units in Scanmask are microscopic juvenile Steinernema on an inert carrier. These are beneficial insect "eating" nematodes. They affect only insects. In a moist dark environment, they kill almost all pest insects. This is ideally suits to combat pests in and on soil and those that bore into wood, trees and shrubs. Earthworms and helpful insects like bees, ladybugs and lacewings are all resistant to this biological control. Scanmask can be stored in its container for seven months at room temperature. In a refrigerator, it can be stored for at least 20 months. After applied to the soil, it can survive over 15 months. One pint Scanmask, $14.95 ppd; 1 quart, $24.95 ppd.

Brier Run Farm, Rt 1, Box 73, Birch River WV 26610. (304) 649-2975. Organic certified (by OCIA—Organic Crop Improvement Association) goat cheese. Certified to contain no residues from herbicides, pesticides or antibiotics. Kinds: Brier Run Chevre; Brier Run Chevre Bleu; Brier Run Chevre Blanc; Brier Run Farm Swiss Style Quark; and Brier Run Farm Chevre

Chapter Ten: Organically Grown

Brier Run Farm
Their Brier Run Chevre was named "Best of Class" in the category of fresh goat cheeses at the recent American Cheese Society annual convention. Judges included experts who are nationally and internationally known in their field. Of the 135 entries of goat's cheese at this competition, Brier Run Chevre received one blue, two red, and one white ribbon.

Fudge that's handmade using organically certified goat's cheese as a base. Their Brier Run Chevre was named "Best of Class" in the category of fresh goat cheeses at the recent American Cheese Society annual convention. Judges included experts who are nationally and internationally known in their field. Of the 135 entries of goat's cheese at this competition, Brier Run Chevre received one blue, two red, and one white ribbon.

Burpee Company, 300 Park Ave, Warminister PA 18974. Mail order source for gardening supplies. Organic gardening materials available: Green Ban herbal insect repellant, 2 1/2 oz bottle, $12.50; RoPel animal and bird repellant has a bitter taste that will keep animals and birds from prized plants, $14.95; Thuricide organic control, a natural microbial insecticide, 4 oz, $4.50; Safer® products such as insec-ticidal soap, fungicide,-miticide, moss & algae killer, grub killer; biological controls include ladybugs, praying mantis egg cases, beneficial nematodes, trichogramma wasps, green lacewings and fly parasites; Soilsaver compost bin is 31" by 28", holds 12 cubic feet, $99.95; Ringer® brown leaf composter maker, $6.95.

Chartrand Imports, PO Box 1319, Rockland ME 04841. (207) 594-7300. Several hundred organic vineyards thrive in Europe, and a handful in the United States. Paul Chartrand is the founder of Chartrand Imports, an organic wine import company. These wines are certified organically grown by independent French agencies or by the Organic Grapes into Wine Alliance of California. Examples of wines handled: Guy Bossard Muscadet Secre et Maine sur lie 1989 ($9.99); Chateau Bousquette St. Chinian Rouge 1988, ($7.49); Guy Chaumont Givry Blanc 1988 ($15.99); Fitzpatrick Wine "Eire Ban" Sauvignon Blanc 1989 ($7.99); many more. In Maine, there are many locations that handle these wines. For other locations, write for list. On West Coast, call Organic Wine Company in San Francisco, 1-800-477-0167.

COGNITION, c/o Tomas Nimmo, COGnition Director of Advertising, Heidelberg, Ontario, Canada N0B 1Y0. (519) 699-4481. FAX # (519) 747-5660.
COGnition is the quarterly educational magazine of the Canadian Organic Growers organization with an esti-

mated 5500+ readers per issue. The magazine is sold in natural foods stores, book stores and other eco-conscious outlets.

Community Mill and Bean, Inc., 267 Rt 89 South, Savannah NY 13146. (315) 365-2664. FAX # (315) 365-2690. Authentic premium organic food products certified by FVO, Farm Verified Organic. Products include: flours (whole wheat, unbleached white, pasts flour, rye, cornmeal, soy, oat, more); grains (spring wheat, corn, rye berries, more); beans (black turtle, garbanzo, great northern, navy, pinto, soybeans, more); mixes (pancake, gingerbread, cornbread, muffin, waffle, more); cereals (oat bran, wheat bran, mighty mush). They will sell wholesale, export, retail, and mail order.

Co-op America, 2100 "M" St NW, Suite 403, Washington DC 20063. (202) 872-5307. Toll-free 1-800-424-2667. This is a non-profit, member-controlled, worker-managed association linking socially responsible businesses and consumers in a national network, a new alternative marketplace. Co-op America allows consumers to align buying habits with values. Basic information found in "Organizations" chapter.

Organic foods from their catalog: Fiddlers Green Farm's organic Maine Breakfast kit, $18 or their organic Emerald Isle Breakfast kit, $17; New Morning Farm of Ohio's organic pasta selection, $20.50; organic cashews from Honduras; Windy River Farm

organic herbs; Once Again Nut Butter mill of New York's organic Valencia peanut butter gift box, $13; Rainforest™ mixed fruit and nuts or cashew nuts; Rainforest Crunch from Community Products, $15 (all profits for Rainforest Crunch are distributed to rainforest preservation projects).

Products from the catalog are found in "Recycling," "Energy Conservation," "Books," " Organically Grown," "Household & Personal Care Products," "Paper Products, " and "Baby & Children's Products" chapters.

Country Grown/ Specialty Grain Company, 12202 Woodbine, Redford MI 48239. (313) 535-9222. Organically grown grains and seeds certified by the Organic Crop Improvement Association. One of their most popular items is their Country Grown® organically grown gourmet popcorn. This is available by the jar (recyclable glass) or as microwave popcorn (packaged in recycled paperboard). Also note: their microwave popcorn packaging contains no susceptors. Susceptors are metallicized plastic film strips that help heat foods but contain chemicals. FDA researchers had found that there is no question that toxic chemicals end up in the food. Therefore, this company does not use susceptors.

Product line includes: grains (buckwheat, sunflower seeds hulled and unhulled, corn, rye, duram wheat, more); seeds (radish, alfalfa, red clover); beans (black turtle, lentil, mung, black-eyed peas, split yellow peas,

Chapter Ten: Organically Grown ★

Erth-Rite has been setting the standard for environmentally safe fertilizers for more than a quarter of a century.

great northern, more); dried fruit (figs, apricots, raisins, more); granola; and snack bars (organic peanut butter, oat bran, spicy raisin, strawberry-banana, toasted sesame).

Crossroads Farms, Box 3230, Jonesport ME 04649-9709. An organic farm that grows over 150 varieties of vegetables, fruits, and flowers. Member of the Maine Organic Farmers & Gardeners Association. Family owned and operated. Storage vegetables can be shipped nationally in the fall (August to November) via UPS. Items that can shipped: squash, dry beans, potatoes, beets, parsnips, cabbage, carrots, artichokes, turnips. Write for free brochure.

Dharma Farma, Ned Whitlock, HC 66, Box 140, Green Forest AR 72638. (501) 553-2550. Organic (certified by Ozark Organic Grower's Association) apples and pears sold by mail order. Apples available: Akane, Gala, Grimes Golden, Liberty, Winesap, Arkansas Black. Write for free price list.

Diamond K Enterprises, RR #1 Box 30-A, St. Charles MN 55972. (507) 932-4308. Organic grains certified by OGBA. Items available: oats (rolled, bran); barley; buckwheat; corn; beans; wheat; sunflowers; flour & cereals. Free brochure.

Dry Creek Herb Farm, 13935 Dry Creek Road, Auburn CA 95603. (916) 878-2441. Shatoiya's handmade all natural skin care products made with organically grown herbs. Includes cleansing grains, herbal splash, dry skin cream, herbal balm, eye care, trauma-aid, and massage oil. Free catalog. See also "Seminars, Speakers & Workshops."

Ecco Bella, 6 Provost Square, Suite 602, Caldwell NJ 07006. (201) 226-5799. FAX # (201) 226-0991. Toll-free 1-800-888-5320. This company manufactures and sells products that are cruelty-free and environmentally sound. The Ecco Bella line of products is extensive and featured in their own catalog, but there are other products featured as well. They carry certified organically grown gourmet coffee in various delicious flavors and also organic popcorn.

More items listed in "Paper Products," "Recycling," "Household & Personal Care Products" and "Energy Conservation" chapters.

Erth-Rite, Inc., RD #1, Box 243, Gap PA 17527. (717) 442-4171. 1-800-332-4171. (Formerly Zook & Ranch Inc) For more than a quarter of a century, Earth-Rite Inc has set the standard for environmentally safe fertilizers. They view organic gardening as more than just an alternative approach to gardening. They believe it is the ONLY safe, practical way to avoid poisoning the environment and food chain. Erth-Rite products are non-leaching, contain no sewage sludge or other potentially hazardous ingredients, are fortified with friendly bacteria, and are non-toxic. Their line of products include garden food, lawn food, greensand, foscal and nitro-super.

Evergreen Bins, PO Box 70307, Seattle WA 98107. (206) 783-7095. Produces a big cedar bin made of 100% waste product for backyard composting. Only $18.75.

Farm Verified Organic™, PO Box 45, Redding CT 06875. (203) 544-9896. FAX # (203) 544-8409. Telex: 204 450 FOODS. FVO is an internationally accepted farm to table product guarantee program that determines the authenticity of organically grown foods. The group is an international network of people dedicated to ecologically sustainable methods of farming, the quality of life and our environment, maintaining integrity and quality within the organic industry, and providing educational events for the public.

Fiddler's Green Farm, RFD 1 Box 656, Belfast ME 04915. (207) 338-3568. Mail order organic baking mixes, hot cereals, flours & grains, baby foods, coffees & teas, potatoes, pasta, jam, syrups, and more. Certified by the Maine Organic Farmers & Growers Association (MOFGA), the Organic Crop Improvement Association (OCIA), the California Certified Organic Farmers (CCOF), the Natural Organic Farmers Association (NOFA), and the Farm Verified Organic (FVO).

Some items in their catalog: toasted buckwheat pancake & muffin mix, 1.5 lbs $2.84; bread & biscuits mix, 1.75 lbs, $3.11; unbleached white flour, 2 lbs, $2.25; dried bean soup mix, 1 lb, $3.25; Simply Pure™ Organic Hot Cereals for Infants & Kids; The Maine Breakfast™ special package; the Happy Birthday Cake Kit™, $9.95; The Maine Pantry™ Sampler with various mixes and treats, $10.95; organic candy bars in three flavors, pg of 6, $5.95.

Also sells Natural Brew unbleached coffee filters, as well are certified organic gourmet coffees.

Their products have been reviewed in *The Boston Globe, The New York Times & The Washington Post.*

Four Chimneys Organic Winery, RD #1, Hall Rd, Himrod NY 14842. (607) 243-7502. Direct mail order source of wines, sparkling wine and grape juice

158

Four Chimneys Organic Winery Reviewers have raved about them. *East West* magazine called Four Chimneys "one of the country's leading organic wineries." *People and Food* and *The Finger Lakes Magazine* also did fine in-depth articles about the winery.

from organically grown grapes. Certified by Natural Food Associates and by the New York State Organic Farmers Association.

The company recently developed America's first organic champagne. They call it "Coronation." They also have a line of white wines, fruit wines, rose wines, red wines, and vinegar.

You may visit the winery when in the Finger Lakes region of New York. Free brochure.

French Meadow Bakery, 2910 Lyndale Ave S, Minneapolis MN 55408. (612) 870-4740. Produces a full line of fresh, hearth baked, organic sourdough breads. These organic gourmet breads are made without cholesterol, dairy, sugar, yeast or preservatives. Made with the simplest, most pure ingredients, these breads are nutritionally superior. They are a complete food, high in bran and fiber, low in calories. Also certified kosher. Large variety: Anaheim Pepper, Austrian Rye, Brown Rice, Date & Almond Brioche, Minnesota Wild Rice, Raisin, Oatmeal

Raisin, Walnut Raisin, Summer, Toasted Sesame, Pumpernickel, Whole Rye, Whole Wheat, Sourdough Batard, Sourdough Baguettes, Sourdough Buns, and more. Founded 1985. Certified organic by the OGBA, the Organic Growers and Buyers Association. Prices range from $2.25 to $14. Sold frozen via distributors, wholesale to retailers, and mail order to the general public.

Frey Vineyards, 14000 Tomki Rd, Redwood Valley CA 95470. Within California 1-800-345-3739. Outside California (707) 485-5177. Producers of organically grown wines certified by the California Certified Organic Farmers.

While in the area (140 miles north of San Francisco) you may tour the winery if you call ahead for an appointment.

Genesee Natural Foods, Inc., RD 2 Box 105, Genesee PA 16923. (814) 228-3200. FAX # (814) 228-3638. Offers organic grains, cereals, beans, flours, fruit, cheese, snacks, baking mixes, breads, pasta, nuts & nut butters, juices. Also listed in "Household & Personal Care Products" for carrying Ecover cleaning products.

Gentle Strength Co-op, 234 West University Drive, Tempe AZ 85281. (602) 968-4831. This store handles many environmentally sensitive lines of products. Organic products: fresh produce when available; herbs, spices, beans, seeds, nuts. Also sold in bulk.

French Meadow Bakery
Their bread has received rave reviews. *Bon Appetit,* April
1990 listed them as one of "The Best: Bread Bakeries."
Other reviews include *Cook's* magazine, *Twin Cities*
magazine, and *Inc.* magazine.

Chapter Ten: Organically Grown ★

Frey Vineyards
These wines have received rave reviews, such as being called "far and away the best producer in the no-chemical arena is Frey Vineyards" by *The Wine Spectator.* The Eugene, Oregon *Register-Guard* said that "Frey Vineyards and Winery of Redwood Valley, California, is this country's best producer of organic wines." Frey wine was selected to be served to the Pope when he visited San Francisco.

More products found in "Household & Personal Care Products," "Baby & Children's Products," "Paper Products," "Books," and "Magazines, Newsletters & Brochures" chapters.

Golden Angels Apiary, PO Box 2, Singers Glen VA 22850. (703) 833-5104. This company products natural honey from the Shenandoah Valley of Virginia. No chemicals are used in any way at any time in any phase of their operation involving either honey or the combs in which the bees store their honey. They do not use moth crystals, sulfur, nor EDB but instead use a biological moth control. They have raw honey from June to October. They also carry their own beeswax, propolis and comb honey, all free from contaminants.

Gold Mine Natural Food Company, 1947 30th St, San Diego CA 92102. (619) 234-9711. 1-800-475-FOOD (3663). Free 40-page organic foods mail order catalog. This extensive catalog has organic & microbiotic foods as well as water purifiers, nontoxic cookware, body care and household supplies. The catalog contains information about using the products, such as recipes, background history of the food, and how to prepare foods. Many of the items are certified Kosher; list is available upon request.

Some of the products available are: organic brown rice, natural grain sweetener; soy sauce; crackers & snacks; miso & condiments; salt plums; vinegar; noodles; mochi, seaweeds; shiitake mushrooms; dried daikon and lotus root; and teas.

Cookware includes: ceramic cooking pot with pressure cooker insert; Genmai Donabe cooking pot; & natural stone pot.

Body care listed in "Household & Personal Care Products" chapter.
See ad page 161.

Gracious Living Organic Farms, c/o Paul Patton, 101 Mountain Parkway, Insko KY 41443. (606) 662-6245. Organic fruits and vegetables sold to members (yearly membership $25): apples, broccoli, cauliflower, green onions, lettuce, peas, tomatoes, sweet potatoes, sweet corn, beans, squash, raspberries, blueberries, watermelons, pumpkins, popcorn, and more. They will grow nearly anything at member's request. They are also distributors for

Nutrition Express health food, cosmetics, stop-smoking Nutri-Cookie, and other products.

Gravelly Ridge Farms, S.R. 16, Elk Creek CA 95939. (916) 963-3216. California certified organic farm is a mail-order source for grains, fruits, and vegetables.

Great Date in the Morning, PO Box 31, Coachella CA 92236. (619) 398-6171. Dates and date products certified organic by the CCOF.

Growing Naturally, PO Box 54, 149 Pine Lane, Pineville PA 18946. (215) 598-7025. FAX # (215) 598-7025. Catalog of products for organic gardening, including: composter and composting tools; natural soil conditioners; Erth-Rite products; predator repellants; insect traps and monitoring systems; biological controls; beneficial insects; botanical controls; fungicides and disease controls; natural pet control products; and gardening accessories. Also "Growing Natural" T-shirt, $9.95.

Hardscrabble Enterprises Inc., Route 6 Box 42, Cherry Grove WV 26804. (304) 567-2727 or (202) 332-0232. Kits for growing your own shiitake mushrooms organically on oak or other hardwood logs from trees harvested while thinning your woodlot. Starter kit for 15 3-foot logs is $20 ppd. Also a *Shiitake Growers Handbook: The Art and Science of Mushroom Cultivation,* 217 pgs, $21.95.

Harmony Farm Supply & Nursery, 3244 Gravenstein Hwy North, Sebastopol CA 95472. Mail address: PO Box 460, Graton CA 95444. (707) 823-9125. FAX (707) 823-1734. Extensive 132-page catalog ($2) of products of interest to organic growers. They began in 1980 as a supplier or organic fertilizers, ecological pest controls and IPM (integrated pest management) monitoring tools. They have added irrigation systems. Most of the products they sell meet the requirements of the California Organic Foods Act, and will note which products do not meet these specifications.

Product lines: drip irrigation systems, accessories and design; sprinkler

Chapter Ten: Organically Grown

irrigation systems, accessories and design; ecological pest control and beneficial insects; organic fertilizers, and seeds.

In addition to selling products, they offer design services for irrigation and landscaping, lab services (soil testing, plant testing & water testing); and consulting for irrigation, integrated pest management, and organic farming.

Additional listings in "Workshops, Seminars & Speakers" and "Books" chapters.

Hugh's Gardens, RR 1 Box 67, Buxton ND 58218. (701) 962-3345. Organically grown produce, especially: potatoes, onions, carrots, beets, parsnip, and winter squash.

IFM, 333 Ohme Gardens Rd, Wenatchee WA 98801. (509) 662-3179. 1-800-332-3179. Free catalog called "Products and Services for Natural Agriculture." They offer organic fertilizers and natural pest controls supplies and services. You can monitor your pests using their BioLure® Insect Trapping Kits, $7.49 or EnzyTec® Pesticide Detection Programs (from $110 to $250). Some of their organic pest controls include: Pyrellin™ EC, 1 gal, $79.95; Safer® Garden Insect Killer made with pyrethrum, 42 oz, $4.99; Ryania-50® for codling moth control, 5 lb bag, $20.95; Rotenone-5% kills a variety of insect pests, 4 lb bag $20.95; several more.

Biological pests controls available are: Semaspore™ for grasshopper control, 5 lbs for $24.95; BioSafe™

predatory nematode that controls over 250 kinds of soil inhabiting insects, 1 box, 10 million nematodes, $14.95; more kinds available. Beneficial predators and parasites are available, such as ladybugs, green lacewing, mealybug destroyer beetle, and more.

Organic fertilizers include: Biotera™ organic soil enhancer that is available in several mixtures, according to your soil's needs; Soil Soft; ComPeat that is 50% composted sawdust and 50% peat; Nitron Formula A-35 additive for composts.

Wondering what exactly your soil needs? They offer a soil audit service (first sample $55 fee) and a plant tissue analysis ($27.50).

Organic flea and tick controls available, such as Safer® Insecticidal Pet Soap or Indoor Flea Guard.

IPM Laboratories, Inc., Main St, Locke NY 13092-0099. (315) 497-3129. IPM stands for "Intelligent Pest Management" which is what the company offers. They produce biocontrol products, pest management services (research, bioassays, and consulting) and insect rearing, such as custom rearing.

Their products include fly parasites for fly control in manure, starts at 5,000 for $10 ppd. Other beneficial insects available for greenhouses & nurseries: spider mite predators; thrips predators; whitefly parasites; aphid predators; mealybug predators; beneficial nematodes.

See also "Books" chapter.

 Chapter Ten: Organically Grown

Jaffe Brothers, PO Box 636, Valley Center CA 92082-0636. (619) 749-1133.

Save on bulk buying of untreated dried fruits, nuts, seeds, grains, unrefined oils, wholewheat pastas, organic baby food and other natural foods. In business for 41 years. Free catalog.

Jantz Design & Manufacturing, PO Box 3071, Santa Rosa CA 95402. (707) 823-8834. Organically grown cotton available from this company to other businesses and individuals.

This company sells 100% certified organic cotton futons and pillows. Mattress pads and comforters made with pure, untreated lambswool batting and prewashed muslin. Free catalog.

Joe Soghomonian, Inc., 8624 S Chestnut, Fresno CA 93725. (209) 834-2772, (209) 834-3150. Organic (certified by California Certified Organic Farmers) table grapes and raisins. Label "Three Sisters" brand. Grapes shipped nationally via UPS—must be shipped air freight outside of California in order to ensure freshness. Raisins may be shipped ground service nationally. Family operation that takes pride in its quality-conscious product. Distributor discounts available.

Kinsman Company, Inc., River Road, Point Pleasant PA 18950. (215) 297-5613. Catalog of gardening supplies. Includes Slide-Panel Accelerator Compost Bins to speed composting using natural heat. K6 holds 9 cubic feet, 30" x 32", $59.95; K8 bin has 15 cubic feet

Buying Organic Foods

It is everyone's responsibility to leave this world a habitable place for the generations to come. We must see that our land remains healthy without a buildup of toxic chemicals. One way we can do this is to use our food dollars to buy organic foods—what an impact that has!

According to Organic Farms, by buying organic food you help to:

•➔ Improve the quality and safety of good.

•➔ Contribute to long-term sustainable food production.

•➔ Conserve energy.

•➔ Avoid dependence on expensive and uncertain sources of petrochemical based fertilizers and pesticides.

•➔ Preserve the family farm.

•➔ Increase net farm income by lowering production costs.

•➔ Reduce soil erosion and compaction.

capacity, 36" x 32", $99.95; K10 bin holds 21 cubic feet, 36" x 44", $129.95. ComposTool has long tubular steel handle for introducing more air to the compost, $11.95. Steinmax Electric Chipper Shredders come in various sizes and styles.

Krystal Wharf Farms, Rd 2 Box 2112, Mansfield PA 16933. (717) 549-8194. They offer 40-80 varieties of certified organically grown fresh fruits and vegetables for refrigerated truck delivery. Mail order (UPS) delivery available for fresh produce, dry goods, wild organic herbs and garden seeds.

Lee's Organic Foods, PO Box 11, Wellington TX 79095. (806) 447-5445. They have been organic growers for 30 years. They produce Organic Fruit Jerky in four flavors: Sweet Apple Jerky; Sweet Peach Jerky; Sweet Concord Grape Jerky; and Sweet Wild Plum Jerky. Organic sugar is the only preservative used. The jerky contains no fat, no cholesterol and is high in healthy fiber. It contains 50% organic fruit, sugar, pancake mix, and cornstarch. Price is $4 per pound.

Living Tree Centre, PO Box 10082, Berkeley CA 94709-5082. (415) 528-4467. Sells Living Tree Almonds that are organically grown, 8 lbs $32. Living Tree Almond Butter made with organically grown almonds, 3 lbs for $15. This company also sells live apple and pear trees.

Maestro-Gro, PO Box 310, 121 Lincoln Drive, Lowell AR 72745. (501) 770-6154. All natural/ organic plant food fertilizers. They have blends available for lawn, turf, grasses, houseplants, herbs, gardens, vegetables, flowers, roses, hollies, berries, bushes, shrubs, trees, bulbs and tubers. Technical consulting also available.

Mendocino Sea Vegetable Company, Box 732, Navarro CA 95463. (707) 895-3741. This company sells wildcrafted northern California sea vegetables. To get started, for $20 they will send you 7 assorted one-ounce packages, plus their cookbook and forager's guide. Their product line includes Mendocino Nori; Sea Palm Fronds; Mendocino Wakame; Mendocino Kombu; North Atlantic Dulse (from Nova Scotia); Flaked Nori (from Baja California); Sea Lettuce; Sea Whip Fronds; Mendocino Grapestone; Fucus Tips.

Their 32-page booklet *Sea Vegetable Gourmet Cookbook and Forager's Guide* ($4.95) tells how to harvest sea vegetables ecologically and how to prepare delicious, healthful sea vegetable dishes.

Mercantile Food Company, 4 Old Mill Road, PO Box 1140, Georgetown CT 06829. Source for American Prairie® Canned Organic Beans. These products are 100% organic and certified by Farm Verified Organic-R, an international certification program. The line of products includes: black beans, kidney beans, pinto beans, garbanzos, navy

Mendocino Sea Vegetable Company

They were selected as the "Best Sea Vegetable Line on the Market" by *East West Journal* in 1987 and as the "Best West Coast Sea Vegetable Supplier" by *East West Journal* in 1986.

John & Eleanor Lewallen, the company's owners, spend at least half of their time doing environmental protection work. Eleanor works for ocean sanctuary (permanent ocean protection) including public education and lobbying in Washington and other places. John has been involved with the Forest and Wildlife Protection and Bond Act of 1990 (aka Forests Forever), a California initiative for the 1990 ballot. He is the co-author of the Sierra Club book *The Grassroots Primer*, a guidebook on how to protect what you care about. Your purchase of their products supports their environmental work. They will send you a letter a couple times a year with a seaweed report and an update about their environmental work.

beans, great Northern beans; almonds, raisins; soups; hot breakfast cereals, and cold breakfast cereals.

Also available are organic wafers, imported from Holland. Types: maple, barley, and apple-pear-spice.

See also "Household & Personal Care Products" chapter.

Mountain Ark, 120 South East Ave, Fayetteville AR 72701. (501) 442-7191. 1-800-643-8909. Free catalog of organic and macrobiotic foods, including: grains, beans, dried fruits, nuts & seeds; organic noodles, snacks; sea vegetables; traditionally-made miso and soy sauce; healthy teas and beverages. Also gourmet cookware, books, water purifiers and more. Each seasonal catalog has descriptions of healthy products for natural living with recipes and articles as well.

Mountain Springs, 356 West Redview Drive, Monroe UT 84754. 1-800-542-2303. Rainbow trout fillets that are quality monitored. Mountain Springs intentionally selects their rainbow trout from farms with clean water. They monitor water quality by looking for the presence of chemicals such as pesticides. They choose only trout grown where no pesticides are present in the water supply. The trout are packaged free of bones, free of skins and free of anything that might detract from their taste and purity. Available regular or smoked. They offer a 100% satisfaction guarantee. Mail order available, credit cards accepted.

Natural Organic Farmers Association, c/o Hawson Kittredge, RFD #2, Sheldon Rd, Barre MA 01005. (508) 355-

Mountain Springs quality-monitored rainbow trout fillets are available in regular or smoked flavor.

2853. Promotes organic agriculture. They have a map of organic growers in these states: MA, NH, VT, CT, RI, NY, NJ, Ontario. Provides organic certification of farms.

Nature's Control, PO Box 35, Medford OR 97501. (503) 899-8318. FAX # (503) 899-9121. Offers beneficial insects for natural pest control. They have predatory mites for spider mite control; whitefly parasites; green lacewing larvae; ladybugs; and mealybug predators. They also offer Safer® Agro Insecticidal soap.

Nitron Industries, Inc., PO Box 1447, 4605 Johnson Road, Fayetteville AR 72702. (501) 750-1777. 1-800-835-0123. Manufacturer and distributor of natural fertilizers and soil conditioners. All of these products are available at retail through the nationally distributed gardening catalog as well as to dealers and wholesalers through their wholesale program. The natural fertilizers are Bat Guano, Soft Rock Phosphate,

Earthworm castings, Fish Meal and many more in all sizes from 20-lb bags to truckloads. Also distributes Diatomaceous Earth and Diatomaceous Earth with Pyrethrins for natural insecticide control. Wet-Flex Hose is available for irrigation, which saves water. FREE catalog by calling toll-free number.

Other services include books on farming and gardening, an annual organic growing seminar, composting information, and other technical information for organic growers.

Ohio Earth Food, Inc, 13737 Duquette Ave NE, Hartville OH 44632. (216) 877-9356. This family business has dealt exclusively in organic fertilizers and livestock supplements for farmers and gardeners. They provide retail sales, mail order sales, wholesale distribution, consultation, and soil testing services. Some of the products in their catalog: ErthRite compost plus; ReVita compost plus; rock phosphate; Jersey greensand; Plant Right pelleted organic fertilizer; Sea-Min kelp meal; Maxicrop liquified seaweed; rotenone; diatomaceous earth; Red Arrow insect spray (pyrethrum base); Safer® insecticidal soap; Safer® flea soap; Rapidtest soil test kit; and many more products.

Organic Foods Express, Inc., 11003 Emack Rd, Beltsville MD 20705. (301) 937-8608. Mail order source for organic foods, including: vegetables; fruit; whole wheat pasta; sweeteners (honey and preserves); snacks (potato chips, rice cakes, wafers and more); oil; cheese; juices; baked goods from organic grains; seeds; dried beans; flour; nuts; dried fruit; grains; soups, nut butters; coffee, and more.

Organic Gardening®, Box 3, Emmaus PA 18099-0003. Organic Gardening is the magazine for organic gardeners. Ten issues per year, $19.50.

Ringer Corporation, 9959 Valley River Road, Eden Prairie MN 55344. (612) 941-4180. FAX # (612) 941-5036. 1-800-654-1047 for ordering. Manufacturers of products for the organic gardeners. People-safe, pet-safe, natural products for a healthier lawn and garden.

Lawn Restore® is a fertilizer that is a slow-release, non-burning formulation of microorganisms, enzymes and natural nutrient sources that work deep in the soil, feeding hungry lawns. Once activated by watering and rainfall, the organisms themselves reproduce natural nitrogen, phosphorus and potassium. 25 lb bag, $24.98.

Flower Garden Restore® uses beneficial Ringer microorganisms that improve soil conditions so plant develop deeper root growth for better moisture retention. 10 lb bag, $19.98; 25 lb bag, $32.98.

Compost Plus® is a compost activator to quickly break down compost piles to usable humans. Takes only 5-8 weeks to decompose even toughest materials. Combines microorganisms, enzymes and nutrients to hasten decomposition of materials like wood-chips, twigs, pine needles and kitchen waste. 10 lb bag, $23.98; 25 lb bag,

$35.98.

Compost Master™ is a heavy duty chipper, shredder, and garden mulcher. $899. Yard Guard™ back yard composter that keeps leaves and grass clippings from blowing away. 36" x 29" and holds 12 bushels, $49.98. World Class Thermal Composter turns grass clippings, leaves, weeds and kitchen scraps into beneficial humus and mulch in just 5-8 weeks. Measures 37" x 32" and holds 13 bushels, $159.98.

Write for their 32-page color catalog of gardener's supplies. More in "Household and Personal Care Products" chapter.

Rising Sun Organic Produce, Box 627 I-80 and PA 150, Milesburg PA 16853. (814) 355-9850. Providers of wholesome food grown by farmers who use organic or biodynamic methods. These farmers use natural pest control techniques and crop rotations to avoid disease. Fresh organically grown produce is their specialty. Items available: fruits & vegetables; dried fruits; nuts and seeds; grains; flours; cereals; pasta; juices; oils; baby food; prepared fruit; sweeteners; snacks; dairy products; soy products; coffee; bread; sea vegetables; Neolife cleaning products; Dorsey non-toxic household products.

Some interesting & hard-to-find organic products include: wild rice ($8.75 lb); veggie spirals pasta ($1.85 lb); American Prairie cereals; organic whole wheat flour (80¢ lb); brown rice syrup ($3.95/ 16 oz); organic corn tortillas—blue or yellow; Cascadian

Farms organic pickles; TOL pasta sauce; organic vinegar ($3.34 qt).

Ronninger's Seed Potatoes, Star Route, Moyie Springs ID 83845. (208) 267-7938. Very large selection of organically grown seed potato varieties and also seeds for cover crops (clover, peas, alfalfa and more). Catalog $1.

Seventh Generation, Colchester VT 05446-1672. (802) 655-3116. FAX toll-free # 1-800-456-1139. Order toll-free 1-800-456-1177. Customer service toll-free 1-800-456-1197.

Seventh Generation is one of the most well-known companies for environmentally safe consumer products. Their 48-page catalog "Products for a Healthy Planet" ($2) contains an extraordinary variety of products. They also practice what they preach. For instance, they recycle their office paper, and reuse cardboard boxes for shipping. They have a 1% fund that goes to environmental organizations.

Organically grown products in the catalog include: coffee; soups (navy bean, carrot, pea, vegetable); popcorn; fruit juices; applesauce; dates; raisins; baby food and baby juice.

There are so many products in this catalog that additional information can be found in these chapters: "Baby and Children's Products," "Books," "Educational Materials," "Paper Products," "Recycling," "Energy Conservation," and "Household & Personal Care Products."

Simply Delicious, 243-A North Hook Rd, PO Box 124, Pennsville NJ 08070. (609) 678-4488. This is a retail natural food store that offers organic cereals, grains, beans and more from Health Valley, Arrowhead Mills and other major product lines. Also listed in "Household & Personal Care Products" and "Paper Products" chapters.

SM Jacobson Citrus, 1505 Doherty, Mission TX 78572. (512) 585-1712. They grow oranges and grapefruits organically certified by the Texas Department of Agriculture. They will mail order direct to your home or business. They keep a mailing list, respond to all inquiries, and will notify you of crop availability.

Spalding Laboratories, 760 Printz Rd, Arroyo Grande CA 93420. (805) 489-5946. This company has developed biological fly control with environmentally safe Fly Predators®. This is an alternative to pesticides for controlling manure and filth breeding flies using tiny beneficial insects which provide low cost, long term, biological control without adverse side effects for dairies, stables, feedlots, poultry, swine, sheep, kennels, etc. Prices start at $2.64 per 1,000. Minimum order 5,000.

Sprout House, 40 Railroad St, Great Barrington MA 01230 (413) 528-5200. Kits and courses for growing organic foods at home. Introductory course ($79) gives you an indoor vegetable kit; 2 flaxseed sprout bags; a book *Recipes from the Sproutman*; the be-

★ Chapter Ten: Organically Grown

Sprout House has kits and courses for growing organic foods at home.

ginners dozen seeds (in half pound bags); and the book *Growing Vegetables Indoors*. A complete course ($139) adds 7 guidebooks and 8 classes on audio cassette. Individual audio cassettes are available for $9 each and includes titles such as "Juice Fasting I"; "Vegetarianism"; "Indoor Gardening." Individual kits are available, such as Flaxseed Sprout Bag ($12.95) which is a bag made from the natural, raw linen fibers of the flaxseed plant and perfect for growing sprouts; or the Indoor Vegetable Kits ($29.95) that contains seeds and custom-designed bamboo sprouters. Organic, chemical-free seeds available: jumbo alfalfa ($3.95 lb); crimson clover ($4.95 lb); Alaskan green pea ($1.95 lb); green lentil ($2 lb); much more.

Books available: *Recipes from the Sproutman* ($7.95) with recipes for spout breads, cookies, crackers, soups, dressing, dips, more; *Juice Fasting* ($7.95) about types of fasts, pre-fasting diet, how and when to fast, liver flushes, and menus; *Growing Vegetables Indoors* ($6.95) that is a training course for growing miniature vegetables indoors—all without soil; *Making Sprout Bread* ($4.95) with step-by-step preparation and advantages of sprout bread; and more titles.

The Sprout House Newsletter is published 5 times a year ($10). Contains information about new seeds, how to maintain the best sprouts, clean water information; workshop sched-

Chapter Ten: Organically Grown

ules; more.

Weiss's Kiwifruit, 594 Paseo Companeros, Chico CA 95928. (916) 343-2354. Organically grown (certified by California Certified Organic Farmers) kiwifruit shipped with free delivery anywhere in continental United States by UPS. Shipped direct from grower to you. Available in October and November (December except cold climate areas). Gifts packs are 2 1/2 lb (10-12) for $8.75; 5 lb (20-24) for $13.75. Tips for using kiwis and recipes included.

This we know,
the earth does not belong to man;
man belongs to the earth.
All things are connected
like the blood which unites one family.
Whatever befalls the earth,
befalls the sons of earth.
Man did not weave the web of life.
He is merely a strand of it.
Whatever he does to the earth,
he does to himself.

**Chief Seattle to President
Franklin Pierce in 1855.**

Chapter Eleven: Organizations

There are numerous environmental organizations today, both nationally and internationally. Many groups are becoming more international in their scope particularly because of their concern to save the world's rainforests and endangered species. There are also regional groups, which are trying to save endangered wetlands, rivers and streams, and other natural resources. These groups also have a great deal to offer in the way of information. Public education is often one of their priorities.

The Acid Rain Foundation, Inc., 1410 Varsity Drive, Raleigh NC 27606. (919) 828-9443. Founded to foster a greater understanding of the acid rain problem and to help bring about its resolution. Their projects: The Acid Rain Resources Directory, a listing of current literature and other materials; International Speakers Bureau lists over 300 scientists, analysts, educators, and researchers; Expert Referral Service to help people get the answers they need to their questions about acid rain; Informational packets; and Reference lists.

They have also developed curriculum for kids: Quiz for Kids, grade 4-8,

$5.95; Word Find, grades 4-8, $7.95; Science Projects, grades 5-12, $9.95; The Air Around Us, grades 5-12, $9.95; Curriculum, acid rain, grades 4-8, $19.95; and more, including puzzles and posters.

Publications: Acid Rain in Minnesota '89, $8.95; Acid Rain in North Carolina, 2 for $1; Report on Effects of Acidifying and Other Air Pollutants on Forests (UN report), $9.94; Resource Director '86 (International), $10; Speakers Bureau, $9.95.

They have a list of audio-visual materials (slides, audio cassettes, video cassettes, films, filmstrips, transparencies) available on the acid rain problem. Membership $25, includes a sub-

scription to the quarterly newsletter.

Adirondack Mountain Club, Inc., RR 3 Box 3055, Lake George NY 12845. (518) 523-3441. (518) 668-4447. A non-profit membership organization with chapters throughout New York, New Jersey, and Pennsylvania, dedicated to broadening public appreciation for the New York State Forest Preserve, to providing opportunities for environmentally-responsible outdoor recreation, and for retaining the wilderness by working on conservation issues.

Countless outdoor activities are provided all year long, such as backpacking and day trips. The club provides guidebooks that are a recognized source of information for the Adirondacks. Volunteer activities also available, such as trial maintenance, out-

house installation, erosion control, relocation & revegetation. Several lodges open to the public are located in the Adirondacks.

Membership includes ten issues of the *Adirondack Magazine,* discounts on books and publications, discounts on lodging, and reduced rates for educational programs. Basic individual membership is $30; various rates available.

Also listed in "Books," "Seminars, Speakers & Workshops" and "Ecotourism" chapters.

Adopt-A-Stream Foundation, PO Box 5558, Everett WA 98206. Founded to ensure that Northwest streams continue to provide spawning and rearing habitat for salmon, steelhead and trout and that these streams continue to serve a recreational function. They wish to restore to

 Chapter Eleven: Organizations

health those waterways damaged by man or nature. They assist others to become actively involved in stream enhancement and environmental education. The goal of the foundation is to have every Northwest stream adopted by schools, community groups, sports clubs, civic organizations or individuals. "Adoption" of a stream means that the parent group will provide the long term care of the stream and establish community wide stream restoration and environmental education activities.

The organization has conducted two International Environmental Education Conferences and has conducted biannual "Clean Water" Teacher Workshops.

They published the book *Adopting a Stream: A Northwest Handbook*. It is available from University of Washington Press, $9.95, call toll-free 1-800-441-4115 for ordering. The group distributed the book *Adopting a Wetland: A Northwest Handbook,* $5 each.

General membership is $25.

The Alliance to Save Energy, 1725 "K" St NW, Suite 914, Washington DC 20006-1401. (202) 857-0666. FAX # (202) 331-9588. An association dedicated to increasing the efficiency of energy use. They conduct research, provide information on new products and efficiency opportunities, and help design and promote sound public policy on energy efficiency issues. Efficiency is a sound system for achieving vital goals, such as a clean environment.

Current project include: promoting

the use of compact fluorescent light bulbs; promoting the improvement of energy efficiency in federal buildings; and researching the positive impact of energy efficiency on the global competitiveness of the US economy.

Membership is $25 for an individual.

Publications are available to the public and listed in "Magazines, Newsletters and Brochures" chapter.

American Cave Conservation Association, Inc., PO Box 409, Horse Cave KY 42749. (502) 786-1466. Dedicated to protecting and preserving caves, karstlands and related groundwater resources. Projects: The American Cave and Karst Center and Museum; the Cave Vandal Reward Program; the Caveland Solid Waste Management Initiative; the National Cave Management Training Seminar Program; and various cleanup projects. Brochures available to the public: American Cave Conservation Association brochures; Karst brochure; Some Facts About Caves brochure; and the National Cave Management Seminar brochure. Membership is $25 per year and includes occasional publications such as the *American Caves* magazine and the ACCA newsletter.

American Forestry Association, PO Box 2000, Washington DC 20013-2000. Many Americans have heard of the Global Releaf program, but not all are aware that the program is from the American Forestry Association. This group has been working for more and better trees and forests since 1875. They have played a major role in the creation of America's system of public lands and parks. They have stopped indiscriminate logging and uncontrolled wildfires. Today they promote conservation action globally.

Their best known project, Global Releaf, has captured the attention of citizens and even other non-profit organizations worldwide. This project creates opportunities for individual action through tree planting, legislative reform and involvement in local and national conservation activities. To find out how you can do your part, call 1-900-420-4545. The cost of the call is $5 and pays for planting a tree. They will also send you additional information on Global Releaf and how you can become involved.

Other project of the American Forestry Association are: Forest Conservation; Friends of the National Forests; Urban & Community Forestry; The National Register of Big Trees (the official list of the largest of every species in the United States!!); Environmental & Forestry Education.

Subscribing membership is $24 per year and entitles member to: subscription to the bimonthly magazine *American Forests;* advice and information on trees and tree planting; wilderness adventures opportunities; special tours; and discounts on books, publications, gifts and services.

American Rivers, 801 Pennsylvania Ave SE, Suite 303, Washington DC 20003-2167. (202) 547-6900. De-voted exclusively to preserving the nation's outstanding rivers and their landscapes. Their goal is to protect 180,000 miles of free-running rivers by the early part of next century. Their river protection program has three parts: federal protection agenda; state rivers protection; and their National Center for Hydropower Policy. Basic membership is $20; benefits include the quarterly newsletter *American Rivers;* action alerts; listings of river outfitters and retailers who support conservation and sometimes they offer discounts; and an application for The American Rivers Card™ MasterCard.

American Solar Energy Society, 2400 Central Ave, B-1, Boulder CO 80301. (303) 443-3130. A national society for professionals and others involved in the fields of solar energy. This group provides a variety of forums for exchange of information on solar energy applications and research. They address critical national issues for which solar energy technologies offer significant contributions. ASES has 6 divisions: Solar Buildings, Solar Electric, Solar Thermal, Solar Fuels and Chemicals, Renewable Resource and Solar Education. There's an annual National Solar Energy Conference that typically includes over 200 paper presentations.

They have a 16-page publications list that offers books, research reports, conference proceedings, & newsletter back issues. For a list of books, see the "Book" chapter. Standard membership-at-large is $50 (other rates available) and includes the bimonthly

GREEN EARTH RESOURCE GUIDE

newsletter *Solar Today,* discounts on publications and conferences, and networking opportunities.

America's Clean Water Foundation, Hall of the States, 4444 N Capitol St NW, Ste 330, Washington DC 20001. (202) 624-7833. An organization dedicated to the preservation of clean water resources and to the education of the public about these valuable natural resources.

Basic Foundation, Inc./Basic Publishing & Promotions, PO Box 47012, St. Petersburg FL 33743. (813) 526-9562. The Basic Foundation was founded in 1970 to discover and foster worldwide efforts to balance population growth with natural resources. They support research activities, exhibits, publications, conferences, lectures and nature tours that educate the public on the threat the overpopulation poses to the world's resources. They believe that it is essential for the world community to act to bring the population growth into balance with the world ecosystem.

Their immediate focus is on saving tropical rainforests. Through their partner, Arbofilia, a non-profit organization in Costa Rica, you can plant endangered tropical trees along deforested rivers, on areas of small farms inhabited by wildlife, along rural roads, parks and beaches, or in reforestation projects of schools. For $5 donation to this project you receive a certificate.

Their catalog contains the following items: Rainforest Crunch, tin filled with 1 lb of Crunch, $13; Grateful Dead Rainforest T-shirt, $18.95; other T-shirts; Rainforest Action Network Poster, $10; and a audio tape "Preparing For a Rain Forest Adventure," $9.95.

More in "Eco-tourism" chapter.

BioIntegral Resource Center, PO Box 7414, Berkeley CA 94707. (415) 524-2567. Dedicated to least-toxic pest management. Projects: BIRC field station; international information gathering program; data bases; integrated pest management design. Members can receive free advice as well as periodicals, booklets and directories. Also listed in the "Organically Grown" chapter.

California Certified Organic Farmers, (CCOF), PO Box 8136, Santa Cruz CA 95061-8136. (408) 423-2263. This organization promotes healthful, ecologically accountable and permanent agriculture. It develops standards and certification programs for organic farming and programs for verifying those standards. They have farm inspector trainings, retailer seminars, local fairs and events and other educational events. Presently over 61,000 acres are in their program. They have been very active in promoting state and national legislation to regulate and aid the organic industry. Membership is $25 for an individual; $40 for organic businesses.

Caribbean Conservation Corp., PO Box 2866, Gainesville FL 32602.

Chapter Eleven: Organizations

(904) 373-6441. Dedicated to the protection and preservation of the marine sea turtle and its habitat, specifically in Costa Rica and the Caribbean. Projects: Adopt-a-Turtle; annual sea turtle tagging program at Tortuguero, Costa Rica; and sea turtle research. *Velador* is the newsletter. Sea turtle video *National Audubon Society Special: Sea Turtle,* 58 minutes, $35.95 plus $3.50 for shipping. Individual membership $35; includes newsletter.

Catalyst, 64 Main St, 3rd Floor, (05602) PO Box 1308, (05601) Montpelier VT . (802) 223-7943. An organization connecting economics, ecology and human rights. Projects: Vermont All Species Project; Grassroots Corporate Action Campaign; Hydro-Quebec action; corporate research and more. Basic membership is $25; benefits include the 28-page magazine *Catalyst: Economics for the Living Earth.*

More information in "Environmental Investing" chapter.

Center for Marine Conservation, 1725 DeSales St NW, Washington DC 20036. (202) 429-5609. Dedicated to worldwide protection of marine wildlife and their habitats and to conserving coastal and ocean resources. More than 110,000 members worldwide. Activities: conducts policy-oriented research; promotes public awareness through education; involves citizens in public policy decisions; supports domestic and international conservation programs for marine species and their habitats.

Specific projects: worked with scientists in the Caribbean to establish a sanctuary for critically endangered humpback whales; coordinates volunteers to clean up beaches; helps establish marine sanctuaries; leads efforts to prevent accidental entanglement and drowning of marine animals in debris (plastics) and fishing gear; forced the federal and state regulations requiring Turtle Excluder Devices on shrimp nets to prevent drowning of thousands of endangered sea turtles; thwarts efforts to increase trade in endangered sea turtle products; forced Exxon to set up rescue and rehabilitation efforts for sea otters after the Alaska oil spill.

Basic membership starts at $20 and all members receive the *Marine Conservation News,* a quarterly newsletter featuring updates on their programs. Members also receive discounts on merchandise in their "Whale Gifts" catalog.

Center for Plant Conservation, 125 Arborway, Jamaica Plain MA 02130-3520. (617) 524-6988. Dedicated to saving the rare and endangered plants native to the U.S. through integrated conservation methods. The Center has created the largest living collection of plant germ plasm of its kind and is backed by seeds stored in the USDA National Seed Storage Service in Fort Collins, Colorado. In just four years, the Center has brought over 300 kinds of rare and endangered native plants into cultivation or seed storage. There's a computerized database that enables the Center to share information with conservation agencies, natural resource managers, and horticulturalists.

There is no membership structure, but contributions are encouraged. They publish a quarterly newsletter *Plant Conservation*. They also have an extensive bibliography of articles and papers by Center staff.

Center for Science in the Public Interest, 1875 Connecticut Ave NW #300, Washington DC 20009. (202) 332-9110. FAX # (202) 265-4954. CSPI was founded by three scientists who wanted to bring the scientific perspective to bear on consumer advocacy issues. Today, the group focuses on food and nutrition, food safety and agriculture, and alcohol policies. The issues they are presently working on are organic and sustainable agriculture, food additives, nutrition and ingredient labeling, deceptive food and beverage advertising, fast food, and serves as a watchdog of government and industry.

Each year the "Americans for Safe Food" project sponsors a national conference on organic and sustainable agriculture.

Books, slides, posters, slide charts, computer software and videos are available. The publication list is available upon request. Books listed in "Books" chapter. Additional materials listed in "Educational Materials" chapter.

Membership is $19.95 and members receive the *Nutrition Action Healthletter* ten times a year, copies of the "Chemical Cuisine" and "Nutrition

Scoreboard" posters, and a 10% discount on product purchases.

Citizen's Clearinghouse for Hazardous Wastes, 2315 Wilson Blvd, Suite A, PO Box 657, Arlington VA 22216. (703) 276-7070. This is a grassroots movement started by Lois Gibb in 1981 to fight the hazardous waste problem at Love Canal. The lesson of Love Canal was how effective citizen action could be, so Lois founded CCHW to help citizens speak out for themselves against local toxic hazards. The Clearinghouse now serves over 5,000 grassroots environmental organizations. Its main function is to help people help themselves. Training conferences held periodically.

Resources available from the group: *Love Canal: My Story* by Lois Gibb, $12.95; *Fight to Win: A Leader's Manual,* $7.50; *Making a Difference,* $1.50; *Research Guide for Leaders,* $3.50; *Love Canal: A Chronology of Events that Shaped a Movement,* $9.95; *Environmental Testing: Where to Look, What to Look For, How to Do It and What It Means,* $8.95; *Reduction of Hazardous Waste: The Only Serious Option,* $8.98; *Safety Plans: What You Need to Know,* $6.95; *Recycling: The Answer to Our Garbage Problem,* $8.95; *Solid Action Guidebook,* $8.98; *History of the Grassroots Movement for Environmental Justice,* $8.50; and many more.

Toxic Waste Site Lists available for each state, $2.50 each state. T-shirts: "Incinerators Burn Me Up," "Toxic Wastes Shouldn't Be in Anyone's

Ziggy ©1990, Ziggy & Friends, Inc./ Distributed by Universal Press Syndicate. Reprinted with permission. All rights reserved.

Backyard," "Wastebuster," "Clean Water, We All Live Downstream," "People United for Environmental Justice," $10 each.

Basic membership is $25; includes bimonthly magazine *Everyone's Backyard,* 10% discount on T-shirts and publications, 10% discount on training conferences and events; discounts on water testing from Water Test Corp; 15% discount on Ecodex Radon test kits; 20% off five titles from Island Press.

Citizen's Coalition for Energy Efficiency, Southeastern Pennsylvania Energy Center, 100 North 17th St, Third Floor, Philadelphia PA 19103. (215) 563-3989. This group has developed and advocated energy programs and policies in Southeastern Pennsylvania for the past ten years. Current

projects are: energy training for teachers and educational groups; Southeastern Pennsylvania Energy Center; Affordable Comfort Conference; energy surveys and technical assistance. Send for publications list.

Clean Sites, 1199 North Fairfax St, Alexandria VA 22314. (703) 739-1275. FAX # (703) 548-8773. Nonprofit organization dedicated to solving America's hazardous waste problem. They work toward fair and effective public policy and also become involved in the cleanup process themselves. In five years, the group has been active at 60 sites. They review the technical studies at hazardous waste sites, they help in the management of the cleanups, and they help resolve disputes between involved parties. The organization is funded by reimbursement for services, government and foundation grants and

 Chapter Eleven: Organizations

private contributions. There is no membership structure.

Climate Institute, 316 Pennsylvania Ave SE, Suite 403, Washington DC 20003. (202) 547-0104. FAX # (202) 547-0111. Telex 214 858 CLIMAT UR. Committed to protecting the balance between climate and life on earth. This group is a catalyst for international cooperation for scientists, business leaders and policy makers. It has organized a series of conferences on regional implications of climate change: 3 in North America; an Africa conference; an Arctic conference; and the Cairo World Conference on Preparing for Climate Change. Publications are available that report on the findings of these conferences. Public education is one of its ongoing programs.

Regular membership is $35; benefits include: subscription to the quarterly *Climate Alert* and discount on conference *Proceedings*.

Concern, Inc., 1794 Columbia Rd NW, Washington DC 20009. (202) 328-8160. A non-profit organization that provides environmental information to help communities find solutions to local problems that are environmentally safe, economically sound & that safeguard the public health. They sponsor training programs on Drinking Water & Household Waste, the VA Solid Waste Project, a Community Outreach Program.

Booklets available listed in "Magazines, Newsletters & Brochures" chapter.

Conservation & Renewable Energy Inquiry & Referral Service (CAREFIRS), PO Box 8900, Silver Spring MD 20907. 1-800-523-2929. CAREFIRS is operated by Advances Sciences Inc, under contract by the US Department of Energy to aid technology transfer by responding to public inquiries on the use of renewable energy technologies and conservation techniques for residential and commercial needs.

The goal of this organization is to assist the general public in determining the feasibility of using these technologies by providing basic and special information. For more technical information, CAREFIRS maintains and refers people to an extensive network of government agencies and organizations whose areas of expertise cover the entire range of energy technologies. The group operates a nationwide toll-free telephone services and a post office box to receive public inquiries.

Topics covered by CAREFIRS include: active and passive solar heating; photovoltaics; wind energy; biomass conversion; solar thermal electric; geothermal energy; small-scale hydroelectric; alcohol fuels; wood heating; ocean energy; and all energy conservation technologies. CAREFIRS provides more than 150 publications, fact sheets, and bibliographies; many are furnished and approved by government organizations.

Co-op America, 2100 "M" St NW, Suite 403, Washington DC 20063. (202) 872-5307. Toll-free 1-800-424-

2667. This is a non-profit, member-controlled, worker-managed association linking socially responsible businesses and consumers in a national network, a new alternative marketplace. Co-op America allows consumers to align buying habits with values. Through Co-op America, consumers have access to quality products from all over the world made by people whose products reflect their values. These people use their collective buying power to change the American economic system. One of the values strongly reflected is environmental sensitivity.

Membership ($20) benefits are: health and life insurance group plans; travel service and a free Travel-Links phone number; updates on major boycotts to force corporations to stop their dangerous practices; Financial Planning Guide to help plan socially responsible investing, Co-op America's quarterly magazine *Building Economic Alternatives* that is filled with articles on strategies for changing the injustice of our economic system, and Co-op America Catalogs that are full of useful, hard-to-find products and valuable information.

Products from the catalog are found in "Recycling," "Energy Conservation," "Educational Materials," "Books," " Organically Grown," "Household & Personal Care Products," "Paper Products," and "Baby & Children's Products" chapters.

Council on Economic Priorities, 30 Irving Place, New York NY 10003.

(212) 420-1133. Toll-free 1-800-822-6435. This organization researches corporate social responsibility, environmental issues and national security. Many consumers have adapted their shopping and investing habits according to socially-responsible ideals, and states and cities are also adopting "principled purchasing" programs, and much of the information available has come from this organization. CEP has published more than 1,000 studies and reports on such issues as pollution by the paper industry, the status of women in corporations, child care, hazardous waste disposal and the transportation of nuclear waste.

Their highly acclaimed book *Shopping for a Better World* has been adopted by many other nonprofit organizations and is available from CEP or other environmentally-responsible catalog companies. This book is a handy pocket size so that you can carry it shopping. This guide is great! It has chapters for shopping to end animal testing, shopping for energy alternatives, shopping to end apartheid, shopping for equal opportunity, shopping for a cleaner world, and more!! They even rate gas & oil companies. There's a form at the end of the book so you can request ratings of companies from which you generally buy products.

Membership to the organization is $25 and all members receive a free "Shoppers Guide" every year.

Cultural Survival, Inc., 53 Church St, Cambridge MA 02138. (617) 495-2562. This organization was founded in 1972 to help vulnerable cultures survive the rapid changes created by the encroachment of governments, businesses and others. The group supports projects on five continents that help indigenous peoples retain their rights and cultures as they learn to live with the modern world. On going projects include: a marketing program for harvested tropical forest products from Latin America, Africa and Asia; teaching Latin American indigenous groups about natural resource management; helping the resettlement and cattle project for the !Kung San in Namibia; supporting a Mayan weavers' cooperative in Mexico; leading an educational campaign to aid Kurds in the Middle East; and more.

Rainforest Crunch is the most well-known product that has resulted from this organization. It can be ordered directly for $42 per dozen boxes or $17.50 per pound in the tins. Brazil nuts are $132 per 44 pounds; cashews $175 per 50 pounds; and cashew fruit $5 per pound. Order address is: Cultural Survival, 11 Divinity Ave, Cambridge MA 02138.

Basic membership starts at $25; benefits include a year's subscription to the *Cultural Survival Quarterly* magazine and the opportunity to volunteer for Community Survival projects in your community.

More information in "Magazines, Newsletters & Brochures" and "Books" chapters.

Desert Tortoise Council, PO Box 1738, Palm Desert CA 92261. To pro-tect endangered desert tortoises.

Ducks Unlimited, Inc., One Waterfowl Way, Long Grove IL 60047. (708) 438-4300. Nonprofit, nonpolitical membership corporation, organized to perpetuate waterfowl and other wildlife on the North American continent, principally by development, preservation, restoration, management, and maintenance of wetland areas on the Canadian primary breeding grounds, which produce the majority of the continental waterfowl; in prime waterfowl nesting, resting and wintering areas of the US; and in the nesting and wintering areas of Mexico. Establishes, promotes, assists and contributes to conservation, restoration and management of waterfowl habitat. The organization has completed more than 5,000 wetland habitat projects in North America, positively impacting 5.3 million acres. They support a number of research projects relative to wetlands/waterfowl conservation.

Organized in 1937. Membership totals 550,000. Annual basic membership of $20 entitles the member to six issues of *Ducks Unlimited* magazine, a membership card, and a window decal. Other membership levels available. Brochures available upon request.

Earth Action Network, Inc., 28 Knight St, Norwalk CT 06851. (203) 854-5559. Non-profit organization that publishes *E, The Environmental Magazine*. This bimonthly full-color magazine was formed for the purpose of acting as a clearinghouse of information, news, and commentary on environmental issues for the benefit of the general public and in sufficient depth to involve dedicated environmentalists. Available on some newsstands. Magazine address: PO Box 5098, Westport CT 06881.

Earth Island Institute, 300 Broadway, Ste 28, San Francisco CA 94133. (415) 788-3666. FAX # (415) 788-7324. This is a radical environmentalist group, but they prefer networking and research to civil disobedience tactics. Presently there are about twenty projects in progress. Some of the main projects are: The Dolphin Project, forcing tuna companies to become dolphin safe through legislation, letter-writing and occasional demonstrations; the Endangered Sea Turtles Project, trying to save the habitats, includes letter-writing to the Mexican government to obtain their cooperation as well; the Central America project is trying to link peace, justice, nonintervention and ecology issues. Volunteers are needed.

Base membership is $25; subscription alone is $15. Their publication is the award-winning quarterly *Earth Island Journal.*

EarthSave, 706 Frederick St, Santa Cruz CA 95062. (408) 423-4069. Founded to show how the current meal & dairy-based American diet is affecting the environment and health of this country. Projects: a PBS documentary on "Diet for a New America" in 1991; school nutritional program called "Healthy People—Healthy Planet";

sponsor for the "Y.E.S. Tour" (Youth for Environmental Sanity), a group of students touring high schools across the country speaking about environmental issues. Basic individual membership is $20; members receive the newsletter and discounts on books and products.

EarthWatch, PO Box 403, 680 Mt. Auburn St, Watertown MA 02272. (617) 926-8200. This organization sends volunteers to work with scientists around the world who are trying to preserve the rainforests, endangered species, and other environmental problems. Basic membership is $25.

Ecology Center, 2530 San Pablo Ave, Berkeley CA 94702. (415) 548-2220. A non-profit education and recycling organization that has served the Bay area since 1969. They operate the oldest on-going recycling program in the state, as well as a comprehensive environmental information service. The Center offers a unique mix of services to the area, such as environmental information, library of environmental books & periodicals, a farmer's market, an ecology center store (with such items as books, periodicals, organic gardening supplies, recycled paper products, T-shirts, gifts, bumper stickers, more), and classes.

The educational needs of the community are served by classes in gardening and related subjects.

Basic membership starts at $20 at year; members receive a monthly newsletter and special discounts.

 Chapter Eleven: Organizations

EcoNet Canada, 456 Spadina Ave, 2nd floor, Toronto, Ontario, Canada M5T 2G8. (416) 929-0634. FAX # (416) 925-7536. Modem: (416) 925-0400. Telex: 063270997. This is an on-line computer environmental information service that can be used by educational organizations, environmental groups, government agencies, businesses, researchers, and others. Rates start at $15 per month.

Energy Federation, Inc., 354 Waverly St., Framingham MA 01701. (508) 875-4921. FAX # (617) 451-1534. Toll-free 1-800-876-0660 outside Massachusetts. Toll free eastern Massachusetts 1-800-752-7372. The organization was formed in 1982 by 6 non-profit community energy organizations to coordinate bulk purchases of quality energy conservation materials. Since then, the group has focused on providing superior service and skilled technical assistance to its customers. Additional information found in "Energy Conservation" chapter.

Energy Probe Research Foundation, 225 Brunswick Avenue, Toronto, Ontario, Canada M5S 2M6. (416) 978-7014. This is an environmental watchdog organization whose goals are: to educate Canadians to the benefits of conservation and renewable energy; to help Canada secure long-term energy self-sufficiency; and to help Canada contribute to global harmony and prosperity.

The organization's achievements include Canada's first radioactive cleanup of a contaminated town (1975) after they publicized gross violations; a cancellation of a utility project that would have contributed to acid rain; tightening of radiation safety standards nationally; and compensation for citizens' groups intervening under Ontario's Environmental Assessment Act.

Current priorities include: the ongoing court challenge of the Nuclear Liability Act; opposition of Ontario Hydro's plan to transport and sell radioactive tritium; bringing attention to the greenhouse effect; and launching a campaign to expose the nuclear industry's abuse of public funds for propaganda purposes.

The group is active in media appearances, articles, legislative lobbying, handling information requests, and mailings of informative brochures.

The organization is divided into three areas: Energy Probe Research Foundation, Probe International, and Environment Probe, each of which has had numerous achievements and each of which is working on current projects. Each division also has its own publications list.

Examples from the Environment Probe publications list: *The Price of Preservation: The Value of timber in the Carmanah Valley Watershed* by Adam White provides a social cost-benefit analysis of logging in British Columbia, $5; *Enlisting Trees in Canada to Fight the Greenhouse Effect* by Wendy Hawthorne, $5; *How You Can Help Fight the Greenhouse Effect* is a free pamphlet that contains ideas for projects that can be carried out around the home and in the community; *How Trees Can Help Fight the Greenhouse Effect* is a free factsheet about the Canadian potential to become a net absorber rather than a net emitter of carbon dioxide.

Environmental Action Coalition, 625 Broadway, New York NY 10012. (212) 677-1601. Has been providing New Yorkers with active projects in recycling and environmental education opportunities for 20 years—beginning with the first Earth Day in 1970. Current projects: the Institutional Recycling Program to help office paper recycling for offices, schools, libraries, government agencies, and hospitals; the Recycling Education Program for teacher-training in New York; New York Releaf program to plant trees to combat the effects of global warming.

Members receive *Cycle*, an 8-page quarterly newsletter with information about their projects and profiles of what people are doing to protect the environment. Membership starts at $20 for an individual.

More information in "Educational Materials" chapter.

Environmental Action Foundation/ Environmental Action, 1525 New Hampshire Ave NW, Washington DC 20036. (202) 745-4870. This organization's work is to protect the health and welfare of present and future generations through pollution prevention. They played a strong role in the passage of a strong Superfund law and

in the federal Right-To-Know law. Through its political action committee, the group supports strong environmental candidates and puts legislators with poor environmental records on its famous "Dirty Dozen" list.

Present projects include: Solid Waste Alternatives Project; Energy Conservation Coalition; Toxics Project; Energy Project.

Basic membership is $25; benefits include the bimonthly *Environmental Action Magazine.*

Publications found in "Magazines, Newsletters and Brochures" chapter.

Environmental Defense Fund, National Headquarters, 257 Park Ave, New York NY 10010. Their main project has been to save seals, sea birds, rare sea turtles, and other marine life from death-dealing plastics at sea. Although legislation has been passed making it unlawful for any US vessel to dump plastic into the ocean, there is still work to be done to be sure this law is enforced. They are also fighting the other threats to marine life: garbage in general, acid rain.

Environmental Hazards Management Institute, 10 Newmarket Rd, PO Box 932, Durham NH 03824. (603) 868-1496. FAX # (603) 868-1547. This organization provides environmental information to private citizens, industry, non-profit agencies, government, and schools. They provide training programs, conferences, and information systems including an environmental database of technical experts in nearly every environmental area.

Their most widely-known educational tool has been the "Environmental Educational Wheels." These educational wheels are eye-catching, informative and easy-to-use. There are three kinds: "Recycling Wheel™" "Household Hazardous Waste Wheel™" and "Water Sense Wheel™". For example, the Recycling Wheel has on one side the categories of items that can be recycled (plastic, glass, paper, etc) and as you turn the wheel to that category, it will tell you about options for recycling that product, how it's collected for recycling, what recycled products can be made from it, the percentage that product occurs in the waste stream, and more. On the backside, there's another group of categories with additional information. These wheels are $2.75 each, quantity discounts available.

Forum International (Worldwide) Inc., 91 Gregory Lane, Suite 21, Pleasant Hill CA 94523. (415) 671-2900. FAX # (415) 946-1500. Founded in 1956 by Dr. Nicolas Hetzer, Forum International is dedicated to creating a worldwide forum for education, research and action on a transdisciplinary, supranational and ecosystemic basis. Forum Travel International and Eco-Tourism International have become the professional travel branch for many programs, conferences, field studies, and other travel-related activities which have been developed. Membership includes the *Ecosphere* magazine.

Freshwater Foundation, PO Box 90,

"Household Hazardous Waste" educational wheel from Environmental Hazards Management Institute.

Navarre MN 55392. (612) 471-8407. Formed to keep water usable for human consumption, industry and recreation through education and research. The organization built and equipped the Gray Freshwater Biological Institute and gave it to the University of Minnesota in 1976. Since that time, the group has supported research at the GFBI and produced conferences, publications, and other educational materials and programs to help people understand our growing water problems. It has provided consulting regionally on water issues with such organizations as the Montana Flathead Basin Commission, Great Lake groups, and the National Water Alliance.

All members receive the newsletter *Facets of Freshwater*; contributing members and above also receive the monthly *US Water News*. Discounts are available to members on Foundation publications, conferences, classes and field trips. Basic membership starts at $25.

Publications available to the public include: *Agrichemicals & Groundwater: Perspectives & Solutions,* an overview of concerns and responses related to the potential of agrichemicals for contaminating groundwater, seeks an awareness of possible solutions, $10; *Understanding Your Shoreline: Protecting Rivers, Lakes & Streams,* 30¢; *Waste is a Water Problems: What You Can Do About Solid Waste,* 30¢; *Groundwater: Understanding Our Hidden Resource,* 30¢; *Water Filters: Their Effect on Water Quality,* 30¢; *Hazardous Waste in Our Homes—and in Our Water,* 30¢; *Understanding Your Septic Systems, 30¢; Nitrates & Groundwater: A Public Health Concern,* a 13-page brochure, 50¢; *A Citizens' Guide to Lake Protection,* $2; more. Quantity prices available.

Videos available include: *When the River Runs Dry* (grades 5-9), comes in a packet with teaching guide & a 4-color poster, $50; *How to Protect Your Private Water Well,* $37; *Water Pollution ... Where Does It Come From?* $37.

Friends of the Earth, 218 "D" St SE, Washington DC 20003. (202) 544-2600. FAX # (202) 543-4710. EcoNet ID—foedc. Friends of the Earth is a merger of three organizations: Friends of the Earth (founded 1969); Environmental Policy Institute (founded 1972); and Oceanic Society (founded 1972). There are 50,000 members and supporters and 37 international affiliates. This organization is an independent global advocacy organization that is dedicated to: protecting the planet; preserving biological, cultural and ethnic diversity; and empowering citizens to have a voice in the decisions that affect their environment and lives.

Current projects include: protecting the ozone layer; saving tropical rainforests; preserving oceans and marine life; and improving East-West relations. Their emphasis is on how environmental problems and policies affect people—their health, their livelihood and their quality of life.

Products available from the organization: "Save Trees" address labels, $3 for a pad of 100 labels, add $1.25 for shipping/ handling; "Ten Things You Can Do to Fight Global Warming" poster, $12 postpaid; "Save the Rainforest" T-shirt, $22 postpaid. Publications listed in "Magazines, Newsletters & Brochures" chapter.

Basic membership is $25; benefits include: subscription to the magazine *Friends of the Earth* published 10 times a year; membership kit that highlights current projects and tells about their Activist Members Program; discounts on products and publications.

Funding Exchange, 666 Broadway, 5th floor, New York NY 10012. (212) 529-5300. A funding organization for grassroots movements doing socially and environmentally responsible work.

The Funds for Animals Inc., 200 West

57th St, New York NY 10019. (212) 246-2096 or (212) 246-2632. An animal protection organization dedicated to ending the exploitation and abuse of animals both wild and domestic. The organization is primarily concerned with addressing hunting and trapping issues and they are involved in all areas of the animal rights arena. Projects: actively involved in getting a ban on bowhunting; stopping bear hunting; stopping the bison hunt in Montana; and using the legislative process to strengthen and further animal protection laws.

Publications available to the public: fact sheets on hunting, the book *The Cat Who Came for Christmas* by Cleveland Amory; the book The *Cat and the Curmudgeon, and Man Kind?* by Cleveland Armory; and *The Bowhunting Alternative* by Adrian Benke.

Individual membership is $25; other types of memberships available; newsletters mailed to members.

George Miksch Sutton Avian Research Center, Inc., PO Box 2007, Bartlesville OK 74005. (918) 336-7778. A non-profit research center to conduct scientific studies, conservation projects and educational programs on avian species worldwide. Projects: Southeastern Bald Eagle Restoration Project; Eagle Education program; Indian Government avian consultation project; research on Bald Eagles, Peregrine Falcons, Loggerhead Shrikes, Andean condor, rare birds of the Oklahoma panhandle. Various donor categories, from $10 student/ senior to $25 individual and on up. Bird-related merchandise available: T-shirts, calendars, etc.

Goldman Environmental Foundation, 1160 Battery Street, Suite 400, San Francisco CA 94111. (415) 788-1090. FAX # (415) 986-4779. This foundation sponsors the Goldman Environmental Prize, which is given each year to 6 environmental heroes, one from each of 6 continental regions. Each recipient receives a $60,000 award funded by the foundation. The prizes are awarded for important efforts to preserve or enhance the environment. Certain criteria are important to the prize jury: private citizens and grassroots initiatives are given priority over scientific, academic or governmental activities; and recent achievements are the basis of recognition.

Nominations are accepted from only two sources: a network of 15 internationally known environmental organizations (including Sierra Club, National Audubon Society, World Wildlife Fund, Rainforest Action Network, Nature Conservancy, Environmental Defense Fund, and more); and a confidential panel of environmental experts from 20 nations.

Final selections are made the the Goldman Environmental Prize Jury, which consists of such recognized persons as Bruce Babbitt, former governor of Arizona and Joan Martin Brown, director of the Washington DC office of the United Nations Environment Programme.

Chapter Eleven: Organizations ★

Prize winners have included Lois Gibbs, who organized a grassroots movement and led community efforts at Love Canal, New York, where 22,000 tons of toxic waste were buried beneath the school. She went on to found the Citizens Clearinghouse for Hazardous Wastes (CCHW) and is the author of *Love Canal, My Story.*

Brochure available to the public about the award.

Great Bear Foundation, PO Box 2699, Missoula MT 59806. (406) 721-3009. Dedicated to the conservation of bears and their habitat. Projects: monitoring government agencies responsible for land management decisions that affect bear survival; reimbursing ranchers in selected areas for livestock lost to grizzlies; $100,00 financed a traveling educational exhibit about bears; donates books about bears to rural libraries in order to educate people about both caution and understanding; maintains an information clearinghouse about bears. All members receive *Bear News,* a quarterly newsletter that is a source of information about issues that affect bears and their habitat. Regular individual membership is $20.

Great Lakes United, Cassety Hall, State University College at Buffalo, 1300 Elmwood Avenue, Buffalo NY 14222. (716) 886-0142. Organized to coordinate and promote the efforts of citizens and organizations in the US and Canada to protect and restore the Great Lakes and St. Lawrence River. The ecosystem of these natural resources

has been threatened by toxic chemicals from leaking dumps, discharge from pipes, and rain contamination from pollution. The contamination of the area calls for international cooperation and coordinated citizen action.

The group sponsors workshops, seminars, & public hearings on water quality issues. Information is available to the public on the Great Lakes-St. Lawrence River water quality, citizen guides to legislations and cleanup plans. Membership is $20 for an individual; includes the newsletter *The Great Lakes United* and *Action Updates.* For $10, a donor will receive a Great Lakes wildlife poster.

Green Cross Certification Company, 1611 Telegraph Avenue, Suite 1111, Oakland CA 94612-2113. 1-800-829-1416. This organization provides a list of products that are independently certified to meet environmental standards. One of the standards is to use the highest achievable level of post-consumer recycled content using high-level technology. Certification includes site visits, documentation reviews, and where appropriate, laboratory testing. Certified products are allowed to carry the Green Cross emblem. **Profiled in Part I of this book.**

Greenpeace, USA, 1436 "U" St NW, Washington DC 20009. (202) 462-1177. This international organization campaigns for worldwide legislation to protect the environment. They support bans on commercial whaling; the ban on dumping radioactive wastes; and protest nuclear testing. They are involved with marine animal protection, ocean ecology, toxic waste reduction and nuclear disarmament. The group publicly protested an ENSCO toxic waste disposal plant near Mobile, Arizona. This is an activist society with 2 million US members, 5 million worldwide.

Membership ($20) includes bimonthly *Greenpeace Magazine,* which focuses on issues like habitat loss, global warming, and pollutants. The magazine is now also available on newsstands.

Publications include the brochure *Greenpeace Guide to Paper*, a very informative booklet about why paper manufacturing causes so much damage to the environment and why recycled, unbleached paper is so much better. Also from Greenpeace is *Stepping Lightly on the Earth, Everyone's Guide to Toxics in the Home.*

Grow, Inc., (Grass Roots the Organic Way), 38 Llangollen Lane, Newtown Square PA 19073. (215) 353-2838. Dedicated to informing people about the misuse and overuse of pesticides and to offer alternatives that really work. They also work to influence legislation on the local, state and federal levels pertaining to the spraying of toxic pesticides on lawns, shrubs and trees in residential areas. They offer suggestions on how to protect your lawn and your family at the same time. Fact sheet available which informs people about the various products that they feel are safer for the environment. Membership

is $15 and includes newsletters, various catalogs and articles that deal with effective alternatives to pesticides.

Household Hazardous Waste Project, 901 South National Ave, Box 108, Springfield MO 65804. (417) 836-5777. This is Missouri's project for community education about the safe use, storage and disposal of hazardous products commonly found in and around the home. Local resources are used whenever available. For instance, local businesses are contacted about accepting waste motor oil, batteries, transmission fluid, paint, and other recyclable wastes. Educational institutions, health organizations, and the media are used to disseminate information to the public. This project is a program of Missouri's Environmental Improvement and Energy Resources Authority and the Southwest Missouri State University. It is not a membership organization.

Their booklet *Guide to Hazardous Products Around the Home* has been recognized and used throughout the United States and by the United Nations Environment Programme. It has also been endorsed by Greenpeace, The Cousteau Society, Seventh Generation and *McCall's* Magazine. This manual helps you understand product labels, helps you select safer products before bringing toxic chemicals into your home, helps minimize waste leaving your home, and helps you located recycling options in your community for some types of hazardous waste. $9.95, 178 pages.

Additional resources listed in "Educational Materials" or "Magazines, Newsletters & Brochures" chapters.

Illinois Environmental Protection Agency, 2200 Churchill Rd, PO Box 19276, Springfield IL 62794-9276. (217) 782-2829. Projects: Household Hazardous Waste Pick Up; Volunteer Lake Monitoring Program. Publications listed in "Magazines, Newsletters & Brochures" chapter.

INFACT, National Field Campaign Office, PO Box 3223, South Pasadena CA 91031. (818) 799-9133. This group builds international campaigns to stop the abuses of transnational corporations which endanger the health and survival of people all over the world. Its current campaign is on nuclear weaponmakers to stop the production and promotion of those weapons. Presently, the focus is on General Electric and they request a boycott of all GE products and services. Basic membership is $15 per year.

INFORM, 381 Park Avenue South, New York NY 10016. (212) 689-4040. An environmental organization researching: toxic waste; waste management; air pollution; and water resources. The group does not lobby or litigate but spends its energy on research, reports and communications. Staff members regularly participate in seminars and conferences.

Publications available are listed in "Magazines, Newsletters & Bro-

chures" chapter. *Inform* is a quarterly newsletter that reports on their latest research projects. Basic membership is $25.

The Institute for Earth Education, PO Box 288, Warrenville IL 60555. (708) 393-3096 or (509) 395-2299. Since 1974, Earth Education has been in the process of helping people live more harmoniously and joyously with the natural world. This organization is composed of people who work at trying to live more lightly on the earth. They emphasize environmental learning programs: Sunship Earth®; Earthkeepers®; Earth Caretakers®; and SUNSHIP II®. These programs have information packets ($1 each) to explain how the programs work. The organization sponsors International Earth Education Conferences in which children and adults can experience the various programs and catch up on latest developments in newer programs. Membership starts at $20 and includes the quarterly publication *Talking Leaves*.

Write for free catalog "The Earth Education Sourcebook," which tells about their organization, their programs, and has various interesting products for sale, such as: books, activities, supplemental educational materials, props, posters, seals, cassette tapes, and T-shirts. Many of the materials are designed for children as well as adults. One interesting book title is *The Earth Speaks* ($10.95) by Steve Van Matre and Bill Weiler. This is a collection of images and impressions by those "who have listened to the earth with their hearts," including Rachel Carson (author of *Silent Spring*), poet Walt Whitman, essayist Henry David Thoreau, naturalist John Muir, and more.

An interesting product offered is "Earthwalks" ($10.95) which is a packet of nature activities, applicable for children as well as adults. There's also an "Earth Education Slide Show" ($100) that contains 120 slides and lasts 20 minutes. Designed for 10-12 year olds. T-shirts ($11.50) include such mottos as "Your Mother [earth] is in Trouble," and "This Body is Made out of 100% Recycled Materials." Many more services available, including workshops and speakers. (Also listed under "Educational Materials" chapter and "Seminars, Workshops, and Speakers" chapter.)

Institute for Local Self-Reliance, 2425 18th St NW, Washington DC 20009. (202) 232-4108. FAX # (202) 332-0463. This organization as formed to promote environmentally sustainable community economic development by investigating examples of closed-loop manufacturing, materials policy, materials recovery, energy efficiency, and small scale production. They have done research on recycling technologies, scrap-based manufacturing, and alternative fuels and industrial products from plant matter.

One of their projects has been procuring equity in scrap-based manufacturing by community organizations. Staff members have provided assistance to *Sesame Street* programmers on ecological educational goals. The group conducts the annual National Citizens Training Conference, which focuses on solid waste management for entrepreneurs, citizen and environmental leaders. They also have local workshops.

Books available listed in "Books" chapter.

Institute for Transportation and Development Policy, PO Box 56538, Washington DC 20011. (301) 589-1810. FAX # (301) 589-3453. Promotes alternative, non-motorized transportation in the US and abroad through projects as well as policy advocacy. Projects: Bikes not Bombs (Nicaragua); Bikes for Africa (Mozambique); Mobility Haiti; Transportation Alternatives Project. This group has donated over 4,000 bicycles to overseas development projects. They work with the Peace Corps and other grassroots development groups supplying overseas volunteers with bicycles and training in basic mechanics. Basic membership is $30. Newsletters are sent to all donors and interested parties.

Institute of Scrap Recycling Industries, Inc., 1627 "K" St NW, 7th floor, Washington DC 20006-1704. (202) 466-4050. FAX # (202) 775-9109. TWX 710 822 9782. EasyLink 620 23427. ISRI is the North American trade association of the scrap processing and recycling industry. It represents 1,800 companies that process, broker and consumer scrap commodities, including metals, paper, plastics, glass and textiles. Suppliers of equipment and services to the industry are also members. A primary objective of this association is to bring about a greater awareness of the industry's role in conserving the future through recycling and in increasing recycling by promoting the program Design for Recycling™.

The group provides public education about the benefits of recycling. Publications available to the public: *The Scrap Map: An Environmental Publication for Grades K-6,* a colorful 6 x 9 brochure that explains the concept of recycling and illustrates recycling of automobiles, aluminum cans and newspapers, $15 for package of 30; *The Scrap Map Teachers' Kit,* includes one copy of *The Scrap Map* and also an environmental poster with bulletin board suggestions, Teachers' Guide, information brochures, a list of ISRI chapters, and the booklet *Scrap: America's Ready Resource,* $5 per kit to teachers, schools, libraries and nonprofit organization. Write order on organizational letterhead and enclose payment.

Phoenix: Voice of the Scrap Recycling Industries is a magazine covering recycling processing activities and issues. Published 2-3 times a year; free to government officials, educators, libraries and environmentalists. Write subscription request on organizational letterhead.

"Who is Making a World of Difference for Our World?" brochure available to the public; single copies free.

International Fund for Animal Welfare, 411 Main St #2, PO Box 193, Yarmouth Port MA 02675. (508) 362-6487. FAX # (508) 362-5841. Their mission is to promote and ensure the just and kind treatment of animals and to improve the quality of the lives of animals. They strive to preserve animals from extinction, to prevent and abolish animal cruelty, and to ensure that the offshore Canadian and Norwegian hunt for harp and hood seals in the Atlantic is brought to an end.

The organization was started by Brian Davies in 1969 with the goal of ending the Canadian seal hunt, a goal for which they have made great strides. In 1987, the Canadian government imposed a ban on the commercial hunt of baby whitecoat harp seals. In Europe in 1989, they have voted against the import of any baby sealskins and any products from baby sealskins.

Future projects include: persuading cosmetic companies to end animal experimentation and testing; encouraging South Korea to introduce tough anti-cruelty laws; protecting the elephants of Africa. The organization does not believe in violence as a way to change things for animals. Rather, they encourage people to become aware and write, write, write to legislators and others in power to make the changes. "Action cards" are often included in their mailings and they are pre-addressed to an appropriate individual.

The organization has grown to over 650,000 supporters and has offices in England, Germany, Holland, the Philippines, and Hong Kong as well as

SHOPPING FOR A BETTER WORLD

A QUICK & EASY GUIDE
TO SOCIALLY RESPONSIBLE SUPERMARKET SHOPPING

Updated & Expanded
1990
EDITION

This easy-to-use guide is enormously popular. Available from Council on Economic Priorities.

headquarters in the US. Members receive several newsletters a year keeping them informed of the group's activities.

International Institute for Energy Conservation, 420 "C" St NE, Washington DC 20002. (202) 546-3388. FAX # (202) 546-6978. Telex: 249114 IIEC UR. This organization strives to foster sustainable development through energy efficiency in developing nations. They act as a broker between institutions with experience in energy efficiency technologies and institutions in developing countries with the need for such experience.

Their three major project areas are:

1. Information Dissemination—workshops, conferences and seminars to provide decisionmakers in developing countries with hands-on experience with energy efficiency.

2. Demonstrations—to show energy efficiency. These activities show how a particular efficiency strategy is feasible technologically and financially.

3. Development of Local Energy Conservation Business Activity—Helping foster the growth of businesses with a vested interest in energy conservation.

Izaak Walton League of America, 1401 Wilson Blvd, Level B, Arlington VA 22209. (703) 528-1818. This organization's purpose is to enjoy & defend America's soil, air, woods, waters and wildlife. Special projects include: "Save Our Streams (SOS)," a citizen stream protection program; "Adopt a Wetland;" "Wetland Watch;"

Bumper sticker from the Land Stewardship Project.

and "Outdoor Ethics Program." They provide special reports on air pollution's impact on crops, acid rain and waterfowl, energy efficient lighting, pesticides and wildlife. Their publication list is available upon request. Their membership is $20 and includes a subscription of *Outdoor America* magazine.

The Land Institute, 2440 East Water Well Rd, Salina KS 67401. (913) 823-5376. A private, non-profit organization devoted to sustainable agriculture and good stewardship of the earth. The goal of study and research is to help transform agriculture in order to protect the long term ability of the earth to support a variety of life and culture. Located along the Smoky Hill River southeast of Salina, Kansas.

Projects: education and outreach in the forms of numerous publications listed later; the Prairie Festival, an annual celebration with workshops and arts events; the Land Stewardship Program has a travelling one-act play "Planting in the Dust" that shows the consequences of treating land as a commodity; a community garden that shows the principles of sustainable organic gardening; an internship program (explained in "Educational Materials" chapter).

Publications: *The Land Report* is a 36-40 page journal published three times a year about the Land Institute; *The Land Institute Research Report,* an annual compilation of research results, $3; numerous articles from and about the Land Institute, most about $1. Send for publications list.

Membership starts at $15; all donors of $15 or more receive *The Land Report*.

See also "Educational Material" chapter.

Land Stewardship Project, 14758 Ostlund Trail North, Marine on St. Croix MN 55047. (612) 433-2770. FAX # (612) 433-2704. Supports sustainable agriculture and land stewardship ethics through a variety of services: completion of a 3-year model county stewardship program in Winona County, Minnesota; the formation of Sustainable Farmers Associations with on-farm experimentation and demonstration in SE and western Minnesota; formation of a citizen's campaign urging farmland owning insurance companies to implement conservation practices.

The organization developed the Farmland Stewardship Center, which is an educational and demonstrational showpiece for stewardship farming techniques located near the Twin Cities.

There is no membership structure,

but those who contribute receive a quarterly 20-page newsletter *The Land Stewardship Letter* and those who contribute to the newsletter receive discounts on products in their catalog. The catalog contains books, videos, cultural programs, music, T-shirts and bumper stickers ("Let's Stop Treating Our Soil Like Dirt").

More information in "Educational Materials" and "Books" chapters.

LightHawk, PO Box 8163, Santa Fe NM 87504. (505) 982-9656. Lighthawk provides the advantages of flight to conservation & environmental groups in the US and abroad in order to show an aerial view of environmental problems, especially clearcutting of national forests, to lawmakers, the media and concerned citizens. Their major focus is to halt deforestation in our own country as well as the tropical rainforests. One of their projects is a National Initiative/ Letter-writing Campaign to encourage Congress to fly the Pacific Northwest forests with Lighthawk and see the destruction first-hand.

The group has for sale T-shirts in various colors, $10; The Ancient Forests: A Call to Action video, $14; and various free articles and pamphlets about forest issues. Membership is $35 for an individual. Benefits include a quarterly   12-page newsletter, a bumper sticker, and regular updates of their work by request.

Malachite School & Small Farm, ASR Box 21, Pass Creek Rd, Gardner CO 81040. (719) 746-2412. They teach about leading a sustainable lifestyle and becoming a more responsible citizen of the world. Their programs teach about conservation, waste reduction, recycling practices, self-reliant food sources, and energy efficient homes. Programs available are: field trips, Malachite Elderhostel, Malachite farmstays, Malachite retreats, Malachite weeks, Malachite hostel program; and Malachite internships.

Malachite recently sponsored an educational presentation for Gardner School. Students learned about global warming, acid rain, endangered animals, and rain forest destruction.

Malachite is an educational organization and welcomes donations. Newsletters sent to all donors.

Marine Mammal Stranding Center, PO Box 773, Brigantine NJ 08302. (609) 266-0538. Rescues stranded whales, dolphins, seals and sea turtles that was ashore on New Jersey beaches. Whenever possible, the animals are brought back to the Center for rehabilitation and eventual release. The museum is open weekends for tours. Volunteers are welcome. Individual membership is $15.

National Arbor Day Foundation, 211 North 12th St, Lincoln NE 68508. (402) 474-5655. Dedicated to tree planting and conservation. Projects: Tree City USA which has helped over 1000 American cities establish their own comprehensive urban forestry tree-care programs; Conservation

Chapter Eleven: Organizations

Trees demonstrates the long-term value of planting, managing and preserving trees; Celebrate Arbor Day! an annual observation across 50 states plus several other countries; Trees for America program has planted more then 10 million trees in America; and "Grow Your Own Tree" and "Trees are Terrific" educational programs designed for grades K-6.

Introductory membership is $10 and the member receives 10 Colorado blue spruce trees as well as a subscription to the bimonthly *Arbor Day* publication. The magazine is packed with how-to tips such as how to become fuel-wood self-sufficient, how to water a tree to maintain its health and vigor, how to keep a Christmas tree fresh and fragrant, and how proper mulching will improve tree growth.

National Audubon Society, 950 Third Ave., New York NY 10022. (212) 832-3200. This organization's purpose is to conserve native plants and animals and their habitats, to protect life from pollution and toxic substances, to seek solutions to global environmental and population problems, and to promote the use and development of renewable energy sources. Since 1905, this group has provided publications, scientific investigations, educational services, lobbying efforts, nature centers, and television programs. There are now over 550,000 members, 510 local chapters, 9 regional offices, and 370 staff members nationwide.

The Audubon Society has been actively involved with policymakers,

not only nationally, but internationally. They support the United Nation's Environmental Programme.

They protect wildlife and natural areas through a system of 80 sanctuaries. They have a permanent staff of scientists that keep their facts up-to-date. Members and the public has been provided with information about environmental issues. Six education centers conduct outdoor classes, community outreach programs, and workshops for training leaders. Travel-study programs are also offered, as well as field seminar on specific skills.

Presently, their high-priority campaigns include: the ancient forests of the Northwestern United States and the animals that face extinction along with the forests; Arctic National Wildlife Refuge to preserve wilderness that may be lost to oil development; saving the wetlands of the United States; and saving the Platte River wildlife areas of Nebraska.

For just $20 the first year (introductory rate), individuals can become members of the Society and receive their bimonthly magazine *Audubon.* Other membership benefits include membership in one of the 500 local chapters; free or reduced admission to Audubon nature centers; invitations to their ecology camps, workshops, and tours; and discounts on nature books, collectibles and gifts.

Other publications of the society include *American Birds,* an ornithological journal; *Audubon Activist,* a monthly newsjournal available to all those who wish to join Audubon's

Activist Network and make a commitment to take action; *Action Alerts* for the activists to advise them of pending legislation; and the annual *Audubon Wildlife Report* that examines federal and state agencies responsible for the management of natural areas and wildlife.

Free to the public are: the Audubon Fact Sheet which describes the organizations philosophy and activities; and Conservation Notebook sheets, one called "Planet Earth: Coming to the Rescue," and another called "Global Climate Change and What You Can Do About It."

National Coalition Against the Misuse of Pesticides (NCAMP), 701 E Street SE, Washington DC 20003. (202) 543-5450. Formed in 1981 as a national network committed to pesticide safety and the adoption of alternative pest management strategies which reduce or eliminate a dependency on toxic chemicals. The organization's primary goal is to effect change through local action and to provide individuals with information on the hazards of toxic pesticides. NCAMP has also sought to bring about federal policy changes. Information about the organization is provided through their newsletters, *Pesticides and You* (about 5 times a year) and *NCAMP's Technical Report* (monthly). A recent issue of *Pesticides and You* included pesticide statistics update, setback for victim rights, a notice that toxic pest strips have returned to the market, more news clips, "chemicalWATCH", and a list of

resources. A compilation of back issues is available. Other publications include a *chemicalWATCH* that tracks chemical effects and alternatives, and *State & Local Pesticide Ordinances: A Compilation of Legislation and Regulation Regarding Pesticide Right-to-Know and Posting and Notification,* which includes laws from 16 states. Brochures include "Least Toxic Control of Lawn Pests" and "Pesticides and Your Fruits and Vegetables."

NCAMP held the Seventh National Pesticide Forum in Washington DC, in March, 1989. The annual event brought together over 200 people from across the country as an opportunity for an exchange of information pertaining to pesticide hazards. In addition, networking is one of the function of the organization, putting people in touch with each other.

The organization has joined an effort with the Trial Lawyers for Public Justice to protect the rights of those poisoned by pesticide to obtain compensation for their injuries. NCAMP has also testified before federal agencies and has published various articles in local and national publications.

Individual regular memberships are $20.

National Parks & Conservation Association, 1015 31st St NW, Washington DC 20007. (202) 944-8530. Dedicated to the protection and improvement of the National Park System. They have developed a Park System Plan: a comprehensive guide to management of our national parks.

Chapter Eleven: Organizations

Books and videos available at their Park Education Center. Membership is $25 and members receive the magazine *National Parks* and the opportunity to be involved in citizen action for park protection.

National Wildflower Research Center, 2600 FM 973 North, Austin TX 78725. (512) 929-3600. Created by Lady Bird Johnson in 1982. Purpose: to conduct research on the conservation and use of wildflowers and native plants and to promote their use in planned landscapes. Using wildflowers and native grasses in public spaces and roadways can reduce the need for other high-cost maintenance and restores the unique, regional character of the habitat. The organization's current research projects include germination experiments, the study of seed mixes, the generation of more information about native seed crop production, and land restoration projects, among others.

The organization maintains a clearinghouse of information on native plants. Materials available include over 250 fact sheets (there's a fact sheet order form). The Center's library contains numerous volumes on native plant propagation, landscaping, and identification. Slides are available for use in publications and programs. The Public Information Office fields thousands of questions annually and assists media as well as individuals.

Major events at the Center include special spring and fall tours, although if you're in the area, they welcome visi-

tors year-round. There's a daily self-guided tour. They also host "Wildflower Days" festivals, with lectures, workshops, arts and crafts. Spring and fall landscaping seminars are conducted each year.

Publications include the membership newsletter *Wildflower* and the magazine *Wildflower, Journal of the National Wildflower Research Center,* published 6 times annually. These are available only to members. Basic individual membership fee is $25. 17,000 members worldwide.

A gift catalog is available. Interesting items in this catalog include alphabet T-shirt for kids (with a different wildflower for each letter) $10.95; wildflower coasters, 4 for $22.95; notecards, 10 for $7; handcrafted leather wildflower pins, $12.50 each; and a hand-enameled copper box, $120. Books also available.

National Wildlife Federation, 1400 16th St NW, Washington DC 20036-2266. Organized to protect our country's natural resources and wildlife. Also fighting for clean air and water.

Natural Organic Farmers Association, c/o Hawson Kittredge, RFD #2, Sheldon Rd, Barre MA 01005. (508) 355-2853. Promotes organic agriculture. They have a map of organic growers in these states: MA, NH, VT, CT, RI, NY, NJ, Ontario. Provides organic certification of farms.

Natural Resource Defense Council, 40

West 20th St, New York NY 10011. (212) 727-2700. Membership department, zip 10114-0466. This organization has worked for 20 years—through effective litigation, persistent advocacy, and hard-hitting research—to protect our air, water and food supplies. The NRDC has led the fight against acid rain, has fought for enforcement of the Clean Air Act, and has been dedicated to improving the quality of the urban environment. There are over 130,000 members.

Their "Mothers and Others for Pesticide Limits" program was instrumental in gaining the ban against the use of the pesticide Alar on apple crops. This project publishes a newsletter called *tlc: truly loving care for our kids and our planet*. The newsletter focuses on ideas for a healthier planet, gives update news on their programs, includes resources, and has activities for kids.

The NRDC has programs in energy efficiency and energy conservation. They also practice what they preach. Their New York office features state-of-the-art energy conservation technology.

The NRDC has a "Rainforest Rescue Catalog" which features items such as: "Rescue the Rainforest" T-shirts (adult $14.95, child $12.95); *Amazon Days, Amazon Nights* audio tape recorded on location in Brazil's Amazon jungle ($7.95); *The Rainforest Book: How You Can Save the World's Rainforests* for people who want to translate their concern into action ($5.95); and *Color the Rainforest* coloring book ($4.95). All proceeds from these NRDC sales go to rainforest protection programs.

Members receive four issues of *The Amicus Journal,* an award-winning magazine of environmental thought and opinion, and five issues of the *NRDC Newsline,* which keeps you informed of NRDC programs and publications. In addition, members receive timely alerts and updates on NRDC work so that you can help influence important environmental policies.

Nature Conservancy, 1815 N. Lynn St, Arlington VA 22209. (703) 841-5300. This group works to preserve nature sanctuaries, such as wetlands, forests, prairies, and tropical rainforests. They purchase land, encourage protection from private land owners, and manage more than 1,000 preserves. They have protected over 3.5 million acres. They have a database and a national inventory of species found in each state. Membership is $15; benefits includes bimonthly *The Nature Conservancy Magazine* and chapter information.

New Alchemy Institute, 237 Hatchville Rd, East Falmouth MA 02536. (508) 564-6301. Dedicated to an ecological future. Located on a 12-acre farm on Cape Cod, Massachusetts, New Alchemy serves students, teachers, gardeners, small-scale farmers and communities with research and education projects on food, energy, water and waste treatment systems. Their research, education and networking agenda seeks to build and strengthen the connections essential to balanced, healthful farms and ecosystems, neighborhoods and communities. They choose to develop food-producing systems that work with and emulate natural processes, and are devoted to land stewardship, resource conservation, recycling, and bioregionally appropriate design.

Current projects focus on landscape design, organic market gardening, greenhouse horticulture, integrated pest management, composting and cover crops.

Educational programs include on-site tours, courses, school and community programs and publications. Internships are available, as well are volunteer opportunities. Their Green Classroom is a garden-based science program in the Falmouth, Massachusetts, schools. This program can be used throughout New England. A teachers' manual is available.

Membership is $35 and includes a subscription to the New Alchemy Quarterly, free admission for tours, reduced tuition for courses and special events, and a 10% discount on books and products in their store.

New Jersey Environmental Federation, 808 Belmar Plaza, Belmar NJ 07719. (201) 280-8988. Statewide organization fighting to protect natural resources and clean up pollution sources. Membership includes 45 groups and over 60,000 people. The organization encourages consumers and businesses to switch to environmentally-sensible products; they work for strict laws reducing the use of toxic pesticides; and they are pushing for waste reduction and recycling efforts.

This organization has helped pass important federal and state laws, including the Superfund, Clean Water and Clean Air Acts. They started the Home SAFE Home program to educate consumers about environmentally-wise products. This program can be rented from the organization and set up as a house tour with 22 household products, folding panel exhibits, and instructions. The organization has also educated voters on the records of candidates for public office, and they have

Chapter Eleven: Organizations

joined labor unions to win citizen suits that protect both factory workers and the environment.

Publications include their quarterly newsletter *Clean Water Action,* which comes with subscribing membership ($24) and monthly New Jersey updates, which come with sustaining membership ($60). Other membership fees includes $2 for a four-month membership (no newsletter) and $6 for annual dues (no newsletter). Another publication is the "Home SAFE Home Chart of Household Alternatives," an 11 x 17 chart that lists safe alternatives for 20 categories of household products. $2 each, group discounts available. "Lawn Care Without Toxic Chemicals," a letter-size flyer gives information on non-toxic lawn care including a supplies source list for central New Jersey. 25¢ each, group discounts available. "Every Citizen's Environmental Handbook," is a 44-page illustrated handbook expanding the information on the Home SAFE Home chart, listing steps consumers can take to further protect the environment, including environmental shopping. There are charts that show specific brand names that are toxic. (Examples: Easy-Off oven cleaner is listed as toxic; Arm & Hammer washing soda is non-toxic and environmentally safe.) Price: $5, quantity discounts available.

North American Native Fishes Association, 123 West Mt. Airy Ave., Philadelphia PA 19119. (215) 247-0384. Founded to bring together people interested in fishes native to this continent for conservation, and aquaristic appreciation of native fishes through observation, study and research; and to assemble and distribute information on native fishes. NANFA provides a networking of people around the continent about who is interested in what. They have a readily available computerized, regularly-updated list of North American fish species listed by federal, state, and provincial governments as endangered, threatened, or special-status; and a directory of native fish articles that appeared in aquarium publications 1946-1981.

American Currents is a quarterly magazine featuring articles on finding, collecting, keeping, observing, conserving, and breeding North American fishes; and news about aquaristics, laws, the environment, scientific literature and developments, and other sources of information. *Darter* is a newsletter published approximately six times a year. Membership to NANFA is $11 year, includes the magazine and newsletter.

Nukewatch, PO Box 2658, Madison WI 53701. (608) 256-4146. Provides education about—and non-violent resistance to—nuclear weapons. Special projects include the Missouri Peace Planting Direct Action, mapping of nuclear weapons, and mapping of H-Bomb truck routes. Publications available are: *Nuclear Heartland* (book); *Prisoner's on Purpose* (book); *Crossing the Line* (book) and maps of land-based nuclear weapons locations. Also available are T-shirts and postcards.

PRC Introduces New Bag

PRC has introduced a new cloth shopping bag for environmentally concerned shoppers.

The bag, which is made of sturdy canvas, comes in two sizes, 13" x 15" ($6.95) and 15" x 20" ($9.95).

The larger bag holds slightly more than a large kraft bag. To order, send checks for the appropriate amount to PRC, P.O. Box 88, Media, PA 19063.

Suggested membership is $20 per year.

One Person's Impact, PO Box 751, Westborough MA 01581. (508) 366-0146. This organization's goal is to provide the resource to enable individuals and organizations to incorporate social, economic and environmental responsibility into all aspects of life. Their projects include: the bimonthly newsletter *One Person's Impact: Practical Actions for Conscious Living;* LIFEtracks workshops for groups and businesses; special reports and guides such as "Environmental Basics for Business" with Resource Directory; "One Kid's Impact;" "Changing Diapers" survey and results; "Earth Year Action Guide;" and an information referral service. Individual membership is $24.

Pan North America Regional Center, 965 Mission St #514, San Francisco CA 94103. (415) 541-9140. FAX # (415) 541-9253. Telex: 15683472

PANNA. Econet: PANNA.

This is the Pesticide Action Network (PAN) which is a worldwide coalition of over 300 non-governmental organizations in more than 50 countries working to stop pesticide misuse and global pesticide proliferation. Local groups can become affiliates of this organization. Affiliate organizations receive a subscription to the *Global Pesticide Campaigner* newsletter and a 10% discount off other publications they distribute.

This group is the coordinator of the Dirty Dozen Campaign, a long-term international public education vehicle targeting selected "Dirty Dozen" pesticides. Elimination of the Dirty Dozen will represent both significant reductions in hazard and a powerful demonstration of the power of individual and collective efforts.

Their quarterly newsletter is the *Global Pesticide Campaigner* and their bimonthly publication is the *PANNA Outlook.*

Poster & charts available are:

"Circle of Poison: What Goes Around Comes Around" by Doug Minkler, 20' x 26', $18; "Pesticides Don't Know When to Stop Killing" the official "Dirty Dozen" International Campaign poster, also available in Spanish, 17' x 22', $5; "Demise of the Dirty Dozen" is a chart listing bans and severe restrictions of Dirty Dozen pesticides in 60 countries, includes resource list and action ideas, $3.

Books available from them are listed in "Books" chapter.

Pennsylvania Resources Council, PO Box 88, Media PA 19063. (215) 565-9131. 1-800-GO-TO-PRC. This is an environmental group known for: recycling and waste reduction expertise; technical and educational publications; conferences, videos & seminars; materials for teachers; and an environmental shopping campaign. They conduct an annual national environmental shopping conference and organize the largest annual recycling conference in the East. They have provided networking for buyers and sellers of recyclables.

Individual membership is $30; benefits include: Environmental Shopping Update; publications free or at cost; reduced fees for seminars; technical assistance; and reduced rate subscription to *Resource Recycling* and *Biocycle.*

Many resources listed in "Educational Materials" and "Magazines, Newsletters & Brochures" chapters.

Additional items available from the organization: Environmental Shopping Poster, 17" x 22", outlines the 4 R's of Environmental Shopping: Reduce, Reuse, Recycle and Reject, $1.25; Become An Environmental Shopper button, 20¢; Environmental Shopping Kit has handbook, products list, poster, button and shopping update, $5; Environmental Shopping Reusable Bag in canvas, two sizes; Recycling button, green on white 1" button with "Recycling Makes ene," 20¢; Recycling stickers, 3.5" x 7.5", 25¢; Recycling pin with state of Pennsylvania with gold recycling logo, $2.50; "I Pledge Not to Litter" button, 20¢; "Don't Be a Litterbug" sign, 11" x 14", free with $5 order on request.

People for the Ethical Treatment of Animals, (PETA), PO Box 42516, Washington DC 20015. (301) 770-7444. This group works for more humane treatment of animals. They have focused on the exploitation of animals for laboratory use. They have an anti-fur campaign and a vegetarian campaign. Basic membership is $15 and includes the bimonthly *PETA News.*

Planet Drum Foundation, Box 31251, San Francisco CA 94131. (415) 285-6556. Founded in 1974 to provide an effective grassroots approach to ecology that emphasizes sustainability, community self-determination and regional self-reliance. Planet Drum developed the concept of a bioregion: a distinct area with coherent and interconnected plant and animal communities that is a whole life-place with unique requirements for human habitation so that it will not be disrupted. Planet Drum's Green City Program puts together representatives from business, government, and activist organizations to put forth recommendations for changes in municipal policy. This program that serves the San Francisco area has been a model for other regions.

The organization's publications include *A Green City Program for San Francisco Bay Area Cities and Towns* by Peter Berg, Beryl Magilavy and Seth Zuckerman, $5.95. This book provides agendas for short- and long-range changes, and visions of what a green city would be like. Their book *Reinhabiting a Separate Country: A Bioregional Anthology of Northern California* by Peter Berg, $7, is a collection of essays, natural history, biography, poems and stories revealing Northern California as a distinct bioregion.

The group has a "Catalogue of Bioregional Primary Sources," which contains 22 bioregional reprints, ranging in price from 35¢ to $3.15 each. Includes such titles as "Bioregional Green" by Kirkpatrick Sale, "Living There" by Seth Zuckerman, "Why I am a Bioregionalist" by Gene Marshall.

The San Francisco office contains a fine library of bioregional references and other ecology-related material. The organization provides networking services to start new bioregional groups and to find resources. The group maintains a directory of bioregional groups. Planet Drum is planning to open a Green City Center (pro-

jected date fall 1991), which will be a place to demonstrate techniques and activities of urban sustainability and which will educate the public about them and influence municipal policies.

Staff members, especially Peter Berg, Director of Planet Drum Foundation, and Judy Goldhaft, present talks and conduct seminars and workshops on bioregional topics for community, college and activist groups. Some typical workshops are: Reinhabiting a Life-Place; How to Start and Maintain a Bioregional Group; How to Educate Others About Bioregionalism. Some typical topics for talks include: Bioregional Life-Place Politics; Bioregions as the Basis of Community Consciousness; and Urban Dwelling from a Bioregional Perspective.

Special Performances. Peter and Judy are both performers who have worked with the San Francisco Mime Troupe, and are available for special performances within their topics. Recently Judy created "Water Web," a 20-minute rap and movement about water cycles and our relationship to them. "Water Web" premiered to a standing ovation at a recent bioregional workshop in Anchorage, Alaska. Peter performs a 45-minute eco-comedy routine that is in constant demand.

Membership to Planet Drum is $20 (U.S.) for one year and includes 2 issues of the newsletter *Raise the Stakes,* the book *Devolutionary Notes,* and *Ecocity Conference 1990.*

Population Reference Bureau, 1875 Connecticut Ave NW, Suite 520,

Washington DC 20009. (202) 483-1100. Population Reference Bureau is a private, nonprofit scientific and educational organization that gathers, interprets and disseminates information about population. The group seeks to increase awareness and understanding of population trends and their implications.

Publications for sale: *Food and Population: Beyond Five Billion*, 40 pages; *World Population in Transition*, 52 pages; *Population Resources, Environment: An Uncertain Future*, 44 pages; *Africa's Expanding Population: Old Problems, New Policies*, 52 pages; *Population Pressures in Latin America*, 50 pages.

Basic individual membership is $45.

Programme for Belize, PO Box 1088, Vineyard Haven MA 02568. (508) 693-0856. FAX # (508) 693-6311. Toll-free 1-800-343-8009. They actively purchase acres of jungle in the 110,000 Rio Bravo Conservation Area in northwestern Belize, Central America. Their "Gift for the Planet" program offers interested parties the chance to protect an acre of tropical forest in Belize for a contribution of $50. The contribution is acknowledged with a frameable certificate of appreciation, made out to the name you choose. It could be used as a gift for someone who has everything else. Free information available.

Additional materials from the organization: "Tropical Forest" is a 17" x 13" color poster, $22; slide show available that shows the tropical area and explains the Programme.

Rainforest Action Movement, 430 E University, Ann Arbor MI 48109. (313) 662-0232. This is a community and University based group committed to educating and raising awareness about tropical and temperate rainforests in an effort to prevent their destruction. They are working to effect change by educating people to the fact that it is in our common interest to preserve these forests. They have lobbied copy stores to carry recycled paper products; they have planted thousands of trees on private and public land in Michigan. They educate individuals on consumer and personal habits that will save trees. The organizations gives an annual $500 grant to an undergraduate or graduate student for research on rainforest-related issues. A T-shirt is available with a colorful rainforest scene on the front, and bulldozer clearing a forest on the back. Each T-shirt is $12 and purchases and protects 10% of an acre of rainforest.

Publication: *Tropical Echoes* 16-page quarterly newsletter, very informative. One recent issue included such articles as: "Hawaii: Is Geothermal Development Really Needed?"; "Mitsubishi: On the Wrong Road," about the company's use of exotic woods and urging boycott of their products; information on Georgia-Pacific and Weyerhauser companies and their importation of exotic hardwoods; "The Ongoing Struggle of the Yanomami," about this Brazilian tribe's struggle for existence.

Chapter Eleven: Organizations

Brochure: "7 things you can do to help save the rainforests." Membership is $10 for one year and includes newsletter; $20 gives you one year membership plus a T-shirt.

Rainforest Action Network, 301 Broadway, Suite A, San Francisco CA 94133. (415) 398-4404. FAX # (415) 398-2732. This is a non-profit activist organization working to save the world's rainforests. RAN works internationally in cooperation with other environmental and human rights organizations on major campaigns to protect rainforests. Eight active campaigns include: US tropical timber imports; Japanese corporations in the rainforests; Sarawak Malaysian rainforests; Hawaiian rainforests; World Bank/ MDBs in the rainforests; tribal crisis in the rainforest; oil exploration in the rainforest.

They publish a resources list that tells where you can obtain books and educational materials about the rainforests. From them you can obtain: T-shirts, "Save the Rainforest," "Iguana on the Pocket," "Rainforest Action Network" with their panther logo or with a leopard face; The 1990 Rainforest Wall Calendar, $9.95; Hugg-a-Planet, a soft globe for children, $18.95; "Save the Rainforest" or "Red-eyed Tree Frog" poster, Rainforest Action Network stickers, roll of 25 for $4.95.

Basic membership is $14; benefits include Monthly Action Alerts and the quarterly *World Rainforest Report*.

Rocky Mountain Institute, 1739 Snowmass Creek Rd, Old Snowmass CO 81654. (303) 927-3128. This is a non-profit resource center concerned with energy conservation and renewable resources such as sun, wind, and water. Publication list available.

Save Mt. Graham Fund, PO Box 15451, Phoenix AZ 85060-5451. This organization is fighting against the astronomy site established on Mount Graham by the University of Arizona (Tucson). According to this group, the area has 18 plants and animals found nowhere else in the world, and the development of the astronomy site has endangered these species. They have begin a lawsuit and legislation to require Endangered Species Act compliance on Mount Graham.

Save the Dunes Council, 444 Barker Rd, Michigan City IN 46360. (219) 879-3937. Formed by concerned citizens of Indiana in 1952 for the preservation and protection of the Indiana Dunes for public use and enjoyment, the Council has been involved in a long battle against industrial interests. Finally, in 1966, legislation was passed that established the Indiana Dunes National Lakeshore. But still the battle is not won, because transforming the law into the reality of a national park has not occurred. The Council is still working to acquire more lands, to build more hiking and biking trails, and to urge members to pressure elected officials to support the dunes projects. Benefits of membership include newsletters, spe-

 Chapter Eleven: Organizations

cial alert notices, and two banquets a year with guest speakers.

Sea Shepherd, PO Box 7000-S, Redondo Beach CA 90277. They wish to halt the killing of whales, seals, dolphins and all endangered marine wildlife. They are activists & lobbyists. You may have seen them on TV—they were the first to paint seal pups to protect them from club swinging sealers. They have been involved in active confrontations with whaling ships, going as far as ramming the sides of guilty ships. They have put seven illegal whaling ships out of business, seven of which were sunk. (They have injured no people in these activities.) They have blockaded Canadian sealing ships to keep them from the seals. Basic membership starts at $25.

Sierra Club, 730 Polk Street, San Francisco CA 94109. (415) 776-2211. This organization's purpose is to explore, enjoy, and protect the earth. Their members are often adventurists who, because of their love of their outdoor activities, have become environmentalists as well. Sierra Club arranges organized trips and outings, such as trips to the Arctic Wildlife Refuge, to California's Kings Canyon Park, or to the Himalayas. Nationally, more than 250 outings are offered annually, and local chapters offer more than 8,000 outings annually. A program called "Inner City Outings" provides outdoor experiences for urban youth and disabled persons.

Members are also conservational-

ists, being at the forefront of environmental action. Sierra Club was an early leader in the fight against the use of DDT and played a role in passing the critical Superfund legislation.

Sierra Club Books provides education through nearly 350 titles. The Sierra Club Books address is: 100 Bush St., 13th Floor, San Francisco CA 94104. (415) 291-1600.

Their publications include the magazine *Sierra,* which has been published since 1893 and is an award-winning, four-color publication filled with environmental articles, commentary and photography. Members receive this magazine 6 times a year. Other publications are the *National News Report,* which is a summary of legislative news concerning the environment; *Source Book,* their catalog of brochures, books, videos, posters and other products; and local chapter newsletters. The brochure "Sierra Club Environmental Resources" is an order form for books and brochures with two prices—one for nonmembers, and a discounted price for members. Categories of publications that can be orders from this form are "Be an Environmental Activist," "Politics and the Environment," "Environmental Education," "Air Pollution," "Protecting America's Public Lands," "Global Warming," and more. One brochure that can be ordered for 50¢ is about environmental educational materials (item #206). You can order a clean air poster for $5 (item #303). For $1 you can order "What You Can Do to Save Tropical Rainforests" (item

#530).

Individual memberships start at $33 with discounts for seniors, students, and limited income members.

Society for Ecological Restoration, 1207 Seminole Hwy, Madison WI 53711. (608) 262-9547. Involved with such project as the Winagre Basin Project that encourages the public to develop a positive relationship with the natural landscape by such activities as girdling trees and collecting seeds in the University of Wisconsin—Madison Arboretum. Basic individual membership starts at $30. Members receive twice-a-year journal, quarterly newsletter, networking data base, and conference invitations.

Soil & Water Conservation Society, 7515 Northeast Ankeny Rd, Ankeny IA 50021. A nonprofit scientific and educational association dedicated to the promotion of wise use of land and water resources worldwide. Source for the brochure "Treasure of Abundance—or Pandora's Box? A Guide for Safe, Profitable Fertilizer and Pesticide Use;" free.

Student Conservation Association, PO Box 550, Charlestown NH 03603. (603) 826-4301. FAX # (603) 826-7755. SCA is an educational organization that provides high school and college students as well as others with the opportunity to volunteer their services for the better management of parks and public lands. The group is a provider of a highly regarded professional training program for thousands of young people.

Special projects include the Resource Assistant Program (about 800 positions available yearly), High School Work Groups (groups of 6-10 participants working on trail construction, wildlife habitat improvement, archaeological field survey work, etc), and the Yellowstone Recovery Project (helping repair damaged trails, campsites, etc that occurred from the 1988 fire). Each year Wilderness Work Skills Training Workshops are conducted at 10-15 locations across the nation. Environmental subjects studied are conservation, nature study, river preservation, and wildlife.

Publishes *Job Scan,* a monthly environmental & natural resource job listing. Subscription is 6 months for $22 (discounted to $18 for members).

Student Pugwash USA, 1638 "R" St NW, Suite 32, Washington DC 20009. (202) 328-6555 for non-students. For students 1-800-WOW-A-PUG. A non-profit educational organization run by students and young professionals to provide university students with a range of programs to prepare them to better understand the social and ethical dimensions of science and technology. Environmental issues are some that are addressed through conferences, regional and local activities & new careers programs.

Publications include: *Tough Questions,* the quarterly newsletter; *Pugwatch,* the monthly chapter bulletin; and *New Careers: Directory of Jobs and Internships in Technology & Society*, a listing of over 150 organizations across the country which have ongoing needs for students and recent graduates, $20 postpaid.

Membership to the organization is free.

Tranet, PO Box 567, Rangeley ME 04970. (207) 864-2252. A transnational network of, by and for people who are participating in global transformation—people who are changing the world by changing their own lives, people who are adopting alternative technologies. They are promoting an emerging new transnational world order in which people-to-people networks will complement and ameliorate the UN/ nation-state systems: a world order in which each individual will have a multitude of paths through which he can improve his own well-being and participate in global world governance. They believe that the global transition we are in affects every aspect of our lives from our inner spiritual beings to the political organizations of the earth.

Special projects carried out by Tranet are: "The Relevance of A.T. Developments in the USA to the Third World;" "Technology for Rural Development;" "The TRANET Clearinghouse" which answers queries from members and others seeking to share expertise; and other projects.

Their quarterly newsletter contains information on topics such as: biodynamic gardening; personal transformation; homesteading; holistic health; alternative energy sources.

Trees for Life, 1103 Jefferson, Wichita KS 67203. (316) 263-7294. A nonprofit organization that helps people worldwide plant and maintain trees. Planting trees that produce food is one way to fight hunger. They have helped plant over 8 million fruit trees, and before the end of this decade they plant to plant 92 million more.

"Project Trees for Life" creates and awareness and provides trees for the world. This project is for grade school children and includes a planting carton for each child, non-toxic seeds, and a teacher's workbook about hunger facts and planting instructions plus other activities. The cost is $10 postpaid for 15 students, $15 postpaid for 30 students. Sample kit is $2 ppd.

Products available from this organization are: "Let There Be Trees," "Kids Care," or "Trees: Kids Care" buttons, $1 each, minimum order 5— each button purchased helps plant trees; "Let There Be Trees" bumper stickers, $1 each plus 50¢ postage; "Let There Be Trees" T-shirts, various sizes and prices.

Newsletters and information available free upon request.

TreePeople, 12601 Mulholland Drive, Beverly Hills CA 90210. (818) 753-4600. This nonprofit "urban forestry" organization teaches people how to plant and care for trees. The group has planted more than 2 million trees in the Los Angeles area and have been instrumental in the planting of 200 million trees worldwide. Los Angeles school-

Pin and bumper sticker available from Trees for Life.

children have taken part in TreePeople programs. Basic membership is $25; benefits include the bimonthly *Seedling News* and free tree seedlings.

The Trust for Public Land, 116 New Montgomery St, 4th Floor, San Francisco CA 94105. (415) 495-4014. FAX # (415) 495-4103. This organization's purpose is to work with public agencies and citizens' groups to acquire land of scenic, recreational, historical or cultural value for public use in urban, rural and wilderness areas. Since its founding in 1972, the Trust has protected almost 500,000 acres in 37 states and Canada and comprises a network of real estate, finance and law experts.

Committed to sharing knowledge of nonprofit land acquisition techniques and pioneering new methods of land conservation and environmentally sound land use, the Trust provides training for, and collaborates with, community land trusts—nonprofit community conservation groups that preserve cherished local landscapes.

Their magazine *Land & People* is published three times a year and is available at no cost to donors. This magazine lists the projects by geographical area.

Union of Concerned Scientists, 26 Church St, Cambridge MA 02238. (617) 547-5552. This organization of nearly 100,000 scientists and individuals is concerned about the impact of advanced technology on society. This group is an advocate to energy strategies that minimize risks to public health and safety and minimize damage to the global environment. They have built an extensive and effective lobbying program. They provide expert testimony and analysis to congressional committees and participate in several legislative coalitions. Research and public education are also programs of this group. They organized a week of education on global warming at hundreds of universities in 1989.

More listed in "Magazines, Newsletters & Brochures," "Books" and in "Educational Materials" chapter.

United Nations Environmental Programme, North American Office, Room DC2-803, New York NY

10017. (212) 963-8139. Dedicated to developing and monitoring environmental programs worldwide, particularly in third world countries. Wide variety of brochures available.

University Research Expeditions Program (UREP), University of California, Berkeley CA 94720. (415) 642-6586. This program provides hands-on field research experiences to students, teachers and the general public by supporting important University of California research at sites around the world. There are worldwide field research projects in the natural and social sciences, including environmental studies, animal behavior, archaeology, arts, anthropology and marine studies. Scholarships for teachers and students are available. Free catalog of expeditions and seasonal updates.

U.S. PIRG (The United States Public Interest Research Group), 215 Pennsylvania Ave SE, Washington DC 20003. (202) 546-9707. A national, non-partisan, non-profit research and advocacy organization funded by citizen contributions. Conducts independent research and lobbies for consumer and environmental protections. Recent measures they have helped to pass include: 1986 strengthening of the Superfund; 1986 Safe Drinking Water Act; 1987 Clean Water Act. Their continuing efforts include: calling for drastic cuts in acid rain-causing pollutants with stronger auto emissions standards; working for swift and thorough clean up of toxic waste dumps; supporting

eliminations of CFCs and cutting of carbon dioxide emissions by increasing energy efficiency; controlling use of pesticides and improving food monitoring procedures; working to reduce, recycle and reuse trash.

Publications of this organizations include the quarterly report, *Citizen Agenda,* which is an 8-page newsletter that provides updates on recent legislation, news briefs, state updates, and profiles of individuals who are making a difference.

Membership starts at $15 for an individual 6-month membership; $25 for an individual 1-year membership. Publications available listed in "Magazines, Newsletters & Brochures" chapter.

Washington Citizens for Recycling Foundation, 216 First Ave South #260, Seattle WA 98104. (206) 343-5171. Their mission is to conserve our natural resources by promoting energy and material conservation with emphasis on the most ecologically sound methods of solid and hazardous waste management, especially through promotion of waste reduction, reuse, and recycling. They also wish to educate and encourage action by citizens, government and industry to further these goals.

Accomplishments: they have helped to initiate the first variable garbage can rate in the nation and helped the implementation of Seattle's curbside recycling program; they encouraged the use of refillable bottles by Rainier Brewery; they have products

THE WILDERNESS SOCIETY LOGO

"Packaging Awards and Booby Prizes from an Environmental Point of View" that received national coverage; they implemented a comprehensive recycling program for students in Seattle schools; they sponsored "Recyclathons" at a Washington University. Basic membership is $20 a year and includes a quarterly newsletter.

West Virginia Division of Natural Resources, 1900 Kanawha Blvd, E., Capitol Complex, Building 3, Charleston WV 25305. (304) 348-2754. FAX # (304) 348-2768. Recycling Section: (304) 348-3370. Projects: Youth Conservation Program; Adopt-A-Highway; Litter Control & Recycling. Fourteen state municipalities are currently involved in curbside recycling projects. Brochure available found in "Magazines, Newsletters & Brochures" chapter.

The Wilderness Society, 900 17th St NW, Washington DC 20006. (202) 833-2300. Dedicated to the protection of national forests, national parks and other wild lands. Projects include letter-writing campaigns to the Secretary of Agriculture protesting the "abuse and mismanagement" our national Forests from overcutting, destruction of old-growth forests and fishing grounds, excessive clearcutting and pollution of watersheds. There are more than 400,000 members and supporters. Regular membership is $30; benefits include the quarterly magazine *Wilderness*.

Wilderness Watch, Inc., PO Box 782, Sturgeon Bay WI 54235. (414) 743-1238. Purpose: to promote the sustained use of our sylvan lands and waters, placing ecological considerations foremost.

Wildlife Information Center, Inc., 629 Green St., Allentown PA 18102. (215) 434-1637. Formed to secure and disseminate wildlife conservation, education, recreation, and scientific research information dealing with selective wildlife issues and opportunities. Advocates of wildlife protection and nonkilling uses such as observation, photography, sound recording, drawing and painting and wildlife tourism. Especially involved with birds of prey.

The Center is actively involved in public lectures and wildlife walks. There are courses for public school teachers dealing with hawk migrations, urban wildlife, world wildlife conservation and other topics. Hundreds of teachers have completed one or more of these courses. In 1987 the Center hosted a national conference with the theme of raptors and public education.

The Center works for wildlife protection by petitioning Federal agencies, by testifying at public hearings, and by meeting with wildlife officials.

Research has been sponsored on the autumn hawk migration at Bake Oven Knob, Pennsylvania, on the famous Kittatinny Ridge hawk migration flyway.

Wildlife Protector is a computer software prepared as a HyperCard stack for Macintosh users. Seven basic sections are: about the Wildlife Information Center; CITES; endangered species; hunting; laws & enforcement; reading list; and wildlife. Member's price, $15; non-member, $25; corporation price, $35.

Reports available from the organization include: "Pole Traps & Raptors: A Protection Crisis," 10 pgs, $5; "Tundra Swan Hunting: A Biological, Ecological and Wildlife Crisis," 9 pgs, $6; "Wildlife in Traveling Animal Shows: An Examination and Critique," 12 pgs, $7.

Books available are: *The Migrations of Hawks* by Donald S. Heintzelman, 369 pgs, $35; *A Guide to Hawk Watching in North America* by Donald S. Heintzelman, 284 pgs, $10; *A Manual for Bird Watching in the Americas* by Donald S. Heintzelman, 255 pgs, $8.

Membership to the organization starts at $25 for an individual.

THE WORLD WILDLIFE FUND LOGO

Windstar Foundation, 2317 Snowmass Creek Rd, Snowmass CO 81654, (303) 927-4777. Dedicated to the belief that responsible personal action will be important for creating a global future. Conducts research and educational programs. Basic membership is $35; benefits includes the quarterly *Windstar Journal*.

World Wildlife Fund, 1250 24th St NW, Washington DC 20037. (202) 293-4800. Telex: 64505 PANDA. Dedicated to protecting wildlife worldwide by protecting their habitats and by directing more than 500 scientifically based projects such as: studying the effects of deforestation on migratory birds; studying gorilla conservation in Rwanda; examining the contribution of wild plants and animals to industrialized society; panda research. The organization has 28 affiliates across 5 continents. They have had projects

Chapter Eleven: Organizations

such as emergency rescue programs, habitat protection, conservation education, and direct land acquisition.

Xerces Society, 10 SW Ash St, Portland OR 97204. (503) 222-2788. Dedicated to the preservation of global invertebrate biodiversity. Projects: The Monarch Project (conserving Monarch butterflies); Oregon Butterfly Mapping; International Conservation Register of Invertebrate Specialists (a computerized database of the expertise available in science and conservation concerning invertebrates); The Madagascar Program.

Products that can be ordered: The Monarch Project sweatshirt (adult $26.95, youth $21.95); Monarch Project T-shirt, $16.95; The Monarch Project bumper sticker, $1.75; greeting cards featuring endangers butterflies, $10.45 per pkg of 12 cards.

Regular membership is $25; benefits: *Wings: Essays on Invertebrate Conservation* three times a year; discounts on Xerces books and gifts; participation in annual 4th of July butterfly count.

More information in "Books" and "Educational Materials," chapter.

Using recycled paper goods will help prevent the continued deforestation of our pacific Northwest. This photo was taken recently on the northwest corner of the Olympic Peninsula east of Seattle. There were miles upon miles of areas plundered like this.

 Chapter Eleven: Organizations

Chapter Twelve: Paper Products

Paper goods of all kinds are now available made from recycled materials: facial tissue, bathroom tissue, paper towels, napkins, printing paper, copier paper, laser paper, computer paper, stationary, envelopes, notecards, and even wrapping paper. There's a nice selection of paper goods in this chapter. Remember, if you're not buying recycled goods, you're not really recycling.

Acorn Designs, 5066 Mott Evans Rd, Trumansburg NY 14886. (607) 387-3424. Their products are notecards, bookmarks, bumper stickers, stationary, notepads, gift tags, T-shirts, and more. Examples: Whales & Dolphins notecards printed on 100% recycled paper, 2 each of 4 designs, $6; "Why Not World Peace?" notecards, 8 for $6; "Recycle" bumper sticker, $1.50; "Save the Humans" bumper sticker, $1.50; "Why Not World Peace?" T-shirt, $12.50; handmade recycled paper/ envelopes, $12; "Save the Humans" tote bag, $14. **An environmental excellence profile of this company appears on page 109.**

Ashdun Industries, Inc., 400 Sylvan Avenue, Englewood Cliffs NJ 07632. (201) 569-3600. FAX (201) 816-0188. They market a line of paper products under the brands C.A.R.E. (Consumer Action to Restore the Environment), Envirocare, Aware, Enviroquest, Project Green, and S.A.F.E. (Sound Alternative For the Environment). An example of their products is their paper towels, which uses 100% recycled waste paper with a post consumer content of 25% to 45% depending on which plant it comes from. Soon they expect the post-consumer waste content will be raised to 70% which would set an industry standard. No fragrances are used. Any printing that appears uses either water-based ink or vegetable dyes.

Ashdun Industries COMPRESSED™ roll of paper towels. Ashdun supports Global ReLeaf, a program of the the American Forestry Association, whose goal it is to plant one hundred million trees by 1992.

A new product from Ashdun Industries is the COMPRESSED™ roll of paper towels. The air has been taken out of the roll and 200 sheets have been put onto one roll. The diameter of the roll is the same as other leading brands with only 80 to 120 sheets. One roll of COMPRESSED is equal to 2 to 3 rolls of other leading brands. If all towels were compressed such as this, a minimum of 600,000 trees could be saved just in corrugated shipping cases. This company also uses less cores and less packaging.

The company has recently introduced new products: trash segregation bags, non-phorous and non-polluting household cleaning aids, bio-degradable laundry products, baby wipes, recycled stationary, cat litter, and recycled paper lunch bags.

Ashdun supports Global ReLeaf, a program of the American Forestry Association, whose goal it is to plant one hundred million trees by 1992.

Atlantic Recycled Paper Company, PO

Box 39096, Baltimore MD 21212. (301) 323-2676. Toll-free 1-800-323-8211. Offers Recyconomic and Domtar recycled copy and printing paper. Recyconomic is made from unbleached, 100% recycled (50% post consumer waste) and can be used in any copy machine or laser printer. Domtar printing paper is non-deinked and made of 100% post consumer waste. Other recycled paper products available: computer paper; fax paper; envelopes; stationary; legal pads; mailing labels; paper towels; napkins; facial tissue; and toilet paper.

Confab Companies, 2301 Dupont Drive, Suite 150, Irvine CA 92715. (714) 955-2690. Today's Choice™ paper towels, napkins, bath tissue, facial tissue, all 100% recycled content. Certified by Green Cross Certification.

Co-op America, 2100 "M" St NW, Suite 403, Washington DC 20063. (202) 872-5307. Toll-free 1-800-424-2667. This is a non-profit, member-controlled, worker-managed association linking socially responsible businesses and consumers in a national network, a new alternative marketplace. Co-op America allows consumers to align buying habits with values. Basic information found in "Organizations" chapter.

Paper products from catalog: "Calligraphy" or "Wildflower" design handmade journals of recycled newspaper, $18.95; notecards with 6 in each set and enveloped on recycled paper in styles Winterweave, African Dignity,

Star of Peace, Christmoose, Happy Sun, any 2 packs for $10.95; Earth-Note Cards from Earth Care Paper Company are printed on 100% recycled paper and have matching recycled envelopes in these styles: Polar Bears, Poinsettias, Cardinal, Holding Hands, Geese, Pine Trees in Snow, Bare Trees in Snow, Swans, Owl and Moon, any 2 sets for $13; ecological gift wrap in these styles: Constellations, Pine Trees and Snow, Peace on Earth, Snowflakes, Caribou, 3 gift wraps for $12.75.

Household paper products made of 100% recycled wastepaper from Conservatree Company: facial tissues, paper towels, toilet paper.

Products from the catalog are found in "Recycling," "Energy Conservation," "Books," " Organically Grown," "Household & Personal Care Products," and "Baby & Children's Products" chapters.

Earth Care Paper Inc., Box 14140, Madison WI 53714. (608) 277-2900. Free 40-page catalog of recycled paper products: notecards; stationary; gift wrap; printing paper; copy paper; and computer paper.

Ecco Bella, 6 Provost Square, Suite 602, Caldwell NJ 07006. (201) 226-5799. FAX # (201) 226-0991. Toll-free 1-800-888-5320. This company manufactures and sells products that are cruelty-free and environmentally sound. The Ecco Bella line of products is extensive and featured in their own catalog, but there are other products

Chapter Twelve: Paper Products

**Notecard design from Good Nature Designs.
Created by wildlife artist Jane Gaston.
You ought to see this one in color—it's great!**

featured as well. Recycled paper products available: bathroom tissue; facial tissues; paper towels; dinner napkins; wildlife notecards in a variety of styles; holiday cards in various styles; writing papers; notepads; copier paper; computer paper; and gift wrap (styles: Pine Cones, Penguins, Caribou, Forest, Leaves, Dove, Constellations), any 2 gift wrap styles for $8. Also available are Melitta cotton coffee filters to save paper filters.

More items listed in "Household & Personal Care Products," "Recycling," "Organically Grown" and "Energy Conservation" chapters.

EcoSource™, 9051 Mill Station Road Bldg #E, Sebastopol CA 95472. (717) 829-7957 or (707) 829-8345. Catalog

of products for a cleaner, safer world. Recycled papers products include toilet paper, 12 rolls, $7; paper towels, 6 rolls, $7.50; paper plates, 125 dinner plates for $14.95; facial tissue, 6 boxes for $5.75; computer paper, 2500 sheets for $34.80; printing paper includes various color, $7.10 ream; letterhead paper, $4.95 ream; business envelopes, various sizes, start at $12.65.

More products listed under "Books," "Recycling," "Energy Conservation," "Clean Air, Clean Water," "Household & Personal Care Products" and "Educational Materials" chapters.

Gentle Strength Co-op, 234 West University Drive, Tempe AZ 85281.

 Chapter Twelve: Paper Products

(602) 968-4831. This store handles many environmentally sensitive lines of products. Paper products: recycled bath tissue, facial tissue and paper towels; Today's Choice women's hygiene products made with unbleached, recycled materials.

More products found in "Household & Personal Care Products," "Organically Grown," "Baby & Children's Products," "Books," and "Magazines, Newsletters & Brochures" chapters.

Good Nature Designs, 1630 E 2nd St, Dayton OH 45403. (513) 253-2722. FAX # (513) 254-9638. High quality note cards, stationary, wrapping paper and art posters, all printed on recycled paper using soybean inks. Several styles to choose from. For example, note cards come in these interesting designs: "Wild About the World" series shows wildlife with the logo "Wild About the World" above a globe; "Farm Folks" series was inspired by traditional American folk art designs; "Elegant Earth" line explore natural shapes and textures; "Native American Collection" is inspired by traditional Navajo patterns; "Colorful Creature" line is derived from contemporary American Southwestern folk art, and there's a dazzling series of wildlife prints from artist Jane Gaston. A new Christmas card's message is "May Your World Be Ever Green."

Jade Mountain, PO Box 4616, Boulder CO 80306. (303) 449-6601. FAX # (303) 449-8266. Toll-free 1-800-442-1972. Large selection of energy saving and appropriate technology products. Paper products include 100% recycled toilet paper, paper towels, facial tissue, napkins, and paper towels. There's also 100% recycled copy paper, 50% recycled copy paper, 50% recycled envelopes, 50% enveloped with cellulose windows; 50% recycled FAX paper; 50% high quality white bond computer paper.

Newsletter/catalog (80-page) subscription, $3 for one year. Also listed in "Energy Conservation," "Household & Personal Care Products," "Clean Air, Clean Water" chapters.

Karen's Nontoxic Products, 1839 Dr. Jack Road, Conowingo MD 21918. (301) 378-4621. 1-800-KARENS-4. Write or call toll-free number for catalog of truly natural, environmentally-safe, cruelty-free and energy building items for family, home and health. Recycled paper products include: stationary, various styles, $5 for 15 sheets and 15 envelopes; notecards, various styles, $4.50 for 10 cards and 10 envelopes; Envision™ toilet paper (70¢), tissue paper (85¢), napkins ($3.25) and paper towels ($1.25).

See also "Books" and "Household & Personal Care Products" chapters.

Orchids Paper Products Company, 5911 Fresca Drive, La Palma CA 90623. (714) 523-7881. Manufacturers of HOPE™ and START™ paper towels, napkins, bath tissue and facial tissue, all 100% recycled content. Certified by Green Cross Certification.

**Notecard design by Orr Enterprises.
Artwork by Catherine D. Hamilton**

Orr Enterprises, PO Box 1717, Monrovia CA 91017, (210 N Madison Ave, Monrovia CA 91016.) (818) 301-0950. Toll-free 1-800-525-8191. They have 8 wildlife notecard designs (kangaroo, leopard, seal, wolf, chimp, wild goat, panda, eagle), on recycled paper. Price: $5.95 package of 10/ all one design or $4.75 for assortment of 8. Also 2 "thank you" note cards and 2 stationary designs, all on recycled paper. They donate a percentage of all sales to environmental organizations.

Pope & Talbot, Inc., 1500 SW 1st Avenue, Portland OR 97201. (503) 228-9161. Manufacturers of Capri™, Pert™, Nature's Choice™, Surety™, Gentle Touch™, and Sun Glory™ paper towels, napkins, bath tissue and facial tissue, all 100% recycled content,

certified by Green Cross Certification.

Real Goods Trading Company, 966 Mazzoni St, Ukiah CA 95482. (707) 468-9214. FAX # (707) 468-0301. Order toll-free 1-800-762-7325. This company has an extensive 106-page catalog full of energy-saving equipment and supplies. Paper products include: 100% recycled Envision brand toilet paper, paper towels, and facial tissue. More items listed in "Books," "Energy Conservation," "Household & Personal Care Products," "Clean Air, Clean Water," "Baby & Children's Products" and "Recycling" chapters.

Recycled Paper Company, Inc., 185 Corey Road, Boston MA 02146. (617) 277-9901. FAX # (617) 738-4877.

This company provides businesses with quality recycled office paper products. They represent most manufacturers of recycled paper in the US and Canada. Product line includes: computer paper; copy paper; labels; envelopes; FAX paper; file folders; legal pads; stationary; printing paper. Minimum order is one full carton; sells to customers in NE United States only.

Set Point Paper Company, 31 Oxford Rd, Mansfield MA 02048. (508) 339-9300. Producers of the Earth Bag™ that is a paper refuse bag that can be used for leaf and yard waste composting, newspaper recycling, aluminum recycling, household trash, and other recycling projects.

Seventh Generation, Colchester VT 05446-1672. (802) 655-3116. FAX toll-free # 1-800-456-1139. Order toll-free 1-800-456-1177. Customer service toll-free 1-800-456-1197.

Seventh Generation is one of the most well-known companies for environmentally safe consumer products. Their 48-page catalog "Products for a Healthy Planet" ($2) contains an extraordinary variety of products. They also practice what they preach. For instance, they recycle their office paper, and reuse cardboard boxes for shipping. They have a 1% fund that goes to environmental organizations.

There's an extensive line of paper products available in their catalog: unbleached 100% recycled toilet paper, paper towels, facial tissue, napkins and paper plates. They have a "Household

Paper Delivery Service" where they will automatically deliver toilet paper, paper towels, and facial tissue every month. There's also writing paper, stationary, notepads, "Rainflower" stationary set, unbleached and recycled computer paper, holiday cards, birthday cards, note cards, and recycled wrapping paper.

There are so many products in this catalog that additional information can be found in these chapters: "Baby and Children's Products," "Books," "Educational Materials," "Household & Personal Care," "Recycling," "Energy Conservation," and "Organically Grown."

Simply Delicious, 243-A North Hook Rd, PO Box 124, Pennsville NJ 08070. (609) 678-4488. This is a retail natural food store that offers organic cereals, grains, beans and more from Health Valley, Arrowhead Mills and other major product lines. Also carries recycled paper products from Envision and Pure Paper. Carries unbleached coffee filters from Natural Brew. Listed in "Household & Personal Care Products" and "Organically Grown" chapters.

Solar Electric Engineering, Inc., 116 4th St, Santa Rosa CA 95401. (707) 542-1990. FAX # (707) 542-4358. This is a publicly owned corporation that has been committed to bringing to the marketplace environmentally sound products at affordable prices to the consumer. They have a 40-page "Environmental Catalog," with recycled paper products, including: Natural Brew® unbleached coffee filters, 100 per package, 8" size, $1.95; 100% recycled dinner napkins, toilet paper, facial tissue and paper towels.

More items listed in "Energy Conservation," "Recycling," "Energy Conservation," "Household & Personal Care Products," "Clean Air, Clean Water," "Baby & Children's Products," and "Magazines, Newsletters & Brochures."

We Recycle Unlimited™, PO Box 275, Cape Porpoise ME 04014. (207) 282-8880. FAX # (207) 282-9488. Sells 100% recycled paper products: toilet paper by the case, half case, quarter case, from 45¢ to 63¢ per roll; facial tissue by the case, half case, from 53¢ to 59¢ per box; napkins by the case or smaller; paper towels by the case, half case, or less, from 78¢ per roll; copier paper from $4.90 per ream; envelopes from 3¢ each; and yellow or white pads from 80¢.

Reprinted by permission: Tribune Media Services

Chapter Thirteen: Recycling

This chapter contains equipment and supplies for recycling, such as aluminum can crushers, newspaper bundlers, and recycling systems. There is also environmentally sensitive packing materials. Reusable shopping bags are found here and also in the "Household & Personal Care Products" chapter.

Alcoa Recycling Company, 1150 Riverview Tower, 900 S. Gay St, Knoxville TN 37902. (615) 971-1907. Free information about aluminum recycling.

The Bag Connection, Inc., PO Box 817, Newberg OR 97132. 1-800-62BAGIT. They produce the "BAGIT" Recycling Bag, Holder & Stand. The system has a bag holder that can be quickly attached for use in home, apartments, schools, commercial outlets, churches, hotels, restaurants or offices. There are both free-standing holders (available in 1, 2 and 4 bag models) and wall mount holders (for 1 or 2 bag models). The bags you use are reusable and easily cleaned simply by washing.

Cedar-al Products Inc., HCR 63 Box 6, Clallam Bay WA 98326. (206) 963-2601. Toll-free order line 1-800-431-3444 from 8-4 pm Pacific time, Mon-Fri. This company makes Excelsior packing material which is a finely shaved wood fiber which replaces styrofoam peanuts at a reasonable cost. It is available in 30 pound bales for $21 plus shipping and is equivalent to 60 cubic feet of packing material.

For those concerned about the great Northwest old-growth forests, we'd like to add that these products are produced from mill wastes, which previously were burned or buried in landfills. No trees were cut to make these products.

Another listing in "Household & Personal Care Products" chapter.

**"BAGIT" recycling bags
from the Bag Connection.**

Chem-Tainer Industries, Inc., 361
Neptune Ave, North Babylon NY
11704. (516) 661-8300. FAX # (516)
661-8209. Toll-free 1-800-654-5607.
Produces a line of recycling trucks and
containers.

Co-op America, 2100 "M" St NW,
Suite 403, Washington DC 20063.
(202) 872-5307. Toll-free 1-800-424-
2667. This is a non-profit, member-
controlled, worker-managed association linking socially responsible businesses and consumers in a national
network, a new alternative marketplace. Co-op America allows consumers to align buying habits with values.

Recycling products from their catalog: Diversified Recycling Systems
mobile recycling cart with two bins,
this one you can fill and wheel out to the
driveway, bins are made of recycled
plastic. You can buy this with a cart,
two bins, or the bins separately. It also
comes in a three-bin and cart system.

Each bin holds 27 gallons of materials.
For apartments, there's a smaller size:
14-gallon bins, no cart. Also for recycling: can crusher.

Products from the catalog are found
in "Recycling," "Energy Conservation," "Educational Materials,"
"Books," " Organically Grown,"
"Household & Personal Care Products," "Paper Products, " and "Baby &
Children's Products" chapters.

**DLR Design & Development
Corporation,** 44105 Leeann, Canton
MI 48187. (313) 459-0754. FAX #
(313) 459-2610. 1-800-869-9709.
Several recycling products available
from this company. The Recycling
Station™ Expandable Recycling Stand
provides an easy and space efficient
method to separate trash for recycling
by re-using paper and plastic handled
shopping bags. It's easy to set up, has
a tubular construction, and expandable,
$14.95. The Recycling Station™
Newspaper Recycling Stand provides a
simple and convenient method for preparing newspaper for recycling. No
tools needed for assembly; tubular
construction; 5-year limited warranty,
$15.95. The Recycling Station™
Multipurpose Recycling Center is a
combination type recycling center, with
a bag section that will hold standard
trash bags for separating cans, glass &
plastic, and a newspaper section for
stacking papers with two built-in
spools of twine. Modular design, tubular frame, 5-year limited warranty; toll-
free support, $29.95. Additional items
for this product are twine, 2 spools/pkg

**Excelsior packing material is finely shaved wood fiber
which replaces styrofoam peanuts.
Available from Cedar-Al Products.**

$5.95; and quick-clips for holding the bags into place, 7/pkg, $2.95.

Dolco Packaging Corp, 13400 Riverside Drive, Suite #200, Sherman Oaks CA 91413. (818) 995-1238.polystyrene egg carton (non CFC) made of at least 25% recycled content, certified by Green Cross Certification.

E & A Environmental Consultants, Inc., 1613 Central St, PO Box 372, Stoughton MA 02072. (617) 341-1400. FAX # (617) 341-4206. Environmental consultants who are special-ists in: solid waste, recycling, composting, and facility design.

Ecco Bella, 6 Provost Square, Suite 602, Caldwell NJ 07006. (201) 226-5799. FAX # (201) 226-0991. Toll-free 1-800-888-5320. This company manufactures and sells products that are cruelty-free and environmentally sound. The Ecco Bella line of products is extensive and featured in their own catalog, but there are other products featured as well. Recycling products found in the catalog are: Can Cycler for crushing aluminum cans, $19.95; their

Chapter Thirteen: Recycling

The Crusher is an aluminum can crusher that makes recycling easier.

very own "Ecco Bella" canvas shopping bag that is durably designed, $14.95; string shopping bags, 2 for $8.95.

More items listed in "Paper Products," "Household & Personal Care Products," "Organically Grown" and "Energy Conservation" chapters.

Eco Source™, 9051 Mill Station Road Bldg #E, Sebastopol CA 95472. (717) 829-7957 or (707) 829-8345. Catalog of products for a cleaner, safer world. Recycling products include: "The Crusher" for crushing aluminum cans, $19.50; personal recycling file for

home or office, $6.50; stackable recycling bins, $12.50 each or $35 for three; recycle-it containers with decals to show what you are recycling, short 16 inch $6.95, tall 31 inch for $9.95; the paperboy for bundling newspapers, $6.95; the recycle box home organizer made of corrugated cardboard with dividers, $12.95; the recycle sorter made of cardboard and designed to hold paper grocery bags full of recyclable materials, $7.25 each.

More products from their catalog found in "Household and Personal Use," "Books," "Energy Conservation," "Clean Air, Clean Water" and "Educational Materials" chapters.

Gaia™, 1400 Shattuck Ave #15, Berkeley CA 94709. (415) 548-4172. Gaia™ is a store and mail order source that calls itself a center for "global, ecological & spiritual resources." It is primarily New Age oriented, with an emphasis on Gaia, the earth goddess. However, it also carries environmental products, such as the Gaia canvas tote bag, 16" x 16', portion of sale goes to Rainforest Action Network, $18.

Laidlaw Environmental Services, PO Box 210799, Columbia SC 29221. (803) 798-2993. 1-800-356-8570. They offer an integrated network for the processing, recycling and complete destruction of industrial solvents as well as liquid and solid organic hydrocarbon based hazardous waste. They are pioneers in turning hydrocarbon based waste into useful waste-to-energy fuel, recycling materials that once

Lillian Vernon's newspaper stacker.

required shipment to landfills or incineration. They can also handle household hazardous waste, non-hazardous waste management, chemical wastes, reactives and laboratory wastes. Call or write for detailed information about their services.

Lillian Vernon Corporation, 510 S. Fulton Avenue, Mount Vernon NY 10555. (914) 699-4131. Their catalog contains a newspaper rack that's good for stacking newspapers prior to binding for recycling. Also the right size for computer printouts. This rack folds flat to store. Order # 649150, $6.98.

The Nature Company, PO Box 2310, Berkeley CA 94702. 1-800-227-1114. FAX (415) 849-0465. Beautiful full-color catalog full of interesting items for people who love nature. One item offered is the "recycling center" that has 3 separate compartments for sorting and

storing glass, plastic and cans. Comes with 3 washable, easy to transport bags. Plastic tubular frame. $69.95.

Other items in the catalog described in "Books," "Household & Personal Care Products," and "Educational Materials" chapters.

Plasco Press Company, Inc., 16037 Foothill Blvd, Azusa CA 91702. (818) 969-1545. Bottlesack™ plastic shopping bag, 30% recycled content, certified by Green Cross Certification.

Plastican™ Inc., 196 Industrial Rd, Leominister MA 01453. (508) 537-4911. FAX # (508) 537-6376. Manufacturer of a complete curbside recycling product line.

Real Goods Trading Company, 966 Mazzoni St, Ukiah CA 95482. (707) 468-9214. FAX # (707) 468-0301. Order toll-free 1-800-762-7325. This company has an extensive 106-page catalog full of energy-saving equipment and supplies. Products for recycling include: cotton string shopping bag, $5; canvas shopping bag that says "Real Goods," $9; stacking recycling bins, $13 each or set of 3 for $36; can crusher, $17.50; personal recycling file that holds scratch paper or paper ready to be recycled, $6. More items listed in "Books," "Energy Conservation," "Household & Personal Care Products," "Clean Air, Clean Water," "Paper Products" and "Baby & Children's Products" chapters.

Resource Recycling Systems Inc., 310 Miller Ave, Ann Arbor MI 48103. (313) 996-1361. Full service consultants in waste reduction, recycling and composting. They can provide design services, market analysis, and feasibility analysis as well as equipment procurement.

Set Point Paper Company, 31 Oxford Rd, Mansfield MA 02048. (508) 339-9300. Producers of the Earth Bag™ that is a paper refuse bag that can be used for leaf and yard waste composting, newspaper recycling, aluminum recycling, household trash, and other recycling projects.

Seventh Generation, Colchester VT 05446-1672. (802) 655-3116. FAX toll-free # 1-800-456-1139. Order toll-free 1-800-456-1177. Customer service toll-free 1-800-456-1197.

Seventh Generation is one of the most well-known companies for environmentally safe consumer products. Their 48-page catalog "Products for a Healthy Planet" ($2) contains an extraordinary variety of products. They also practice what they preach. For instance, they recycle their office paper, and reuse cardboard boxes for shipping. They have a 1% fund that goes to environmental organizations.

Recycling equipment in the catalog includes: stacking bins, 12.5" x 20" x 15", $16.95 each or 3 for $48; the economical free-standing sorter, 43" x 12.5" x 9", line each compartment with paper bags, $7.95; recycling cabinet on wheels, 36" x 27" x 18", some assembly required, $139; newspaper stacker with a big ball of twine, $24.95; aluminum can crusher, $22.50; composter, $110.

There are so many products in this catalog that additional information can be found in these chapters: "Baby and Children's Products," "Books," "Educational Materials," "Paper Products," "Household & Personal Care Products," "Energy Conservation," and "Organically Grown."

Shamrock Industries, Inc., Recycling Division, 834 N. 7th St, Minneapolis MN 55411-4394. (612) 332-2100. Toll-free 1-800-822-2342. Toll-free in Minnesota 1-800-822-2343. They have recycling containers for curbside recycling in various styles: Stackable Bins; Three-Bagger heavy-duty 21-gallon container; One Step recyclers in 7-gallon, 14-gallon and 26-gallon sizes.

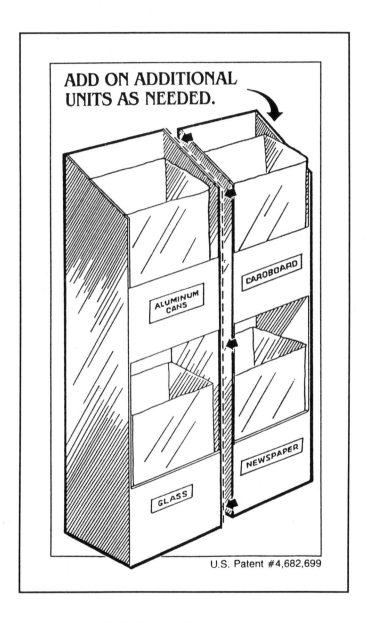

ADD ON ADDITIONAL
UNITS AS NEEDED.

ALUMINUM
CANS

CAROBOARD

GLASS

NEWSPAPER

U.S. Patent #4,682,699

TERC recycling system.

Chapter Thirteen: Recycling ★

Signature Art, PO Box 801, Wilder VT 05088. (802) 295-3291. They produce the award-winning For-The-Earth Bags™ that eliminate the need for plastic shopping bags. These bags are made in the USA of sturdy cotton canvas in natural and bright colors. They feature a large interior pocket for carrying extra bags. The straps are the perfect length for both shoulder and hand carrying. Beautiful nature scenes are silk screened on the side. Businesses may custom order their own logo. These bags are ideal for the beach, gym, school, work, toddler, overnighter, and carry-on, as well as grocery and clothes shopping.

Styles available in these bags are: Lily, Palm Lagoon, Earth, Turtle, Fluorescent Palm Lagon, Sunburst, Penguins, Rainforest and Savanna.

For-The-Earth Bags™ were recently selected by *Ecologue: The Consumer's Guide to Environmentally Safe Products* as one of the top ten products. Signature Art received an *Ecologue* Award for being an "Earth Conscious Company" and for "products and practices for a safe planet."

Another product from the company is a Russian string shopping bag, called "Avoska." These bags are traditionally made by the blind. They have a wide neck opening and are available in cotton and rayon in variety of colors. They fold conveniently to fit into pocket or purse.

The company's goal is to offer environmentally sound alternatives to ecologically damaging behavior patterns, with a focus on shopping habits.

Signature Art contributes 10% of its profits to environmental organizations. Environmental groups receive a 5% discount on their wholesale purchases.

When calling or writing for information, please specify wholesale or retail catalog (minimum wholesale order is 24). Also listed in the "Household & Personal Care" chapter. **See ad page 132.**

Solar Electric Engineering, Inc., 116 4th St, Santa Rosa CA 95401. (707) 542-1990. FAX # (707) 542-4358. This is a publicly owned corporation that has been committed to bringing to the marketplace environmentally sound products at affordable prices to the consumer. They have a 40-page "Environmental Catalog," with recycling products, including: two types of can crushers, The Can Cycler, $17.50 and The Crusher, $19.95; recycling bins that are stackable, each holds 12 1/2 gallons, 1 bin for $9.75 or 3 for $27; reusable canvas shopping bags, $8.95; string shopping bag for bulk foods or vegetables, 2 for $8.95.

More items listed in "Energy Conservation," "Energy Conservation," "Household & Personal Care Products," "Paper Products," "Clean Air, Clean Water," "Baby & Children's Products," and "Magazines, Newsletters & Brochures."

Stamp San Francisco, PO Box 16215, San Francisco CA 94116. (415) 252-5975. This company makes rubber stamps. One of their messages is "Recycle" in a specially designed circu-

Chapter Thirteen: Recycling

lar pattern (different from the recycle emblem you see on packaging.) Other environmental styles available, such as the earth stamp, or "Extinction is forever" with dinosaurs.

TERC—The Ertley Recycling Concept, 699C Friar Ct, Lakehurst NJ 08733. (201) 657-4690. Has patented a household recycling kit consisting of an in-house wall rack that holds paper supermarket bags and a covered in-ground curb box for the proper presentation of recyclables at the curb. This system has been developed so that all recyclable commodities in the residential waste stream can be individually source-separated. This approach to the problem recognizes the existing list of recyclables and allows for expansion as other commodities are added. This project recognizes the tenets of successful recycling: that all recyclables are included; that recycling is a partnership between residents, business and industry, and government agencies; that it does not minimize the responsi-

bility of each partner nor the make-up of the waste stream; and understands that total recycling can be accomplished expeditiously only if an all-inclusive plan is selected, responsibilities defines and continuity maintained. A TERC system is financed by a charge of $2 per week per household. The system has also designed a collecting vehicle, and a drive-thru recycling center.

The Vermont Country Store, Inc., PO Box 3000, Manchester Center VT 05255. (802) 362-2400. Their catalog offers a newspaper stacker that makes it easy to stack up your newspapers and tie them with twine. The device has four raised platforms that leave space underneath for tying up the bundle. Price, $12.95; ball sisal twine, $2.95. The catalog also has a can crusher that includes a magnet for sorting steel from aluminum, $14.95. Purists might object to the fact that these two products are made of plastic.

More items described in "Household & Personal Care Products" chapter.

Chapter Thirteen: Recycling

Chapter Fourteen:
Seminars, Workshops & Speakers

This chapter contains additional ways to learn about solar electricity, sustainable agriculture, healing environments, natural resources, organic gardening, and other environmental topics. Speakers and performers are included.

Adirondack Mountain Club, Inc., RR3 Box 3055, Lake George NY 12845. (518) 523-3441. (518) 668-4447. Offers educational workshop on nature in the Adirondacks, such as "Alpine Flora and Ecology" and "Forest Types and Forest Managements." Other types of classes offered include outdoor skills, backcountry first aid, and week long field programs. An Elderhostel program is offered. These backcountry educational programs are offered so that people can learn to enjoy the outdoors without destroying the environment.

Also listed in "Eco-tourism," "Seminars, Speakers & Workshops" and "Organizations" chapters.

California School of Herbal Studies, PO Box 39, Forrestville CA 9536.

(707) 887-7457. Offers sessions on herbalism including "Environment & Herbs" which explains the ecology and evolution of herbs. Write for brochure.

Carol Venolia, PO Box 694, Gualala CA 95445. (707) 884-4513. An architect who creates healing environments. Also available for consulting and workshops.

Cheesemans' Ecology Safaris, 20800 Kittredge Rd, Saratoga CA 95070. (408) 741-5330. Tours are arranged and led by Doug Cheeseman, Professor of Zoology, Ecology and Gail Cheeseman, naturalist and birder. Doug is the Director of the DeAnza College Environmental Study Area, a native plant garden or arboretum. Doug and Gail have been program chairpersons for the Santa Clara Valley Audubon Society for the past 8 years. Gail is also the co-chairperson of the Environmental Action Committee for that Audubon chapter.

Doug and Gail Cheeseman are available for public speaking and lectures to community groups.

More information in "Eco-tourism" chapter.

Dry Creek Herb Farm, 13935 Dry Creek Road, Auburn CA 95603. (916) 878-2441. Offers classes and apprenticeships in the art of herbology. See also "Household & Personal Care Products" chapter.

Fowler Solar Electric Inc, PO Box 435, 13 Bashan Hill Road, Worthington MA 01098. (413) 238-5974. Paul Jeffrey Fowler, president of Fowler Solar Electric, author of *The Solar Electric Independent Home* book, and designer of solar electric systems, is available to speak about PV (photovoltaic) systems and their design.

See also "Energy Conservation" and "Books" chapters.

Harmony Farm Supply & Nursery, 3244 Gravenstein Hwy North, Sebastopol CA 95472. Mail address: PO Box 460, Graton CA 95444. (707) 823-9125. FAX (707) 823-1734. Extensive mail order catalog ($2) of organic grower's supplies, including irrigation and integrated pest management supplies. This company offers a series of workshop pertaining to organic gardening, irrigation, and more. Ex-

amples: Drip Irrigation, 2 hours; Xeriscape Landscape Design, 2 hours; Greywater Workshop/ Demonstration, 3 hours; Erosion Control, 2 hours; Ecological Pest Controls, 2 hours; Organic Vegetable Gardening, 2 hours; and more. All workshops are free and no reservations are required. More information in "Organically Grown" and "Books" chapters.

The Institute for Earth Education, PO Box 288, Warrenville IL 60555. (708) 393-3096 or (509) 395-2299. Since 1974, Earth Education has been in the process of helping people live more harmoniously and joyously with the natural world. This organization is composed of people who work at trying to live more lightly on the earth. They emphasize environmental learning programs: Sunship Earth®; Earthkeepers®; Earth Caretakers®; and SUNSHIP II®. These programs have information packets ($1 each) to explain how the programs work. The organization sponsors International Earth Education Conferences in which children and adults can experience the various programs and catch up on latest developments in newer programs. Membership starts at $20 and includes the quarterly publication *Talking Leaves*.

Write for free catalog "The Earth Education Sourcebook," which tells about their organization, their programs, and has various interesting products for sale. (Also listed under "Educational Materials" chapter and "Organizations" chapter.)

Many more services available, including workshops and speakers. They have conducted workshops since 1974, and thousands of teachers, naturalists, and outdoor leaders have attended their sessions. If you would like to sponsor a one to two-day training session to prepare your leaders to offer earth education programs, write to them for information.

Steve Van Matre, the chairman and founder of The Institute for Earth Education, is widely known as an author, designer, educator, organizer, and just all-round interesting guy. He is available for speaking engagements. Upcoming workshops and speeches are listed in the SEEDBEDS, a supplement to the *Talking Leaves* newsletter.

Malachite School & Small Farm, ASR Box 21, Pass Creek Rd, Gardner CO 81040. (719) 746-2412. They teach about leading a sustainable lifestyle and becoming a more responsible citizen of the world. Their programs teach about conservation, waste reduction, recycling practices, self-reliant food sources, and energy efficient homes. Programs available are: field trips, Malachite Elderhostel, Malachite farmstays, Malachite retreats, Malachite weeks, Malachite hostel program; and Malachite internships.

Malachite recently sponsored an educational presentation for Gardner School. Students learned about global warming, acid rain, endangered animals, and rain forest destruction.

Malachite is an educational organization and welcomes donations. Newsletters sent to all donors.

National Audubon Society, 950 Third Ave., New York NY 10022. (212) 832-3200. Six education centers conduct outdoor classes, community outreach programs, and workshops for training leaders. Travel-study programs are also offered, as well as field seminar on specific skills. See the "Organization" chapter for complete listing.

Nigra Enterprises, 5699 Kanan Road, Agoura CA 91301-3358. (818) 889-6877. Jim Nigra has helped thousands of people improve the quality of their air and water. He specializes in satisfying the environmental needs of those with chemical sensitivities and traditional allergies. In addition to improving home and office environments, Jim has also been involved in designing systems for a wide variety of other applications, including studios, pet stores, doctors' offices, and music schools.

Jim is available for speaking engagements, especially on a local level. For information about his products, see "Clean Air, Clean Water" chapter.

Nitron Industries, Inc., PO Box 1447, 4605 Johnson Road, Fayetteville AR 72702. (501) 750-1777. 1-800-835-0123. Manufacturer and distributor of natural fertilizers and soil conditioners. Other services include books on farming and gardening, an annual organic growing seminar, composting information, and other technical information for organic growers. FREE catalog by calling toll-free number.

More information in "Organically

Grown" chapter.

Planet Drum Foundation, Box 31251, San Francisco CA 94131. (415) 285-6556. Staff members, especially Peter Berg, Director of Planet Drum Foundation, and Judy Goldhaft, present talks and conduct seminars and workshops on bioregional topics for community, college and activist groups. Some typical workshops are: Reinhabiting a Life-Place; How to Start and Maintain a Bioregional Group; How to Educate Others About Bioregionalism. Some typical topics for talks include: Bioregional Life-Place Politics; Bioregions as the Basis of Community Consciousness; and Urban Dwelling from a Bioregional Perspective.

Special Performances. Peter and Judy are both performers who have worked with the San Francisco Mime Troupe, and are available for special performances within their topics. Recently Judy created "Water Web," a 20-minute rap and movement about water cycles and our relationship to them. "Water Web" premiered to a standing ovation at a recent bioregional workshop in Anchorage, Alaska. Peter performs a 45-minute eco-comedy routine that is in constant demand. More information in the "Organizations" chapter.

Safe Environments, 2512 9th St #17, Berkeley CA 94710. Toll-free 1-800-356-2663. One-day seminars on: Introduction to Indoor Pollution—Guidelines for the Professional; Practical Uses of Indoor Pollution Monitoring Devices; Advanced Indoor Pollution

Monitoring & Diagnostics for Professionals; and Problem Solving in Indoor Pollution. Also listing in "Miscellaneous" chapter.

Sisters' Choice, 1450 6th St, Berkeley CA 94710. (415) 524-5804. Cassette tape called *All In This Together* (Candy Forest, Nancy Schimmel and the Singing Rainbows Youth Ensemble, ages 9-15, with special guests Laurie Lewis & Rosie Radiator) is 15 ecology songs for the whole family. The songs are folk, jazz & rock numbers about the disappearing rain forest, pet overpopulation, endangered species, the urban forests and other songs about the environment. Some of the song titles are: "My Sister's a Whale in the Sea," "Must Be Johnny Appleseed," "Eating Up the Forest." This tape was a 1990 Parents' Choice Gold Award Winner. Cassette is $10.

For Singing Rainbow performances and workshops, call Candy Forest at (415) 550-7752. For storytelling performances and workshops, call Nancy Schimmel at (415) 843-0533.

See also "Baby & Children's" or "Educational Materials" chapter.

Solar Survival, PO Box 250, Cherry Hill Rd, Harrisville NH 03450. (603) 827-3811. The work of this company involves many areas of simple passive solar design involving: house plans; intensive gardening; solar food hydration; domestic water systems; window/shutter systems; and masonry stove systems. Designer Lea Poisson, an incredible child prodigy-turned-solar designer, has patented several products for energy efficiency. One of the most popular of his designs has been the Trisol™ Greenhouse.

The Trisol greenhouse method can be learned one of several ways: through his book *The Solar Greenhouse Book* (Rodale, $10.95); through purchase of a kit ($3500); through a Trisol brochure with floorplans, photographs and descriptive material ($10); through a license and blueprint specifications ($300 for 1200 sq ft model or $350 for 1500 sq ft model); or through a <u>seminar and gardening workshop</u> at the research center in Harrisville, New Hampshire (tuition $30 per person, $50 per couple).

Much more information about this company and their solar designs and products can be found in the "Energy Conservation" chapter.

Sunnyside Solar, RD 4 Box 808, Green River Road, Brattleboro CT 05301. (802) 257-1482 (in Vermont). 1-800-346-3230. Offers a photovoltaic seminar and hands-on workshop. This is a one-day program which includes a full presentation on independent photovoltaic home electric systems and a hands-on workshop building a four-module system. Includes lunch, a full packet of information, and Davidson's New Solar Electric Home. Limited to 8 participants per session. $85. Held 6-7 times a year. Write for dates.

Chapter Fifteen: Miscellaneous

There are some items that cannot be classified under any other category, but deserve to be included in this book. Some of the things found in this chapter are: consultants, rubber stamps, test kits, artificial scrimshaw, environmental clip art, an environmental award, environmental job listings, and a special computer network.

Artek, Inc., PO Box 145, Elm Avenue, Antrim NH 03440. (603) 588-6825. FAX # (603) 588-6894. Manufactures a line of "polymer ivory" scrimshaw reproductions which look exactly like the real thing yet are manufactured using no animal products. They pride themselves in keeping the art of scrimshaw alive while supporting efforts to preserve and protect natural resources and wildlife. These are faithful museum reproductions or facsimiles of actual historic prototypes, and are done with the permission of specific museums. Items available in their "Save the Whale" collection include the whale and walrus teeth, cribbage boards, pendants, nautical key chains, buttons, and jewelry boxes. Blank teeth and tusks are available for hobbyists, as well as scrimshaw kits. Nantucket basket makers can find supplies here.

Carol Venolia, PO Box 694, 38820 S Highway 1, Suite 205, Gualala CA 95445. (707) 884-4513. An architect who creates healing environments. She has studied the effects of environmental light, color, temperature, sound, and plants. Also available for consulting and workshops. Author of the book *Healing Environments: Your Guide to Indoor Well Being* (Celestial Arts, 1988), $9.95. Found under Celestial Arts, "Books" chapter.

Dolco Packaging Corp, 13400 Riverside Drive, Suite #200, Sherman Oaks CA 91413. (818) 995-1238. polystyrene egg carton (non CFC) made of at least 25% recycled content, certified by Green Cross Certification.

EcoNet Canada, 456 Spadina Ave, 2nd floor, Toronto, Ontario, Canada M5T 2G8. (416) 929-0634. FAX # (416) 925-7536. Modem: (416) 925-0400. Telex: 063270997. This is an on-line computer environmental information service that can be used by educational organizations, environmental groups, government agencies, businesses, researchers, and others. Rates start at $15 per month.

Eco Source™, 9051 Mill Station Road Bldg #E, Sebastopol CA 95472. (717) 829-7957 or (707) 829-8345. Catalog of products for a cleaner, safer world. Includes a very interesting "RCI Environmental Test Kit" that contains everything you need to collect samples to find out if you have pollutants in and around your home. After collecting the samples, you mail them to the lab in the containers provided. Kit $49.95.

Environmental Action Foundation/ Environmental Action, 1525 New Hampshire Ave NW, Washington DC 20036. (202) 745-4870. They have a clip art book of hundreds of environmentally-themed art pieces for newsletter and small-magazine editors. Called *Art: For Environment's Sake,* $12 postpaid. More information in "Organizations" and "Magazines, Newsletters & Brochures" chapters.

Franklin Associates, Ltd, 4121 West 83rd St, Suite 108, Prairie Village KS

66208. (913) 649-2225. Environmental consultants.

Goldman Environmental Foundation, 1160 Battery Street, Suite 400, San Francisco CA 94111. (415) 788-1090. FAX # (415) 986-4779. This foundation sponsors the Goldman Environmental Prize, which is given each year to 6 environmental heroes, one from each of 6 continental regions. Each recipient receives a $60,000 award funded by the foundation. The prizes are awarded for important efforts to preserve or enhance the environment. Certain criteria are important to the prize jury: private citizens and grassroots initiatives are given priority over scientific, academic or governmental activities; and recent achievements are the basis of recognition.

Nominations are accepted from only two sources: a network of 15 internationally known environmental organizations (including Sierra Club, National Audubon Society, World Wildlife Fund, Rainforest Action Network, Nature Conservancy, Environmental Defense Fund, and more); and a confidential panel of environmental experts from 20 nations.

Final selections are made the the Goldman Environmental Prize Jury, which consists of such recognized persons as Bruce Babbitt, former governor of Arizona and Joan Martin Brown, director of the Washington DC office of the United Nations Environment Programme.

Prize winners have included Lois

Gibbs, who organized a grassroots movement and led community efforts at Love Canal, New York, where 22,000 tons of toxic waste were buried beneath the school. She went on to found the Citizens Clearinghouse for Hazardous Wastes (CCHW) and is the author of *Love Canal, My Story.*

Brochure available to the public about the award.

Green Cross Certification Company, 1611 Telegraph Avenue, Suite 1111, Oakland CA 94612-2113. 1-800-829-1416. This organization provides a list of products that are independently certified to meet environmental standards. One of the standards is to use the highest achievable level of post-consumer recycled content using high-level technology. Certification includes site visits, documentation reviews, and where appropriate, laboratory testing. Certified products are allowed to carry the Green Cross emblem. **Profiled in Part I of this book.**

The Job Seeker, Rt 2 Box 16, Warrens WI 54666. (608) 378-4290. Publishes a job listing bulletin for the environmental and natural resources fields, including: forestry, biology, wildlife, fisheries, soil and conservation, environmental education, environmental protection/ regulation, parks and outdoor recreation. The bulletin is published twice a month. The listings are quite detailed, giving first the job title, then salary range, location, qualifications needed, duties, how, where, and when to apply. The advertisements are free to those who are seeking employees. The individual subscription starts at $19.50 for 6 issues.

Nigra Enterprises, 5699 Kanan Road, Agoura CA 91301-3358. (818) 889-6877. Jim Nigra has helped thousands of people improve the quality of their air and water. He specializes in satisfying the environmental needs of those with chemical sensitivities and traditional allergies. In addition to improving home and office environments, Jim has also been involved in designing systems for a wide variety of other applications, including studios, pet stores, doctors' offices, and music schools.

Jim acts as an independent agent offering personalized service (starting with a free telephone consultation); a variety of state-of-the-art equipment shipped direct to you from the manufacturer in most cases; discount prices because of low overhead; and return privileges.

He specializes in air and water purification systems, but also can provide a variety of other products: vacuums; face masks; lighting & fixtures; paints; sealants; wood stains; spackle; caulk; waxes; adhesive; cleansers; etc.

Also listed in "Clean Air, Clean Water" and "Seminars, Workshops & Speakers" chapters.

Safe Environments, 2512 9th St #17, Berkeley CA 94710. Toll-free 1-800-356-2663. Provides Home & Office Testing Laboratories for comprehensive, on-site environmental testing, analysis and consulting service. The company currently has teams of investigators in these major cities: New York City, Philadelphia, San Francisco, Los Angeles, San Jose and San Diego. Also listed in "Workshops, Seminars & Speakers" chapter.

Schaefer Applied Technology, 200 Milton St, Unit 8-R, Dedham MA 02026-2917. (617) 320-9900. Order toll-free 1-800-366-5500. Manufactures the Model EM1 Electromagnetic Field Detector, a low-cost, accurate, easy-to-use meter for measuring environmentally-hazardous ELF magnetic fields in and around homes, schools and businesses. Recommended by *Family Circle*. Price: $89.95 plus $5 for shipping. Educational booklet included with product.

Serendipity Systems, PO Box 140, San Simeon CA 93452. (805) 927-5259. This publisher of fiction has books and magazines "printed" on computer disks. These on-disk books can be read and recycled many times, saving trees. They also have software called PC-MEMO and PC-BOOK that can help make a "paperless" office, saving even more trees.

Stamp San Francisco, PO Box 16215, San Francisco CA 94116. (415) 252-5975. This company makes rubber stamps. One of their messages is "Recycle" in a specially designed circular pattern (different from the recycle emblem you see on packaging.) Other environmental styles available, such as the earth stamp, or "Extinction is forever" with dinosaurs.

COMPANY INDEX

7167. 60, 109-110

Arrowhead Mills, Inc., PO Box 2059, 110 S. Lawton St., Hereford TX 79045. (806) 364-0730. 152

Artek, Inc., PO Box 145, Elm Avenue, Antrim NH 03440. (603) 588-6825. FAX # (603) 588-6894. 237

Ashdun Industries, Inc., 400 Sylvan Avenue, Englewood Cliffs NJ 07632. (201) 569-3600. FAX (201) 816-0188. 215, 216

The Athene Series/ Pergamon Press, Inc., Maxwell House, Fairview Park, Elmsford NY 10523. (914) 592-7700. Toll-free for orders only 1-800-257-5755. Telex: 13-7328. 31

Atlantic Recycled Paper Company, PO Box 39096, Baltimore MD 21212. (301) 323-2676. Toll-free 1-800-323-8211. 216

Aura Cacia, Inc., 1401 Main St, PO Box 399, Weaverville CA 96093. (916) 623-3301. FAX # (916) 623-2626. 110

Avon Books, 105 Madison Ave, New York NY 10016. (212) 481-5600. FAX # (212) 532-2172. Toll-free 1-800-238-0658. Telex: 88-0261. 32

Baby Bunz & Company, PO Box 1717, Sebastopol CA 95473. (707) 829-5347. 23

The Bag Connection, Inc., PO Box 817, Newberg OR 97132. 1-800-62BAGIT. 223, 224

Baldwin Hill Bakery, Baldwin Hill Rd, Phillipston MA 01331. (508) 249-4691. 152, 153

Ballantine/ Del Rey/ Fawcett/ Ivy Books, Division of Random House, Inc., 201 E 50th St, New York NY 10022. (212) 751-2600. Toll-free 1-800-638-6460. 32

Basic Foundation, Inc./ Basic Publishing & Promotions, PO Box 47012, St. Petersburg FL 33743. (813) 526-9562. 69, 175

Basil Blackwell, Inc., 432 Park Ave S, Ste 1503, New York NY 10016. (212) 684-2890. 32

Baubiologie Hardware, 207 16th St, Unit B, Pacific Grove CA 93950. (408) 372-8626. 33, 62, 73, 87, 110

Beacon Press, 25 Beacon St, Boston MA 02108. (617) 742-2110. FAX # (617) 367-3237. 33

Beehive Botanicals, Rt 8, Box 8258, Ogren Road, Hayward WI 54843. (715) 634-4274. Toll-free 1-800-283-4274. 111

Ben & Jerry's, Route 100, PO Box 240, Waterbury VT 05676. (802) 244-5641. 14-18, 112

Beneficial Insectary, 14751 Oak Run Road, Oak Run CA 96069. (916) 472-3715. 153

Bikecentennial, PO Box 8308, Missoula MT 59807. (406) 721-1776. 69

BioIntegral Resource Center, PO Box 7414, Berkeley CA

94707. (415) 524-2567. 153, 175

BioLogic, Springtown Rd, PO Box 177, Willow Hill PA 17271. (717) 349-2789. 153

Biological Journeys, 1696 Ocean Drive, McKinleyville CA 95521. Toll-free reservation number 1-800-548-7555. Or make arrangements with Eureka Travel Agency at (707) 445-0861, FAX #(707) 445-5957, 1-800-228-1973, TELEX 4952863. 69

Biomass Publications of America, Box 69333, Portland OR 97201. (503) 246-4436. FAX # (503) 452-0595. 88, 138

Body Love Natural Cosmetics, PO Box 7542, 303 Potrero St #4, Santa Cruz CA 95061. (408) 425-8218. 1-800-873-3076. 112

Botanicus, Inc., 7920 Queenair Drive, Gaithersburg MD 20879. (301) 977-8887. Toll-free 1-800-282-8887. 112

Brier Run Farm, Rt 1, Box 73, Birch River WV 26610. (304) 649-2975. 153, 154

Bumkins International Inc., 291 North 700 East, Payson UT 84651. (801) 465-3995. (801) 465-9330. 23

Burpee Company, 300 Park Ave, Warminister PA 18974. 154

Buzzworm, Inc., 1818 16th St, Boulder CO 80302. (303) 442-1969. 138

California Certified Organic

Farmers, (CCOF), PO Box 8136, Santa Cruz CA 95061-8136. (408) 423-2263. 175

California School of Herbal Studies, PO Box 39, Forrestville CA 9536. (707) 887-7457. 232

Calvert Group, 4550 Montgomery Avenue, 10th floor North, Bethesda MD 20814. (301) 951-4820. 1-800-368-2748. 104

Cambridge University Press, 32 E 57th St, New York NY 10022. (212) 688-8885. 33

Caribbean Conservation Corp., PO Box 2866, Gainesville FL 32602. (904) 373-6441. 74, 175

Carole's Cosmetics—The Caring Catalog, 2973 Harbor Blvd, Suite 174, Costa Mesa CA 92626. (714) 842-0454. 112

Carol Venolia, PO Box 694, 38820 S Highway 1, Suite 205, Gualala CA 95445. (707) 884-4513. 232, 237

Catalyst, 64 Main St, 3rd Floor, (05602) PO Box 1308, (05601) Montpelier VT . (802) 223-7943. 104, 176

Cedar-al Products Inc., HCR 63 Box 6, Clallam Bay WA 98326. (206) 963-2601. Toll-free order line 1-800-431-3444 from 8-4 pm Pacific time, Mon-Fri. 112, 223, 225

Celestial Arts, PO Box 7327, Berkeley CA 94707. (415) 524-1801. FAX # (415) 524-1052. 34

Center for Marine Conservation, 1725 DeSales St NW, Washington DC 20036. (202) 429-5609. 176

Center for Plant Conservation, 125 Arborway, Jaimaica Plain MA 02130-3520. (617) 524-6988. 176

Center for Science in the Public Interest, 1875 Connecticut Ave NW #300, Washington DC 20009. (202) 332-9110. FAX # (202) 265-4954. 34, 74, 177

Chartrand Imports, PO Box 1319, Rockland ME 04841. (207) 594-7300. 154

Cheesemans' Ecology Safaris, 20800 Kittredge Rd, Saratoga CA 95070. (408) 741-5330. 70, 232

Chempoint Products Company, 543 Tarrytown Rd, White Plains Ny 10607. 1-800-343-6588. 113

Chem-Tainer Industries, Inc., 361 Neptune Ave, North Babylon NY 11704. (516) 661-8300. FAX # (516) 661-8209. Toll-free 1-800-654-5607. 224

C.H.I.P. Distribution Company, 1139 Dominquez St., Unit E, Carson CA 90746. (213) 603-1114. 113

Citizen's Clearinghouse for Hazardous Wastes, 2315 Wilson Blvd, Suite A, PO Box 657, Arlington VA 22216. (703) 276-7070. 177

Citizen's Coalition for Energy Efficiency, Southeastern Pennsylvania Energy Center, 100 North 17th St, Third Floor, Philadelphia PA 19103. (215)

563-3989. 178

Clean Sites, 1199 North Fairfax St, Alexandria VA 22314. (703) 739-1275. FAX # (703) 548-8773. 178

Clean Water Tech, PO Box 15330, San Luis Obispo CA 93406. 62

Clean Yield Group, PO Box 1880, Greensboro Bend VT 05842. (802) 533-7178. 105

Climate Institute, 316 Pennsylvania Ave SE, Suite 403, Washington DC 20003. (202) 547-0104. FAX # (202) 547-0111. Telex 214 858 CLIMAT UR. 179

Clothcrafters, Inc., PO Box 176, Elkhart Lake WI 53020. (414) 876-2112. 113

Cloverdale, Inc., PO Box 268, West Cornwall CT 06796. 113

COGNITION, c/o Tomas Nimmo, COGnition Director of Advertising, Heidelberg, Ontario, Canada N0B 1Y0. (519) 699-4481. FAX # (519) 747-5660. 138, 154

Community Mill and Bean, Inc., 267 Rt 89 South, Savannah NY 13146. (315) 365-2664. FAX # (315) 365-2690. 155

Community Products Inc., RD #2, Box 1950, Montpelier VT 05602. (802) 229-1840. 114

The Compassionate Consumer, PO Box 27, Jericho NY 11753. (718) 445-4134. 34, 114

Conari Press, 1339 61st St,

Emeryville CA 94608. (415) 596-4040. FAX # (415) 428-2861. 34

Concern, Inc., 1794 Columbia Rd NW, Washington DC 20009. (202) 328-8160. 139, 179

Confab Companies, 2301 Dupont Drive, Suite 150, Irvine CA 92715. (714) 955-2690. 217

Conscious Connection Magazine, 432 Altair Place, Venice CA 90291. (213) 392-9661. 62

Conservation & Renewable Energy Inquiry & Referral Service (CAREFIRS), PO Box 8900, Silver Spring MD 20907. 1-800-523-2929. 88, 119

Co-op America, 2100 "M" St NW, Suite 403, Washington DC 20063. (202) 872-5307. Toll-free 1-800-424-2667. 23, 57, 74, 88, 114, 155, 179, 217, 224

The Cotton Place, PO Box 59721, Dallas TX 75229. (214) 243-4149. 115

Council of State Governments, Iron Works Pike, PO Box 11910, Lexington KY 40578-9989. (606) 252-2291. 35

Council on Economic Priorities, 30 Irving Place, New York NY 10003. (212) 420-1133. Toll-free 1-800-822-6435. 35, 180, 193

Country Comfort, PO Box 3, 28537 Nuevo Valley Dr, Nuevo CA 92367. (714) 657-3438. 24, 115

Country Grown/ Specialty

Grain Company, 12202 Woodbine, Redford MI 48239. (313) 535-9222. 155

Creative Printing & Publishing, 712 N. Hwy 17-92, Longwood FL 32750. (407) 830-4747. Toll-free outside Florida 1-800-780-4447. 75

Crossroads Farms, Box 3230, Jonesport ME 04649-9709. 156

Cultural Survival, Inc., 53 Church St, Cambridge MA 02138. (617) 495-2562. 36, 139, 180

Dahon, The Folding Bicycle People, 901 Corporate Center Dr, Suite 508, Monterey Park CA 91754. (213) 264-7969. FAX # (213) 264-8042. 89

Dell Publishing Company, 666 Fifth Ave, New York NY 10103. (212) 765-6500. FAX # (212) 492-9698. Toll-free 1-800-223-6834. Telex: 23-8781 DELL UR. 36

Desert Essence Cosmetics, PO Box 588, Topanga CA 90290. (213) 455-1046. FAX # (213) 455-2245. 115

Desert Tortoise Council, PO Box 1738, Palm Desert CA 92261. 181

Deva Lifewear, Box GEF1, Burkittsville MD 21718-0438. (301) 663-4900. FAX # (301) 663-3560. Toll free order line 1-800-222-8024. 115

Devices & Services Company, 10024 Monroe Dr, Dallas TX 75229. (214) 902-8337. 89

Dharma Farma, Ned Whitlock, HC 66, Box 140, Green Forest AR 72638. (501) 553-2550. 156

Diap-Air, 3331 Gold Run Rd, Boulder CO 80302. (303) 442-3334. 24

Discover, 3 Park Ave, New York NY 10016. (212) 779-6200. 139

DLR Design & Development Corporation, 44105 Leeann, Canton MI 48187. (313) 459-0754. FAX # (313) 459-2610. 1-800-869-9709. 224

Dolco Packaging Corp, 13400 Riverside Drive, Suite #200, Sherman Oaks CA 91413. (818) 995-1238. 225, 237

Dona Designs, 825 Northlake Drive, Richardson TX 75080. (214) 235-0485. 116

Dry Creek Herb Farm, 13935 Dry Creek Road, Auburn CA 95603. (916) 878-2441. 116, 156, 233

Ducks Unlimited, Inc., One Waterfowl Way, Long Grove IL 60047. (708) 438-4300. 181

E & A Environmental Consultants, Inc., 1613 Central St, PO Box 372, Stoughton MA 02072. (617) 341-1400. FAX # (617) 341-4206. 225

Earth Action Network, Inc., 28 Knight St, Norwalk CT 06851. (203) 854-5559. 138, 181

Earth Care Paper Inc., Box 14140, Madison WI 53714. (608) 277-2900. 217

 Company Index

Earth Island Institute, 300 Broadway, Ste 28, San Francisco CA 94133. (415) 788-3666. FAX # (415) 788-7324. 182

EarthSave, 706 Frederick St, Santa Cruz CA 95062. (408) 423-4069. 182

Earth's Best, PO Box 887, Middlebury VT 05753. 1-800-442-4221. 24

Earth Science, PO Box 1925, Corona CA 91718. (714) 524-9277. FAX # (714) 524-5705. 116

EarthWatch, PO Box 403, 680 Mt. Auburn St, Watertown MA 02272. (617) 926-8200. 182

The Earthwise Consumer, PO Box 279, Forest Knolls, CA 94933. (415) 488-4614. 36, 139

Earthworks Press, Box 25, 1400 Shattuck Ave, Berkeley CA 94709. (415) 841-5866. 37

Ecco Bella, 6 Provost Square, Suite 602, Caldwell NJ 07006. (201) 226-5799. FAX # (201) 226-0991. Toll-free 1-800-888-5320. 89, 116, 117, 156, 217, 225

Echo Energy Products, 219 Van Ness Ave, Santa Cruz CA 95060. (408) 423-2429. 89

Eco Design Company, 1365 Rufina Circle #1, Santa Fe NM 87501. Telephone orders 1-800-621-2591. 117

The Ecology Box, 425 East Washington, Ann Arbor MI 48104. (313) 662-9131. 117

Ecology Center, 2530 San Pablo Ave, Berkeley CA 94702. (415) 548-2220. 182

EcoNet Canada, 456 Spadina Ave, 2nd floor, Toronto, Ontario, Canada M5T 2G8. (416) 929-0634. FAX # (416) 925-7536. Modem: (416) 925-0400. Telex: 063270997. 183, 238

EcoSafe Products Inc., PO Box 1177, St. Augustine FL 32085. 1-800-274-7387. 117

Eco Source™, 9051 Mill Station Road Bldg #E, Sebastopol CA 95472. (717) 829-7957 or (707) 829-8345. 38, 63, 89, 118, 218, 226, 238

Elemental Enterprises, PO Box 928, Monterey CA 93942. (408) 394-7077. 91

E. L. Foust Company, Inc., Box 105, Elmhurst IL 60126. (708) 834-4952. 1-800-225-9549. 38, 63

Energy Federation, Inc., 354 Waverly St., Framingham MA 01701. (508) 875-4921. FAX # (617) 451-1534. Toll-free 1-800-876-0660 outside Massachusetts. Toll free eastern Massachusetts 1-800-752-7372. 91, 183

Energy Keeper Kap Company, PO Box 2202, Farmington Hills MI 48333. (313) 553-3173. 91

Energy Probe Research Foundation, 225 Brunswick Avenue, Toronto, Ontario, Canada M5S 2M6. (416) 978-7014. 139, 143

Energy Store, PO Box 3507,

Santa Cruz CA 95063-3507. (408) 464-1938. Toll-free 1-800-228-1938. 24, 38, 75, 92-93

Environmental Action Coalition, 625 Broadway, New York NY 10012. (212) 677-1601. 76, 140, 184

Environmental Action Foundation/ Environmental Action, 1525 New Hampshire Ave NW, Washington DC 20036. (202) 745-4870. 140, 184, 238

Environmental Economics, 1026 Irving Street, Philadelphia PA 19107. (215) 925-7168. 39

Environmental Defense Fund, National Headquarters, 257 Park Ave, New York NY 10010. 184

Environmental Hazards Management Institute, 10 Newmarket Rd, PO Box 932, Durham NH 03824. (603) 868-1496. FAX # (603) 868-1547. 76, 184, 185

Environmental Planning Office, Hawaii State Department of Health, 5 Waterfront Plaza, Suite 250, 500 Ala Moana Blvd, Honolulu HI 96813. (808) 543-8337. 141

Environmental Purification Systems, PO Box 191, Concord CA 94522-9964. (415) 284-2129. 1-800-829-2129. 64

Erth-Rite, Inc., RD #1, Box 243, Gap PA 17527. (717) 442-4171. 1-800-332-4171. 156, 157

Evergreen Bins, PO Box 70307, Seattle WA 98107. (206) 783-

7095. 157

Everpure, Inc., 660 Blackhawk Dr, Westmont IL 60559-9005. (708) 654-4000. 64

Explorers at Sea, Inc., PO Box 51, Main St, Stonington ME 04681. (207) 367-2356. 70

Farm Verified Organic™, PO Box 45, Redding CT 06875. (203) 544-9896. FAX # (203) 544-8409. Telex: 204 450 FOODS. 157

F-Chart Software, 4406 Fox Bluff Rd, Middleton WI 53562. (608) 836-8536. 93

Fiddler's Green Farm, RFD 1 Box 656, Belfast ME 04915. (207) 338-3568. 157

Financial Network Investment Corporation, 605 1st Ave, Ste 505, Seattle WA 98104. (206) 292-8483. 105

First Affirmative Financial Network, 1040 S. 8th St, Suite 200, Colorado Springs CO 80906. (719) 636-1045. FAX # (719) 636-1943. Toll-free 1-800-422-7284. 105

Forum International (Worldwide) Inc., 91 Gregory Lane, Suite 21, Pleasant Hill CA 94523. (415) 671-2900. FAX # (415) 946-1500. 70, 185

Four Chimneys Organic Winery, RD #1, Hall Rd, Himrod NY 14842. (607) 243-7502. 157, 158

Fowler Solar Electric Inc, PO Box 435, 13 Bashan Hill Road, Worthington MA 01098. (413)

238-5974. 39, 93, 233

Franklin Associates, Ltd, 4121 West 83rd St, Suite 108, Prairie Village KS 66208. (913) 649-2225. 238

French Meadow Bakery, 2910 Lyndale Ave S, Minneapolis MN 55408. (612) 870-4740. 158, 159

Freshwater Foundation, PO Box 90, Navarre MN 55392. (612) 471-8407. 77, 141, 185

Frey Vineyards, 14000 Tomki Rd, Redwood Valley CA 95470. Within California 1-800-345-3739. Outside California (707) 485-5177. 158, 160

Friends of the Earth, 218 "D" St SE, Washington DC 20003. (202) 544-2600. FAX # (202) 543-4710. EcoNet ID—foedc. 141, 186

Funding Exchange, 666 Broadway, 5th floor, New York NY 10012. (212) 529-5300. 186

The Funds for Animals Inc., 200 West 57th St, New York NY 10019. (212) 246-2096 or (212) 246-2632. 186

Gaia™, 1400 Shattuck Ave #15, Berkeley CA 94709. (415) 548-4172. 39, 226

Genesee Natural Foods, Inc., RD 2 Box 105, Genesee PA 16923. (814) 228-3200. FAX # (814) 228-3638. 118, 158

Gentle Strength Co-op, 234 West University Drive, Tempe

AZ 85281. (602) 968-4831. 25, 39, 118, 141, 158, 218

George Miksch Sutton Avian Research Center, Inc., PO Box 2007, Bartlesville OK 74005. (918) 336-7778. 187

Golden Angels Apiary, PO Box 2, Singers Glen VA 22850. (703) 833-5104. 160

Goldman Environmental Foundation, 1160 Battery Street, Suite 400, San Francisco CA 94111. (415) 788-1090. FAX # (415) 986-4779. 187, 238

Gold Mine Natural Food Company, 1947 30th St, San Diego CA 92102. (619) 234-9711. 1-800-475-FOOD (3663). 119, 160, 161

Good Nature Designs, 1630 E 2nd St, Dayton OH 45403. (513) 253-2722. FAX # (513) 254-9638. 218, 219

Gracious Living Organic Farms, c/o Paul Patton, 101 Mountain Parkway, Insko KY 41443. (606) 662-6245. 160

Gravelly Ridge Farms, S.R. 16, Elk Creek CA 95939. (916) 963-3216. 161

Great Bear Foundation, PO Box 2699, Missoula MT 59806. (406) 721-3009. 188

Great Date in the Morning, PO Box 31, Coachella CA 92236. (619) 398-6171. 161

Great Lakes United, Cassety Hall, State University College at Buffalo, 1300 Elmwood

Avenue, Buffalo NY 14222. (716) 886-0142. 188

Green Cross Certification Company, 1611 Telegraph Avenue, Suite 1111, Oakland CA 94612-2113. 1-800-829-1416. 19-22, 188, 239

Green Fields Inc., 30770 Buck Heaven Rd, Hillsboro OR 97213. (503) 538-8738. 119

Greenpeace, USA, 1436 "U" St NW, Washington DC 20009. (202) 462-1177. 140, 188

Grow, Inc., (Grass Roots the Organic Way), 38 Llangollen Lane, Newtown Square PA 19073. (215) 353-2838. 189

Growing Naturally, PO Box 54, 149 Pine Lane, Pineville PA 18946. (215) 598-7025. FAX # (215) 598-7025. 119, 161

Hardscrabble Enterprises Inc., Route 6 Box 42, Cherry Grove WV 26804. (304) 567-2727 or (202) 332-0232. 161

Harmony Farm Supply & Nursery, 3244 Gravenstein Hwy North, Sebastopol CA 95472. Mail address: PO Box 460, Graton CA 95444. (707) 823-9125. FAX (707) 823-1734. 40, 161, 233

Harper & Row, Publishers, 10 E 53rd St, New York NY 10022. (212) 207-7000. Toll-free 1-800-242-7737. In Pennsylvania toll-free 1-800-982-4377. Telex 12-5741 (US); Telex 6-2501 (International). 40

Healthy Kleaner, PO Box 4656, Boulder CO 80306. (303) 444-

3440. Sales 1-800-EARTH29 (3278429). 119

Heart's Desire, 1307 Dwight Way, Berkeley CA 94702. 119

Heavenly Soap, 5948 E 30th St, Tucson AZ 85711. (602) 790-9938. 119

Heldref Publications, 4000 Albemarle St NW, Washington DC 20016. Subscription toll-free 1-800-365-9753. 142

Home Energy, 2124 Kittredge St, #95, Berkeley CA 94704. (415) 524-5405. 142

Home Service Products Company, PO Box 269, Bound Brook NJ 08805. (201) 356-8175. 120

Houghton Mifflin Company, One Beacon St, Boston MA 02108. (617) 725-5000. FAX # (617) 227-5409. Telex: 4430255. 40

Household Hazardous Waste Project, 901 South National Ave, Box 108, Springfield MO 65804. (417) 836-5777. 40, 77, 142, 189

Hugh's Gardens, RR 1 Box 67, Buxton ND 58218. (701) 962-3345. 162

Humane Alternative Products, 8 Hutchins St, Concord NH 03301. (603) 224-1361. 120

Humane Street USA, Offices & Store: 985 Terra Bella Ave, Mountain View CA 94043. Orders & Mail: PO Box 807, Mountain View CA 94042. (415) 965-8441. 120

The Hummer Nature Works, Reagan Wells Canyon Box 122, Uvalde TX 78801. (512) 232-6167. 120-121

Ida Grae Natures Colors Cosmetics, 424 LaVerne Ave, Mill Valley CA 94941. (415) 388-6101. 121

IFM, 333 Ohme Gardens Rd, Wenatchee WA 98801. (509) 662-3179. 1-800-332-3179. 121, 162

Illinois Environmental Protection Agency, 2200 Churchill Rd, PO Box 19276, Springfield IL 62794-9276. (217) 782-2829. 77, 142, 190

INFACT, National Field Campaign Office, PO Box 3223, South Pasadena CA 91031. (818) 799-9133. 190

INFORM, 381 Park Avenue South, New York NY 10016. (212) 689-4040. 41, 143, 190

The Institute for Earth Education, PO Box 288, Warrenville IL 60555. (708) 393-3096 or (509) 395-2299. 77-78, 190, 233

Institute for Local Self-Reliance, 2425 18th St NW, Washington DC 20009. (202) 232-4108. FAX # (202) 332-0463. 78, 191

Institute for Transportation and Development Policy, PO Box 56538, Washington DC 20011. (301) 589-1810. FAX # (301) 589-3453. 191

Institute of Scrap Recycling

Industries, Inc., 1627 "K" St NW, 7th floor, Washington DC 20006-1704. (202) 466-4050. FAX # (202) 775-9109. TWX 710 822 9782. EasyLink 620 23427. 78, 143, 191

International Fund for Animal Welfare, 411 Main St #2, PO Box 193, Yarmouth Port MA 02675. (508) 362-6487. FAX # (508) 362-5841. 192

International Institute for Energy Conservation, 420 "C" St NE, Washington DC 20002. (202) 546-3388. FAX # (202) 546-6978. Telex: 249114 IIEC UR. 193

IPM Laboratories, Inc., Main St, Locke NY 13092-0099. (315) 497-3129. 41, 162

Izaak Walton League of America, 1401 Wilson Blvd, Level B, Arlington VA 22209. (703) 528-1818. 193

Island Press, PO Box 7, Covelo CA 95428. 42

Jade Mountain, PO Box 4616, Boulder CO 80306. (303) 449-6601. FAX # (303) 449-8266. Toll-free 1-800-442-1972. 64, 79, 93, 121, 219

Jaffe Brothers, PO Box 636, Valley Center CA 92082-0636. (619) 749-1133. 163

Jantz Design & Manufacturing, PO Box 3071, Santa Rosa CA 95402. (707) 823-8834. 122

Jason Natural Products, 8468 Warner Drive, Culver City CA 90232-2484. (213) 838-7543. FAX # (213) 838-9274. 122

The Job Seeker, Rt 2 Box 16, Warrens WI 54666. (608) 378-4290. 239

Joe Soghomonian, Inc., 8624 S Chestnut, Fresno CA 93725. (209) 834-2772, (209) 834-3150. 163

J.R. Carlson Laboratories, Inc., 15 College Drive, Arlington Heights IL 60004. (708) 255-1600. 112

Karen's Nontoxic Products, 1839 Dr. Jack Road, Conowingo MD 21918. (301) 378-4621. 1-800-KARENS-4. 42, 122, 219

Kinsman Company, Inc., River Road, Point Pleasant PA 18950. (215) 297-5613. 163

Kiss My Face Corporation, PO Box 224, Gardiner NY 12525. (914) 255-0884. FAX # (914) 255-4312. 123

Krystal Wharf Farms, Rd 2 Box 2112, Mansfield PA 16933. (717) 549-8194. 164

KSA Jojoba, 19025 Parthenia #200, Northridge CA 91324. (818) 701-1534. FAX # (818) 993-0194. 123

LaCrista, Inc., PO Box 240, Davidsonville MO 21035. (301) 956-4447. 123

Laidlaw Environmental Services, PO Box 210799, Columbia SC 29221. (803) 798-2993. 1-800-356-8570. 226

Lakon Herbals, 4710 Templeton Rd, Montpelier VT 05602. (802) 223-5563. 124

The Land Institute, 2440 East Water Well Rd, Salina KS 67401. (913) 823-5376. 79, 194

Land Stewardship Project, 14758 Ostlund Trail North, Marine on St. Croix MN 55047. (612) 433-2770. FAX # (612) 433-2704. 42, 79, 194

Lee's Organic Foods, PO Box 11, Wellington TX 79095. (806) 447-5445. 164

LightHawk, PO Box 8163, Santa Fe NM 87504. (505) 982-9656. 195

Lillian Vernon Corporation, 510 S. Fulton Avenue, Mount Vernon NY 10555. (914) 699-4131. 124, 227

Living Tree Centre, PO Box 10082, Berkeley CA 94709-5082. (415) 528-4467. 164

Livos Plant Chemistry, 1365 Rufina Circle, Santa Fe NM 87501. (505) 438-3448. See Eco Design Company. 124

Los Alamos Sales Company, PO Box 795, Los Alamos NM 87544. (505) 662-5053. 94

Maestro-Gro, PO Box 310, 121 Lincoln Drive, Lowell AR 72745. (501) 770-6154. 164

Malachite School & Small Farm, ASR Box 21, Pass Creek Rd, Gardner CO 81040. (719) 746-2412. 80, 195, 234

Marine Mammal Stranding Center, PO Box 773, Brigantine NJ 08302. (609) 266-0538. 195

Marvelous Toys Works, 2111 Eastern Ave., Baltimore MD 21231. (301) 276-5130. 25

MasterMedia Ltd., 215 Park Ave South, Suite 1601, New York, NY 10003. (212) 260-5600. Toll-free 1-800-334-8232. 43

Mendocino Sea Vegetable Company, Box 732, Navarro CA 95463. (707) 895-3741. 164, 165

Mercantile Food Company, 4 Old Mill Road, PO Box 1140, Georgetown CT 06829. 124, 164

Mia Rose Products, Inc., 1374 Logan Unit #C, Costa Mesa CA 92626. (714) 662-5465. Toll-free 1-800-292-6339. 125

Microphor, Inc., 452 East Hill Road, PO Box 1460, Willits CA 95490. (707) 459-5563. FAX # (707) 459-6617. 94

Mountain Ark, 120 South East Ave, Fayetteville AR 72701. (501) 442-7191. 1-800-643-8909. 43, 64, 165

Mountain Fresh Products, (formerly Golden Lotus), PO Box 40516, Grand Junction CO 81504. (303) 434-8434. FAX # (303) 434-8395. 125

Mountain Springs, 356 West Redview Drive, Monroe UT 84754. 1-800-542-2303. 165, 166

National Arbor Day Foundation, 211 North 12th St, Lincoln NE 68508. (402) 474-5655. 80, 143, 195

National Audubon Society, 950 Third Ave., New York NY 10022. (212) 832-3200. 80, 143, 196, 234

National Coalition Against the Misuse of Pesticides (NCAMP), 701 E Street SE, Washington DC 20003. (202) 543-5450. 144, 197

National Ecological & Environmental Delivery System (N.E.E.D.S.), 527 Charles Ave., Syracuse NY 13209. 1-800-634-1380. 64-65

National Parks & Conservation Association, 1015 31st St NW, Washington DC 20007. (202) 944-8530. 144, 197

National Wildflower Research Center, 2600 FM 973 North, Austin TX 78725. (512) 929-3600. 144, 198

National Wildlife Federation, 1400 16th St NW, Washington DC 20036-2266. 198

Natural Organic Farmers Association, c/o Hawson Kittredge, RFD #2, Sheldon Rd, Barre MA 01005. (508) 355-2853. 165, 198

Natural Resource Defense Council, 40 West 20th St, New York NY 10011. (212) 727-2700. Membership department, zip 10114-0466. 43, 145, 198

The Nature Company, PO Box 2310, Berkeley CA 94702. 1-800-227-1114. FAX (415) 849-0465. 43, 145, 198

Nature Conservancy, 400 1815 Lynn St, Arlington VA 22209.

(703) 841-8737. 199

Nature's Colors, 424 LaVerne Ave, Mill Valley CA 94941. 126

Nature's Control, PO Box 35, Medford OR 97501. (503) 899-8318. FAX # (503) 899-9121. 166

New Alchemy Institute, 237 Hatchville Rd, East Falmouth MA 02536. (508) 564-6301. 81, 200

New Alternative Fund, 295 Northern Blvd, Great Neck NY 11021. (516) 466-0808. 106

New Jersey Department of Environmental Protection, Division of Water Resources, CN 029, Trenton NJ 08625. (609) 932-1637. 145

New Jersey Department of Environmental Protection, Office of Communications & Public Education, 401 East State St, Trenton NJ 08625. (609) 292-2885. 145

New Jersey Environmental Federation, 808 Belmar Plaza, Belmar NJ 07719. (201) 280-8988. 145, 200

Nigra Enterprises, 5699 Kanan Road, Agoura CA 91301-3358. (818) 889-6877. 65, 234, 239

Nitron Industries, Inc., PO Box 1447, 4605 Johnson Road, Fayetteville AR 72702. (501) 750-1777. 1-800-835-0123. 44, 166, 234

North American Native Fishes Association, 123 West Mt. Airy

Company Index ★

Ave., Philadelphia PA 19119. (215) 247-0384. 146, 201

North Country Soap, 7888 Hennepin County Rd #6, Maple Plain MN 55359. (612) 479-3381. FAX # (612) 476-8527. Orders toll-free 1-800-328-4827 ext 2153. 126

Northeast Publishing, Inc., PO Box 571, Emmaus PA 18049. 44

Northeast Regional Agricultural Engineering Service, 152 Riley-Robb Hall, Cooperative Extension, Ithaca NY 14853. (607) 255-7654. 146

Nukewatch, PO Box 2658, Madison WI 53701. (608) 256-4146. 201

Off the Deep End Travels, PO Box 7511, Jackson WY 83001. (307) 733-8707. Toll-free 1-800-223-6833 outside Wyoming. 71

Ohio Earth Food, Inc, 13737 Duquette Ave NE, Hartville OH 44632. (216) 877-9356. 166

Old Mill Farm School of Country Living, PO Box 463, Mendocino CA 95460. (707) 937-0244. 81

One Person's Impact, PO Box 751, Westborough MA 01581. (508) 366-0146. 202

Orchids Paper Products Company, 5911 Fresca Drive, La Palma CA 90623. (714) 523-7881. 219

Organic Foods Express, Inc., 11003 Emack Rd, Beltsville MD 20705. (301) 937-8608. 166

Organic Gardening®, Box 3, Emmaus PA 18099-0003. 167

Orr Enterprises, PO Box 1717, Monrovia CA 91017, (210 N Madison Ave, Monrovia CA 91016.) (818) 301-0950. Toll-free 1-800-525-8191. 220

Pan North America Regional Center, 965 Mission St #514, San Francisco CA 94103. (415) 541-9140. FAX # (415) 541-9253. Telex: 15683472 PANNA. Econet: PANNA. 44, 202

Papa Don's Toys, Walker Creek Road, Walton OR 97490. (503) 935-7604. 25

PAX World Fund, 224 State Street, Portsmouth NJ 03801. (603) 431-8022. Toll-free 1-800-767-1729. 106

The Peaceable Kingdom, 1902 W 6th St, Wilmington DE 19805. (302) 429-8687. (302) 652-7840. 126

Penguin USA, 1633 Broadway, New York NY 10019. (212) 397-8000. FAX # (212) 397-8273. Telex: 23-6109. 44

Pennsylvania Resources Council, PO Box 88, Media PA 19063. (215) 565-9131. 81, 146, 202, 203

People for the Ethical Treatment of Animals, (PETA), PO Box 42516, Washington DC 20015. (301) 770-7444. 203

Pets 'N People, Inc., 5312 Ironwood Street, Rancho Palos Verdes CA 90274. (213) 373-1559. 26, 126

Photocomm Inc., Consumer Division, 930 Idaho-Maryland Rd, Grass Valley CA 95945. Toll-free 1-800-544-6466. 94

Planet Drum Foundation, Box 31251, San Francisco CA 94131. (415) 285-6556. 45, 82, 146, 203, 235

Plasco Press Company, Inc., 16037 Foothill Blvd, Azusa CA 91702. (818) 969-1545. 127, 227

Plastican™ Inc., 196 Industrial Rd, Leominister MA 01453. (508) 537-4911. FAX # (508) 537-6376. 227

Plenum Publishing Corp, 233 Spring St, New York NY 10013-1578. 94

Pope & Talbot, Inc., 1500 SW 1st Avenue, Portland OR 97201. (503) 228-9161. 220

Population Reference Bureau, 1875 Connecticut Ave NW, Suite 520, Washington DC 20009. (202) 483-1100. 204

Prentice Hall Press, 15 Columbus Circle, New York NY 10023. (212) 373-8500. 45

Prima Publishing & Communications, PO Box 1260PH, Rocklin CA 95677. (916) 624-5718. 46

Programme for Belize, PO Box 1088, Vineyard Haven MA 02568. (508) 693-0856. FAX # (508) 693-6311. Toll-free 1-800-343-8009. 205

 Company Index

Public Broadcasting Service, 1320 Braddock Place, Alexandria VA 22314-1698. (703) 739-5380. 1-800-424-7943.

The Pure Water Place, Inc., PO Box 6715, Longmont CO 80501. (303) 776-0056. 65

The Putnam Berkeley Group Inc., (Perigee Books), 200 Madison Avenue, New York NY 10016. (212) 951-8400. FAX # (212) 213-6706. Toll-free 1-800-631-8571. Telex: 42-2386. 46

PV Network News, Rt 10 Box 86, Santa Fe NM 87501. 147

PV News, Box 90, Casanova VA 22017. 147

Rainbow Concepts, Rt 5, Box 569-H, Pheasant Mountain Rd, Toccoa GA 30577. (404) 886-6320. 127

Rainforest Action Movement, 430 E University, Ann Arbor MI 48109. (313) 662-0232. 12-13, 46, 147, 205

Rainforest Action Network, 301 Broadway, Suite A, San Francisco CA 94133. (415) 398-4404. FAX # (415) 398-2732. 83, 206

Random House, 201 E 50 St, New York NY 10022. (212) 751-2600. FAX # (212) 872-8026. Toll-free 1-800-638-6460. Telex: 12-6575. 46

R. Duck Company, 650 Ward Dr, Suite H, Santa Barbara CA 93111. (805) 964-4343. Toll-free orders 1-800-422-DUCK (3825). 26

Real Goods Trading Company, 966 Mazzoni St, Ukiah CA 95482. (707) 468-9214. FAX # (707) 468-0301. Order toll-free 1-800-762-7325. 26, 46, 65, 94, 127, 220, 227

Recycled Paper Company, Inc., 185 Corey Road, Boston MA 02146. (617) 277-9901. FAX # (617) 738-4877. 220

Refuse Industry Productions, Inc., PO Box 1011, Grass Valley CA 95945. (916) 272-7289. Outside California call toll-free 1-800-535-9547. 83

Resource Recycling, Inc., PO Box 10540, Portland OR 97210. (503) 227-1319. FAX # (503) 227-6135. 1-800-227-1424. 228

Resource Recycling Systems Inc., 310 Miller Ave, Ann Arbor MI 48103. (313) 996-1361. 147

Resources Conservation Inc., PO Box 71, Greenwich CT 06836. (203) 964-0600. FAX # (203) 324-9352. Toll-free 1-800-243-2862. 94

Ringer Corporation, 9959 Valley River Road, Eden Prairie MN 55344. (612) 941-4180. FAX # (612) 941-5036. 1-800-654-1047 for ordering. 128, 167

Rising Sun Organic Produce, Box 627 I-80 and PA 150, Milesburg PA 16853. (814) 355-9850. 167

RMED International Inc., PO Box 3667, 16770 Johnson Drive, Industry CA 91744. (818) 961-7800. FAX # (818) 333-6647. Toll-free 1-800-344-6379. 26

Robbins Engineering, Inc., 1641-25 McCulloch Blvd, #294, Lake Havasu City AZ 86403. (602) 855-3670. 95

Robert Berend, Attorney at Law, Registered Investment Advisor, Stockbroker, 6611 W. 5th St, Los Angeles CA 90048-4601. (213) 651-2375. 106

Rocky Mountain Institute, 1739 Snowmass Creek Rd, Old Snowmass CO 81654. (303) 927-3128. 206

Ronninger's Seed Potatoes, Star Route, Moyie Springs ID 83845. (208) 267-7938. 168

RPL Energy Enterprises Inc., 96 Elgin Ave., Manchester NH 03104. (603) 669-0836. 95

Rutgers Cooperative Extension, Publications Distribution Center, Cook College, PO Box 231, New Brunswick NJ 08903. (201) 932-9762. 147

Safe Environments, 2512 9th St #17, Berkeley CA 94710. Toll-free 1-800-356-2663. 235, 239

Safer, Inc., 189 Wells Ave, Newton MA 02159. (617) 964-2990. 128

Sanctuary Travel Services, Inc., 3701 E Tudor Rd, Anchorage AK 99507. (907) 561-1212. FAX # (907) 563-6747. Toll-free 1-800-247-3149. 71

Save Mt. Graham Fund, PO Box 15451, Phoenix AZ 85060-5451. 206

Save the Dunes Council, 444 Barker Rd, Michigan City IN

46360. (219) 879-3937. 206

Save the Planet Shareware, PO Box 45, Pitkin CO 81241. (303) 641-5035. 83

Save the World, PO Box 84366, Los Angeles CA 90073. (213) 450-3134. 83

Schaefer Applied Technology, 200 Milton St, Unit 8-R, Dedham MA 02026-2917. (617) 320-9900. Order toll-free 1-800-366-5500. 128, 240

Sea Shepherd, PO Box 7000-S, Redondo Beach CA 90277. 206

Sennergetics, 8751 Shirley Ave, Northridge CA 91324. (818) 885-0323. 95

Serendipity Systems, PO Box 140, San Simeon CA 93452. (805) 927-5259. 240

Set Point Paper Company, 31 Oxford Rd, Mansfield MA 02048. (508) 339-9300. 221, 228

Seventh Generation, Colchester VT 05446-1672. (802) 655-3116. FAX toll-free # 1-800-456-1139. Order toll-free 1-800-456-1177. Customer service toll-free 1-800-456-1197. 26, 47, 84, 95, 128-129, 148, 168, 221, 228

Shaker Shops West, 5 Inverness Way, PO Box 487, Inverness CA 94937. (415) 669-7256. FAX # (415) 669-7327. 130

Shahin Soap, PO Box 8117, 427 Van Dyke Ave, Haledon NJ 07538. (201) 790-4296. 130

Shamrock Industries, Inc., Recycling Division, 834 N. 7th St, Minneapolis MN 55411-4394. (612) 332-2100. Toll-free 1-800-822-2342. Toll-free in Minnesota 1-800-822-2343. 228

Shikai Products, PO Box 2866, Santa Rosa CA 95405. (707) 584-0298. Outside California 1-800-448-0298. 130

Sierra Club, 730 Polk Street, San Francisco CA 94109. (415) 776-2211. 47, 148, 206

Signature Art, PO Box 801, Wilder VT 05088. (802) 295-3291. 130, 131

Simmons Handcrafts, 42295 Hwy 36, Bridgeville CA 95526. (707) 777-3280, ext 6074 (radio phone). 65, 132

Simply Delicious, 243-A North Hook Rd, PO Box 124, Pennsville NJ 08070. (609) 678-4488. 132, 221

Sinan Company, PO Box 857, Davis CA 95617-0857. (916) 753-3104. 132

Sisters' Choice, 1450 6th St, Berkeley CA 94710. (415) 524-5804. 27, 84, 235

SM Jacobson Citrus, 1505 Doherty, Mission TX 78572. (512) 585-1712. 168

Snugglups Diapers, PO Box 7BB, St. Francis KY 40062. (502) 865-5501. 1-800-876-0674. 28

Social Responsibility Investment Group, Inc., 127 Peachtree St NE, Atlanta GA 30303. (404)

577-3635. FAX# (404) 577-4496. 107

Social Investment Forum, 430 1st Ave N, Suite 290, Minneapolis MN 55401. (612) 333-8338. 106

Society for Ecological Restoration, 1207 Seminole Hwy, Madison WI 53711. (608) 262-9547. 208

Soil & Water Conservation Society, 7515 Northeast Ankeny Rd, Ankeny IA 50021. 149, 208

Solar Components Corporation, 121 Valley St, Manchester NH 03103. (603) 668-8186. FAX # (603) 627-3110. 96

Solar Development Inc., 3630 Reese Ave, Riviera Beach FL 33404. (407) 842-8935. FAX # (407) 842-8967. 96

Solar Electric Engineering, Inc., 116 4th St, Santa Rosa CA 95401. (707) 542-1990. FAX # (707) 542-4358. 28, 48, 65, 96, 132, 149, 221, 230

Solar Electric Specialties Company, PO Box 537, 101 North Main St, Willits CA 95490. (707) 459-9496. Toll-free 1-800-344-2003. 98

Solarex, (An Amoco Company), PO Box 548, Santa Cruz NM 87567. (505) 753-9699. FAX # (505) 753-8474. 98

Solar Industries, 1985 Rutgers University Blvd, Lakewood NJ 08701. (201) 905-0440. Toll-free outside New Jersey 1-800-227-7657. 98

Solar Research, PO Box 869, Brighton MI 48116. (313) 227-1151. 98

Solar Survival, PO Box 250, Cherry Hill Rd, Harrisville NH 03450. (603) 827-3811. 48, 97, 98, 235

Spalding Laboratories, 760 Printz Rd, Arroyo Grande CA 93420. (805) 489-5946. 168

Spare the Animals, Inc., PO Box 233, Tiverton RI 02878. (401) 625-5963. 132

Specialty Concepts Inc., 9025 Eton Ave, Canoga Park CA 91304. (818) 998-5238. FAX # (818) 998-5253. Telex 662914 SCI CNPK. 99

Sprout House, 40 Railroad St, Great Barrington MA 01230 (413) 528-5200. 48, 85, 149, 168, 169

Stamp San Francisco, PO Box 16215, San Francisco CA 94116. (415) 252-5975. 230, 240

Student Conservation Association, PO Box 550, Charlestown NH 03603. (603) 826-4301. FAX # (603) 826-7755. 208

Student Pugwash USA, 1638 "R" St NW, Suite 32, Washington DC 20009. (202) 328-6555 for non-students. For students 1-800-WOW-A-PUG. 208

Sunelco®, the Sun Electric Company, PO Box 1499, 100 Skeels St, Hamilton MT 59840. (406) 363-6924. FAX # (406) 363-6046. 1-800-338-6844. 99

Sunnyside Solar, RD 4 Box 808, Green River Road, Brattleboro CT 05301. (802) 257-1482 (in Vermont). 1-800-346-3230. 48, 99, 236

Sunrise Lane, 780 Greenwich St., New York NY 10014. (212) 242-7014. 133, 149

Sun Selector, PO Box 1545, Parkersburg WV 26101. (304) 485-7150. FAX # (304) 422-3931. 100

SunTrak™, 2350 E 91st St, Indianapolis IN 46240. (317) 846-2150. 100

SunWatt®, RFD Box 751, Addison ME 04606. (207) 497-2204. 49, 100

Synerjy, PO Box 1854, Cathedral Station, New York NY 10025. 100

Tender Corporation, PO Box 290, Littleton Industrial Park, Littleton NH 03561. (603) 444-5464. FAX # (603) 444-6735. Toll-free 1-800-258-4696. 133

TERC—The Ertley Recycling Concept, 699C Friar Ct, Lakehurst NJ 08733. (201) 657-4690. 229, 231

TESS (Thermal Energy Storage Systems Inc), RR 1 Box 3, Beanville Road, Randolph VT 05060. (802) 728-4485. FAX # (802) 728-9582. 1-800-323-TESS. 100, 101

ThermaFlo, 3640 Main St, Springfield MA 01107. (413) 733-4433. FAX #(413) 733-9267. 1-800-8484-CFC. 66

Thermo Dynamics Ltd, 81 Thornhill Dr, Dartmouth, Nova Scotia, Canada B3B 1R9. Call Collect (902) 468-1001. 100

3-Day Solar Store, (Monday-Wednesday), Box 23, Capella CA 95418. (707) 485-0588. 101

3-M Energy Control Products, Bldg 225-4S-08 3M Center, St. Paul MN 55144-1000. (612) 736-2388. 101

Tranet, PO Box 567, Rangeley ME 04970. (207) 864-2252. 209

Treekeepers, 249 South Hwy 101, Ste 518, Solana Beach CA 92075. (619) 481-6403. FAX # (619) 481-2305. 133, 134

TreePeople, 12601 Mulholland Drive, Beverly Hills CA 90210. (818) 753-4600. 209

Trees for Life, 1103 Jefferson, Wichita KS 67203. (316) 263-7294. 85, 209, 210

The Trust for Public Land, 116 New Montgomery St, 4th Floor, San Francisco CA 94105. (415) 495-4014. FAX # (415) 495-4103. 210

Union of Concerned Scientists, 26 Church St, Cambridge MA 02238. (617) 547-5552. 49, 85, 150, 210

United Nations Environmental Programme, North American Office, Room DC2-803, New York NY 10017. (212) 963-8139. 210

University of California Press,

2120 Berkeley Way, Berkeley CA 94720. (415) 642-4247. 49

University Research Expeditions Program (UREP), University of California, Berkeley CA 94720. (415) 642-6586. 85, 211

U.S. Environmental Directories, PO Box 65156, St. Paul MN 55165. 49

U.S. Fish and Wildlife Service, US Department of the Interior, National Fisheries Contaminant Research Center, Route 2, 4200 New Haven School Road, Columbia MO 65021. (314) 857-5399. 150

U.S. PIRG (The United States Public Interest Research Group), 215 Pennsylvania Ave SE, Washington DC 20003. (202) 546-9707. 149, 211

US Sky, 2907 Agua Fria, Santa Fe NM 87501. FAX # (505) 471-5437. Toll-free 1-800-323-5017. 101

Vanderburgh Enterprises, Inc., PO Box 138, Southport CT 06490. (203) 227-4813. 101

Vermont Castings, Prince St, Randolph VT 05060. (802) 728-3181. 102

The Vermont Country Store, Inc., PO Box 3000, Manchester Center VT 05255. (802) 362-2400. 133, 231

Voyagers International, PO Box 915, Ithaca NY 14851. (607) 257-3091. Telex 887181. FAX # (607) 257-3699. 71

Warm Earth Cosmetics, 2230

Normal Ave, Chico CA 95928. (916) 895-0455. FAX # (916) 342-8223. 135

Washington Citizens for Recycling Foundation, 216 First Ave South #260, Seattle WA 98104. (206) 343-5171. 211

Water Furnace International Inc., 4307 Arden Drive, Fort Wayne IN 46804. (219) 432-LOOP (5667). FAX # (219) 432-1489. 102

The Watt Stopper, 296 Brokaw Rd, Santa Clara CA 95050. (408) 988-5331. FAX # (408) 988-5373. Toll-free 1-800-879-8585. 102

Weiss's Kiwifruit, 594 Paseo Companeros, Chico CA 95928. (916) 343-2354. 170

Weleda Inc., 841 S. Main St, PO Box 769, Spring Valley NY 10977. Pharmacy (914) 352-6145. Bookkeeping, Wholesale, & Inquiries. (914) 356-4134. FAX # (914) 356-5270. 135, 136

We Recycle Unlimited™, PO Box 275, Cape Porpoise ME 04014. (207) 282-8880. FAX # (207) 282-9488. 222

West Virginia Division of Natural Resources, 1900 Kanawha Blvd, E., Capitol Complex, Building 3, Charleston WV 25305. (304) 348-2754. FAX # (304) 348-2768. Recycling Section: (304) 348-3370. 212

Whole Earth Review, PO Box 38 Sausalito CA 94966. (415) 332-1716. 150

Wilderness: Alaska/ Mexico, 1231 Sundance Loop, Fairbanks AK 99709, (907) 452-1821. 72

The Wilderness Society, 900 17th St NW, Washington DC 20006. (202) 833-2300. 212

Wilderness Watch, Inc., PO Box 782, Sturgeon Bay WI 54235. (414) 743-1238. 212

Wildlife Games Inc., PO Box 247, Ivy VA 22945. (804) 972-7016. 28, 86

Wildlife Information Center, Inc., 629 Green St., Allentown PA 18102. (215) 434-1637. 49, 86, 150, 212

William Morrow & Company, Inc., (imprint Quill), 105 Madison Ave, New York NY 10016. (212) 889-3050. FAX # (212) 689-9139. Toll-free 1-800-843-9389. Telex: 22-4063 WILMOR. 49

Windstar Foundation, 2317 Snowmass Creek Rd, Snowmass CO 81654, (303) 927-4777. 213

World Wildlife Fund, 1250 24th St NW, Washington DC 20037. (202) 293-4800. Telex: 64505 PANDA. 213

Working Assets Money Fund, 230 California St, San Francisco CA 94111. (415) 989-3200 (call collect for information). FAX # (415) 989-5920. Toll-free 1-800-533-3863 for Prospectus. 107

Xerces Society, 10 SW Ash St, Portland OR 97204. (503) 222-2788. 50, 86, 214

 Company Index

Zomeworks Corp, PO Box
25805, Albuquerque NM 87125.
(505) 242-5354. FAX # (505)
243-5187. 103

PARENT ALERT!!

Parents' Guide for Helping Kids Become "A" Students

by Anne Farrell, Jacqueline Watson, and Elaine Dundas.
This practical book shows parents how to help their children
develop better study skills. Specific, easy-to-follow ideas
are given for reading math, spelling, writing, homework, more!

Small Press Top 40—September 1990

Saddleback Valley News (Aug 29, 1990)—"A Dianetics for
the parents of school children."

AUTHOR WATSON WILL APPEAR ON CNN'S "DAYWATCH" PROGRAM

0-933025-21-1 $11.95

Available at B. Dalton Booksellers

Company Index ★

ORDER FORM

To order more books from Blue Bird Publishing, use this handy order form.

_____ *Homeless! Without Addresses in America*	$11.95
_____ *Green Earth Resource Guide*	$12.95
_____ *Home Schools: An Alternative* (3rd edition)	$11.95
_____ *Home Education Resource Guide* (revised)	$11.95
_____ *Home Business Resource Guide*	$11.95
_____ *Dr. Christman's Learn-to-Read Book*	$15.95
_____ *The Sixth Sense: Practical Tips for Everyday Safety*	$11.95
_____ *They Reached for the Stars!*	$11.95
_____ *Parents' Guide to Helping Kids Become "A" Students*	$11.95
_____ *Home School Manual*	$15.50

Shipping Charges: $1.50 for first book. Add 50 cents for each additional book.
Total charges for books: _____
Total shipping charges: _____
TOTAL ENCLOSED: _____

NAME:_____
ADDRESS:_____
CITY, STATE, ZIP:_____
Telephone #: _____

**Credit card orders
call toll-free 1-800-654-1993**

Purchase orders may be mailed or sent by FAX # (602) 983-7319. Wholesale and library orders given discount.

Send mail order to:

**BLUE BIRD PUBLISHING
1713 East Broadway #306
Tempe AZ 85282
(602) 968-4088
FAX (602) 983-7319**

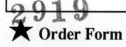

2919
★ Order Form